Staging Indigenous Heritage

Staging Indigenous Heritage examines the cultural politics of four Indigenous cultural villages in Malaysia. Demonstrating that such villages are often beset with the politics of brokerage and representation, the book shows that this reinforces a culture of dependency on the brokers.

By critically examining the relationship between Indigenous tourism and development through the establishment of Indigenous cultural villages, the book addresses the complexities of adopting the 'culture for development' paradigm as a developmental strategy. Demonstrating that the opportunities for self-representation and self-determination can become entwined with the politics of brokerage and the contradictory dualism of culture, it becomes clear that this can both facilitate and compromise their intended outcomes. Challenging the simplistic conceptualisation of Indigenous communities as harmonious and unified whole, the book shows how Indigenous cultures are actively forged, struggled over, and negotiated in contemporary Malaysia

Confronting the largely positive rhetoric in current discourses on the benefits of community-based cultural projects, *Staging Indigenous Heritage* should be essential reading for academics and students in the fields of museum studies, cultural heritage studies, Indigenous studies, development studies, tourism, anthropology, and geography. The book should also be of interest to museum and heritage professionals around the world.

Yunci Cai is Lecturer in Museum Studies and Co-Director of the MA/MSc in the Heritage and Interpretation (Distance Learning) programme at the University of Leicester, UK. She is a critical heritage and museum studies scholar, specialising in the cultural politics and museologies in and of Asia.

Routledge Studies in Culture and Development
Paul Basu, Wayne Modest and Tim Winter, Series Editors

There is a burgeoning interest among academics, practitioners and policy-makers in the relationships between 'culture' and 'development'. This embraces the now well-recognized need to adopt culturally sensitive approaches *in* development practice, the necessity of understanding the cultural dimensions *of* development, and more specifically the role of culture *for* development. Culture, in all its dimensions, is a fundamental component of sustainable development, and throughout the world we are seeing an increasing number of governmental and non-governmental agencies turning to culture as a vehicle for economic growth, for promoting social cohesion, stability and human wellbeing, and for tackling environmental issues. At the same time, there has been remarkably little critical debate around this relationship, and even less concerned with the interventions of cultural institutions or creative industries in development agendas. The objective of the *Routledge Studies in Culture and Development* series is to fill this lacuna and provide a forum for reaching across academic, practitioner and policy-maker audiences.

The series editors welcome submissions for single- and multiple-authored books and edited collections concerning issues such as the contribution of museums, heritage and cultural tourism to sustainable development; the politics of cultural diplomacy; cultural pluralism and human rights; traditional systems of environmental management; cultural industries and traditional livelihoods; and culturally appropriate forms of conflict resolution and post-conflict recovery.

Cultural Diplomacy and the Heritage of Empire
Negotiating Post-Colonial Returns
Cynthia Scott

Staging Indigenous Heritage
Instrumentalisation, Brokerage, and Representation in Malaysia
Yunci Cai

https://www.routledge.com/Routledge-Studies-in-Culture-and-Development/
book-series/RSCD

Staging Indigenous Heritage
Instrumentalisation, Brokerage, and Representation in Malaysia

Yunci Cai

LONDON AND NEW YORK

First published 2021
by Routledge
2 Park Square, Milton Park, Abingdon, Oxon OX14 4RN

and by Routledge
52 Vanderbilt Avenue, New York, NY 10017

Routledge is an imprint of the Taylor & Francis Group, an informa business

© 2021 Yunci Cai

British Library Cataloguing-in-Publication Data
A catalogue record for this book is available from the British Library

Library of Congress Cataloging-in-Publication Data
A catalog record has been requested for this book

ISBN: 978-0-367-14854-6 (hbk)
ISBN: 978-0-429-05362-7 (ebk)

Typeset in Sabon
by codeMantra

This book is dedicated to the Indigenous people and activists of Malaysia, whose tireless dedication to your cultures and your causes has been the most inspiring, and to my family, especially my parents Chua Seo Peng and Pang Kwang Tian, for your love and support over the years.

Contents

List of figures   viii
Preface   xi
Acknowledgements   xv
List of abbreviations   xix

1   Introduction   1

2   Historicising Indigeneity in Malaysia   25

3   Capacity-building as a modern civilising mission   52

4   Indigeneity as an intractable double-bind   89

5   Appropriation, reinvention, and contestation of
    Indigenous heritage   117

6   The big man as arbitrator of heritage   154

7   Conclusion   184

Bibliography   193
Index   216

Figures

1.1 Location of case studies in Malaysia 2

2.1 The National Orang Asli Museum at Gombak in the state of Selangor in Peninsular Malaysia. Photograph: Author 49

3.1 Compounds of the Mah Meri Cultural Village. The Mah Meri Cultural Village is sited on the ancestral lands of the Mah Meri people at Kampung Sungai Bumbun on Carey Island in Peninsular Malaysia. Photograph: Author 53

3.2 A Mah Meri villager with the award-winning Chained Tiger Ancestor woodcarvings on sale at the Mah Meri Cultural Village. Photograph: Author 60

3.3 The craft hut of a Mah Meri woodcarver Gali Adam by the main road leading through Kampung Sungai Bumbun on Carey Island. Photograph: Author 63

3.4 The Mah Meri wedding ceremony of Sharitaudin Bah Tuin and Diana Uju held at Kampung Sungai Bumbun on Pulau Carey in November 2014. The groom and bride are sitting on a dais after the *bersanding* ritual. Photograph: Colin Nicholas from COAC 70

3.5 The Mah Meri craft centre at Kampung Rambai built by JAKOA and visited by tourists of the Mah Meri Cultural Village. Photograph: Author 77

3.6 The Mah Meri annual *Hari Moyang* celebrations at Kampung Sungai Bumbun in March 2015. Photograph: Author 79

4.1 The Orang Seletar Cultural Centre is sited within Kampung Sungai Temon in the state of Johor in Peninsular Malaysia. Photograph: Author 89

4.2 Visitors on a boat trip to see the mangrove swamps at Johore Strait, guided by the Orang Seletar villagers from Kampung Sungai Temon. Photograph: Author 95

4.3 The Orang Seletar villagers at Kampung Sungai Temon performing a dance on stage beside the Orang Seletar Cultural Centre. Photograph: Colin Nicholas from COAC 98

4.4   The wooden houses of the Orang Seletar villagers at
      Kampung Sungai Temon at Danga Bay in Peninsular
      Malaysia. Photograph: Author   100
4.5   The judge and lawyers on a visit to the Orang Seletar
      Cultural Centre situated within Kampung Sungai Temon
      and other sites of customary significance in the vicinity.
      Photograph: Colin Nicholas from COAC   109
4.6   The Orang Seletar plaintiffs at the Johor Bahru
      High Court speaking with their lawyer, Yogeswaran
      Subramaniam. They were wearing leaf-woven headdresses,
      representing their collective cultural identity in their
      assertion of native customary rights. Photograph: Colin
      Nicholas from COAC   110
5.1   Entrance to the Monsopiad Cultural Village. The
      Monsopiad Cultural Village is sited in Kampung Kuai-
      Kadazon in the District of Penampang in the eastern
      Malaysian state of Sabah. Photograph: Author   118
5.2   Forty-two human skulls at the Monsopiad Cultural
      Village. They are installed at the ceiling of the ritual house
      and are the main attraction of the Monsopiad Cultural
      Village. Photograph: Author   124
5.3   The *Magavau* ceremony staged at the *Pesta Kaamatan*
      celebration at the Kadazandusun Cultural Association
      premises in 2015. Photograph: Author   134
5.4   The *Magavau* ceremony staged for the SEAMEO
      SPAFA conference in Bangkok in 2015. Photograph:
      SEAMEO SPAFA   137
5.5   Two *bobohizans*, Adam Gontusan and Kudut, conducting
      the *Modsuung* ritual at the Monsopiad Cultural Village.
      Photograph: Author   140
5.6   The *Gintutun Do Mohoing* menhir at the Monsopiad
      Cultural Village. Photograph: Author   149
6.1   The Lotud longhouse with the exhibition galleries at the
      Linangkit Cultural Village. The Linangkit Cultural Village
      is sited in Kampung Selupoh in the District of Tuaran in
      the eastern Malaysian state of Sabah. Photograph: Author   154
6.2   A Lotud motif on a Lotud costume made with the
      Linangkit needle-weaving technique. Photograph: Author   160
6.3   The newly constructed community hall funded by the
      Sabah State Government at the premises of the Linangkit
      Cultural Village. Photograph: Author   162
6.4   A spirit medium, *libabou*, in trance for the *Monolibabou*
      ritual conducted at the Linangkit Cultural Village. The
      libabou, covered by a purple *sarong*, is chanting softly
      while holding a string of beads. Photograph: Author   167

6.5   The local elites and community leaders sat together around
      a group of shared dishes to symbolise the invitation
      extended to the spirits to partake in the merry-making of
      the *Mohlukas* ceremony held at the Linangkit Cultural
      Village. Photograph: Author   170
6.6   The *tantagas* jingling their *sindavang* during the *Mohlukas*
      ceremony conducted in the garden. Photograph: Author   172
6.7   The *Monolibabou* ritual conducted by the Lotud ritual
      specialists on 13 June 2015. The *libabou* had her hands
      on her head, covered by a *sarong*, as she shook her head in
      trance. Photograph: Judeth John Baptist from Sabah State
      Museum   178
6.8   The *tantagas* and *libabou* in trance for the *Tumabur* ritual
      ceremony. Photograph: Author   181

Preface

My inspiration for this research came from a long-held interest in the museums and museological practices of non-Western and Indigenous cultures. My early foray into Indigenous cultures was inspired by my visits to the Auckland War Memorial Museum and the Museum of New Zealand Te Papa Tongarewa whilst on an Erasmus exchange in New Zealand in 2003. Deeply captivated by the Maori objects, especially the life-size Maori houses, on display at these museums, I came to take an interest in museums and the representation of cultures, especially those in Southeast Asia, a region close to my heart. After working for a few years in the museum sector in Singapore, I came to the University College London (UCL) to do an MA in Museum Studies in 2009. It then dawned on me that the prevailing museum studies literature did not reflect the myriad museological models and practices that I had encountered in Southeast Asia, and I struggled to make sense of these museum developments with the conceptual tools that I had learnt on my courses.

A conversation with Christina Kreps on a bus journey in a rural town of northern Thailand whilst serving as an intern at a field school organised by the Princess Maha Chakri Sirindhorn Anthropology Centre in 2010 ignited my interest in doing research on Southeast Asian museology. I still vividly remember how I had asked Christina if she could write a book on Southeast Asian museology for students from the region like me. To my surprise, she replied, 'This is a book which should be written by people like you, who grew up and work in the region'. Three years later, a generous scholarship from UCL afforded me the opportunity to return to my alma mater to do a PhD research on Southeast Asian museology, supervised by Paul Basu and Rodney Harrison. In 2013, I began my PhD research seeking to explore local museum practices in Southeast Asia.

I soon took an interest in the Indigenous museums in Malaysia, and what I perceived to be a form of Indigenous museology in Southeast Asia. My research objectives were informed by prevalent discourses of Indigeneity, culture for development, community engagement, and non-Western museology. Situated at the nexus of these various discourses, the proliferation of Indigenous cultural villages in Malaysia seemed like a noteworthy museological phenomenon for further exploration. During my exploratory fieldwork from March to May 2014, I visited over ten Indigenous museums[1] in Malaysia to identify suitable case studies for in-depth exploration. Following this exploratory fieldwork, I selected four Indigenous cultural villages as case studies for my comparative research, namely the Mah Meri Cultural Village in Carey Island and the Orang Seletar Cultural Centre in Johor Bahru, both in Peninsular Malaysia, and the Monsopiad Cultural Village and the Linangkit Cultural Village, both in Sabah, East Malaysia. These case studies were selected to reflect diversity in ownership, funding arrangements, and management structures among the Indigenous museums in Malaysia.

This book is a work of museum anthropology on an emergent museum culture in an under-represented region of the world, where I seek to interrogate the place and position of these Indigenous cultural villages within their broader global and national contexts, uncovering the knowledge produced about and by them (Bouquet 2012). For around 15 months between July 2014 and September 2015, I conducted ethnographic fieldwork in Malaysia during which I lived with local communities and volunteered at the four Indigenous cultural villages, spending around three to four months in each community. At the cultural villages, I undertook a variety of tasks, such as observing and participating in cultural performances, minding the reception, hosting guests, cleaning the exhibition galleries and community halls, running programmes for the cultural villages, as well as doing administrative and accountancy work, in order to understand day-to-day operations. In the homes of my host families, I engaged in a variety of tasks, such as cooking, weaving, cleaning, and other housework, in order to understand their everyday cultural practices. Thereafter from 2015 to 2019, I conducted numerous short trips to my fieldsites to update my research participants of my findings and to understand the latest developments at these Indigenous cultural villages.

Primary data for this study was derived from ethnographic research methods such as participant observation, unstructured and semi-structured interviews, as well as focus group discussions with different stakeholders of these Indigenous cultural villages. This ethnographic approach allowed me to develop a nuanced and grounded understanding of heritage discourse and practice in Malaysia by understanding how different people constructed, interacted with, and responded to heritage discursively and materially. An ethnographic approach was chosen, since this gives equal privilege to what research participants say and what they do – and recognises that these are not necessarily consistent. Thus, attention was given to everyday interactions through immersive fieldwork, allowing for the uncovering of unspoken or tacit knowledge that was not easily expressed or codified in language (Marcus 1995). This 'multi-sited ethnography' (Marcus 1995) allowed me to develop a nuanced and grounded understanding of heritage discourse and practice between the processes of heritage instrumentalisation that were being played out among the different Indigenous groups, against the common national context of Malaysia, and the global emergence of the Indigenous rights movement. My fieldwork was also conducted within the parameters of the ethical guidelines on responsible ethnographic fieldwork, such as obtaining free, prior, and informed consent (FPIC) from my research participants.

Davies (2008) calls for an awareness and recognition of the wider politics and power relations in which the research is embedded, which extends from the macro-politics concerning research funding, institutional ideologies, and political influence, to the micro-politics of establishing contacts and gaining consent from research participants through relationship building. I critically reflected on how my professional, ethnic, and gender positions as a female, ethnic Chinese-Singaporean trained in a Western academic institution in London had a bearing on how I perceived the research field, how I was perceived by my collaborators and research subjects in the research field, and the fieldwork data I could or could not access. Recognising that the study of Indigenous issues is always bound up with Indigenous politics and advocacy due to the historical marginalisation of Indigenous people and the global rise of the Indigenous consciousness and rights movements, I actively centre Indigenous agency in my research and recognise Indigenous self-determination. Subscribing to the ethos of anthropological engagements, I expressed a shared commitment to visions of social justice (Low and Merry 2010), in collaborations with prominent non-governmental organisations (NGOs), particularly the Center for Orang Asli Concerns (COAC), the Malaysian Bar Council, and Partners of Community Organisations, Sabah (PACOS) Trust.

Once I became immersed in my fieldsites, it soon became apparent that my assumptions about the positive roles that these Indigenous museums played in the lives of Indigenous people were somewhat naïve, and that the reality on the ground was much more complicated and ambiguous. After observing the day-to-day operation of these Indigenous cultural villages, and interacting with the different stakeholders, I realised that the overwhelmingly positive rhetoric of international agencies such as UNESCO and much of the museological literature paid little attention to the complex motivations and uneven power relations evident in these institutions. So, I decided to turn my ethnographic focus to understanding these complex dynamics and power politics at the four Indigenous cultural villages, and their implications on the lives and cultural heritage of the Indigenous people. My PhD thesis and this book grew out of my experiences of living with and learning from Indigenous communities, Indigenous activists, and museum professionals who have generously given me their time and shared with me their knowledge. I dedicate this book to them.

Note

1 Among the numerous Indigenous museums that have been set up are the Monsopiad Cultural Village, Linangkit Cultural Village, Mari Mari Cultural Village, Borneo Cultural Village, and Sabah State Museum and Heritage Village – all in Sabah; the Sarawak Cultural Village in Sarawak, as well as the National Orang Asli Museum at Gombak, Orang Asli Museum at Melaka, Mah Meri Cultural Village, Orang Seletar Cultural Centre, and Temuan Eco-Culture and Heritage Park in Peninsular Malaysia.

Acknowledgements

I would like to thank my supervisors, Paul Basu and Rodney Harrison, for shepherding me along this intellectual journey of discovery, and encouraging me to explore the complex world around us with enthusiasm and curiosity. My supervisors have gone beyond the call of duty to help me make sense of my complex fieldwork data, as well as read, comment, and edit on many drafts of my work with critical scrutiny. I feel extremely privileged to be able to work under their mentorship and guidance, and to be inspired by their enthusiasm for the subject. I am also very grateful for their care and guidance that extends beyond my PhD study, and their support for my aspirations as I embark on an academic career. I would like to acknowledge the award of the UCL Overseas Research Scholarship (2013–2016) and UCL Graduate Research Scholarship (2013–2016) which funded my studies at the UCL Institute of Archaeology.

This book would not have been possible without the support and assistance of my research sponsors, advisors, and interlocutors in Malaysia, who have generously given their time and resources to support my fieldwork and share their perspectives with me. Fieldwork in Malaysia is a major highlight of my PhD journey, and I relish many friendships I have made whilst on fieldwork in Malaysia. First of all, I would like to thank Judeth John Baptist from the Sabah State Museum for her friendship, guidance, and support. Judeth generously sponsored my research and introduced to her networks, without which my fieldwork in Sabah would not have gotten off the ground. I am also grateful to her colleagues, Robin Lojiwin, Stanley Peter, and Lydia Chua, her family in Tuaran, as well as her team from the Cultural Performing Group, especially Rita Dymphna Tati and Bon Bonny Edip, for supporting my work in many ways. My sincere gratitude goes to Joanna Kitingan, Director of museum, who kindly hosted me at the museum as a visiting researcher.

My sincere gratitude goes to Julinus Jeffery Jimit, Doreen Munting Lansing, and Chloe Tiffany Lee from the Sabah Tourism Board, Anne Lasimbang from PACOS Trust, and Rita Lasimbang from the Kadazandusun Language Foundation. I am grateful to Antakin Andau, Headman of Kampung Bantayan, his wife, and all the Lotud ritual specialists, especially Odun xvi *Acknowledgements*

Badin, Odun Lumanjar, Odun Sobinting, Odun Gading, and Ina Jarambah, for allowing me to document their rituals. I am grateful to Augusta Lojikin, Adam Gontusan, and Ina Gusiti for sharing with me the practices of the Kadazan ritual specialists. I also thank Jacqueline Pugh-Kitingan, Patricia Regis, Masaru Miyamoto, Benedict Topin, Tan Sri Herman Luping, and Eleanor Goroh for their insights on the cultural heritage of Sabah.

At Kampung Kuai-Kadazon in Sabah, I would like to thank Winnie Jimis, her husband, Donald Kely Jitilon, their children, Noel, Deanne, Joanne, and Joey, and my beloved Grandma (Ina), who hosted me at their home. Wildy Moujing, the Headman of Kampung Kuai-Kadazon, and Jack Lettong generously shared with me their ancestral heritage and the history of Monsopiad. At the Monsopiad Cultural Village, I am grateful to Christine Perroud and Herman Scholz, as well as staff especially Elvy Luis and Norhisyam Mohd Sabran (Bob) for facilitating my research.

At Kampung Selupoh in Sabah, I am grateful to Odun Perantis, Odun Ronnie, and Odun Lanjutan, my three sireh-chewing grandmas, and their family members especially Nor Atika Eyka and Alice Li, who hosted me in their home, and took care of me as if I were their granddaughter. At the Linangkit Cultural Village, I would like to thank the late Datuk Patrick Jilan, and his family, especially Alice Teh-Jilan, Elvin Jilan, Jerry Jilan, Czer Jilan, and Jennifer Pondon, for hosting me. My gratitude also goes to Margaret Jilan, the Village Headwoman of Kampung Selupoh, as well as Peter Lintar, Yatie Tie, and Winnie Edwin, for facilitating my research at the cultural village.

In Peninsular Malaysia, I am immensely grateful to Colin Nicholas and Koong Hui Yein from the Center for Orang Asli Concerns, and the pro-bono lawyers from the Malaysian Bar Council, especially Yogeswaran Subramaniam, K. Mohan, Steven Thiru, and Aaron Mathews, for sharing their insights on the Indigenous people in Malaysia. I am deeply indebted to Colin Nicholas and Yogeswaran Subramaniam for generously opening up their networks for my research and for acting as a sounding board for my ideas in the development of this work. I also thank Reita Rahim from Gerai Orang Asli, Wong Yun Yun from Nature Classroom, and Mohd Shahnaz Bin Yazid from the Department of Orang Asli Affairs for sharing their insights.

At the University of Malaya, I am grateful to Kamal Solhaimi Bin Fazal, who sponsored my research permit, Harold Thwaites, who hosted me at the Centre for Creative Content and Digital Innovation, as well as Ramy Bulan, Hanafi Bin Hussin, Rusaslina Binte Idrus, Danny Wong, and Dato Yahya Awang for sharing their knowledge and opening up their networks. I am grateful to Munirah Binte Abdul Manan from the Malaysian Economic Planning Unit for granting my research permit, and my language teacher, Punita Vathi Muniandy, who taught me to speak and write in Malay, and who helped with the translation of my consent forms from English to Malay language. My gratitude also goes to Geoffrey Benjamin, Fausto Barlocco,

Liana Chua, Danny Tan, Farouk Yahya, Karl Anderbeck, and Clare Chan for generously opening up networks and sharing their insights on the Indigenous communities in Malaysia.

At Kampung Sungai Bumbun in Peninsular Malaysia, I would like to thank Diana Uju and her husband Sharitaudin Bah Tuin, Julidah Uju and her husband Gali Adam, Maznah Unyan, Sazali Halim, Junaidah Karim, Reita Uju, Asnika Aibus, and many others, who kindly hosted me. At Kampung Sungai Temon, also in Peninsular Malaysia, I am grateful to Salim bin Palon, the Headman of Kampung Sungai Temon, and his family, especially Eddy bin Salim, Jefree bin Salim, Meeli binte Salim, and Maria Jampo, for hosting me at the Orang Seletar Cultural Centre and sharing many stories about their cultural heritage.

I am immensely grateful to my examiners, Christina Kreps and the late Claire Dwyer, for their insightful questions which gave me many ideas that led to the strengthening of this work, and their helpful advice on my career aspirations. I am deeply saddened by the demise of Claire Dwyer in 2019 and will remember her kindness and generosity when our paths crossed.

At the National University of Singapore, I thank Shirlena Huang and Johan Geertsema for their longstanding support and unwavering belief in my academic abilities. I am grateful to Hamzah Muizaini for his insights on this book manuscript.

At the University of Leicester, I am grateful to my colleagues for their guidance and support, which eased my transition into an academic career, and allowed me to juggle the different demands of the job. Special thanks go to Sandra Dudley, Simon Knell, Lisanne Gibson, Richard Sandell, and Sarina Wakefield for their advice on the development of this manuscript, as well as to Amy Barnes who superbly copyedited the whole manuscript.

I am grateful to the series editors, Paul Basu, Tim Winter, and Wayne Modest, for their insightful guidance, Heidi Lowther and Kangan Gupta, my editors at Routledge, as well as Assunta Petrone, my project manager, for their tireless guidance and support in bringing this book project to fruition. Most importantly, I would like to acknowledge the unwavering love and support of my family, especially my parents Chua Seo Peng and Pang Kwang Tian, and my dearest brother Cai Zhiqin. I would like to thank them for giving me their unreserved support to pursue my passion and interest, providing me with the resources to go as high as I can possibly reach, and encouraging me never to give up when the going gets tough.

Acknowledgement for the use of materials

Figures 3.4, 4.3, and 4.5 are reproduced here with the kind permission of Colin Nicholas from the Center of Orang Asli Concerns. Figure 6.7 is reproduced here with the kind permission of Judeth John Baptist from the Sabah State Museum. Figure 5.4 is reproduced here with the kind permission of

Noel Hidalgo Tan from the Southeast Asian Regional Centre for Archaeology and Fine Arts (SEAMEO SPAFA).

'Between Tradition and Modernity: The Ritual Politics of Indigenous Cultural Heritage in Urbanising Sabah, East Malaysia' by Cai Yunci first appeared in *Routledge Handbook of Urbanisation in Southeast Asia* edited by Rita Padawangi, pp. 179–190. This work is reproduced here with the kind permission of the publisher, Routledge, London and New York.

'Cleansing the Sacred Mountain in the Aftermath of the 2015 Mount Kinabalu Earthquake' by Cai Yunci and Judeth John Baptist first appeared in the *Journal of the Malaysian Branch of the Royal Asiatic Society*. Issue 89, Volume 310, pp. 61–78. This work is reproduced here with the kind permission of the publisher.

'Mohlukas: A Housewarming Ceremony at the Linangkit Cultural Village' by Cai Yunci first appeared in *Sabah Malaysian Borneo*, Issue 180, pp. 10–13. This work is reproduced here with the kind permission of the publisher, Sabah Tourism Board.

'Performing Cultures, Negotiating Identities: The Cultural Politics of Indigenous Cultural Villages in West Malaysia' by Cai Yunci first appeared in *Citizens, Civil Society and Heritage-making in Asia* edited by Hsin-Huang Michael Hsiao, Hui Yew-Foong, and Philippe Peycam, pp. 114–136. This work is reproduced here with the kind permission of the publisher, ISEAS – Yusof Ishak Institute, Singapore, http://bookshop.iseas.edu.sg.

Abbreviations

ACNA	Advisory Council for Native Affairs
AIPP	Asian Indigenous Peoples Pact
ASEAN	Association of Southeast Asian Nations
BERSIH	Coalition for Clean and Fair Elections
COAC	Center for Orang Asli Concerns
FPIC	Free, Prior and Informed Consent
GEF	Global Environment Facility
GIS	Geographic Information System
GPS	Global Positioning System
ICOM	International Council of Museums
IDEAL	Institute for the Development of Alternative Living
IDR	Iskandar Development Region
IDRA	Iskandar Development Region Agency
IPHRD	Indigenous Peoples Human Rights Defenders
JAKOA	Jabatan Kemajuan Orang Asli [Department of Orang Asli Development]
JHEOA	Jabatan Hal Ehwal Orang Asli [Department of Orang Asli Affairs]
JKKK	Jawatan Kuasa Kemajuan dan Keselamatan Kampung [Committee of Village Development and Security]
JKKN	Jabatan Kebudayaan dan Kesenian Negara [National Department for Culture and Arts]
JOAS	Jaringan Orang Asal SeMalaysia [Indigenous Peoples Network of Malaysia]
KDCA	Kadazandusun Cultural Association
KLF	Kadazandusun Language Foundation
KLOSA	Persatuan Komulakan Lotud Sabah [Lotud Youth Association]
MCP	Malayan Communist Party
MHDC	Malaysia Handicraft Development Corporation
MOTAC	Ministry of Tourism, Arts and Culture
MSMS	Malaysian Society of Marine Science
NEP	New Economic Policy

NGO	Non-Governmental Organisation
OECD	Organisation for Economic Co-operation and Development
OHCHR	Office of the United Nations High Commissioner for Human Rights
PACOS Trust	Partners of Community Organisations, Sabah (after Year 2003) / Projects for Awareness and Community Organisations in Sabah (before Year 2003)
PGDK	Panglima Gemilang Darjah Kinabalu [Commander of the Order of Kinabalu]
POASM	Peninsular Malaysia Orang Asli Association
PSB	Parti Bersatu Sabah [United Sabah Party]
RM	Malaysian Ringgit
SEAMEO-SPAFA	Southeast Asian Regional Centre for Archaeology and Fine Arts
SUHAKAM	Suruhanjaya Hak Asasi Manusia Malaysia [The Human Rights Commission of Malaysia]
UKM	Universiti Kebangsaan Malaysia [National University of Malaysia]
UNCSD	United Nations Conference on Sustainable Development
UNDRIP	United Nations Declaration on the Rights of Indigenous Peoples
UNESCO	United Nations Educational, Scientific and Cultural Organisation
UNPFII	United Nations Permanent Forum on Indigenous Issues
USDA	United Sabah Dusun Association
WGIP	Working Group of Indigenous Peoples

1 Introduction

Over the last three decades, the idea that culture can contribute to sustainable development has attracted significant global interest. Within this developmental discourse widely promoted by UNESCO, especially through its establishment of the World Commission on Culture and Development in 1993, culture is a fundamental component of sustainable development that serves both as a means and an end to human development (UNESCO 1995; UNCSD 2012). According to UNESCO's (2010a: 2) rhetoric, 'culture is a powerful contributor to economic development, social stability and environmental protection, [and] defines the way human beings live and interact both at local and global scales'. As cultural institutions, museums can 'contribute to the economy, social capital and the well-being of a local community [by] strengthening creativity, a sense of belonging and civic engagement' (OECD/ICOM 2018: 5).

Staging Indigenous Heritage offers a critique of the 'culture for development' discourse through an in-depth study of four Indigenous[1] cultural villages in Malaysia, namely the Mah Meri Cultural Village in Carey Island and the Orang Seletar Cultural Centre in Johor Bahru, both in Peninsular Malaysia; and the Monsopiad Cultural Village and the Linangkit Cultural Village, both in Sabah, East Malaysia (Figure 1.1). Here I conceptualise 'Indigenous cultural villages' as a form of Indigenous museum, and particularly, a hybrid variation of the open-air historical museum and the eco-museum, which appear to be preserving the 'living' traditions and customs of cultural groups by exhibiting collections of buildings and expressions of cultural heritage in an open-air setting. My central argument is that community-based cultural projects often come to be interwoven with the politics of brokerage and representation that cultivate and perpetuate a culture of dependency between the brokers managing these cultural villages and the local communities that these projects seek to support, leading to the marginalisation of these communities. These brokers can be understood as intermediaries who translate and mediate between different actors in diverse social, political, economic, and cultural systems to facilitate access to resources in different spheres (Simon 2009; Probojo 2010; Stovel and Shaw 2012; Lindquist 2015). It thus calls for reconsideration of how the wider discourses on 'culture for development' can be operationalised by UNESCO, international aid agencies, national governments, and museum

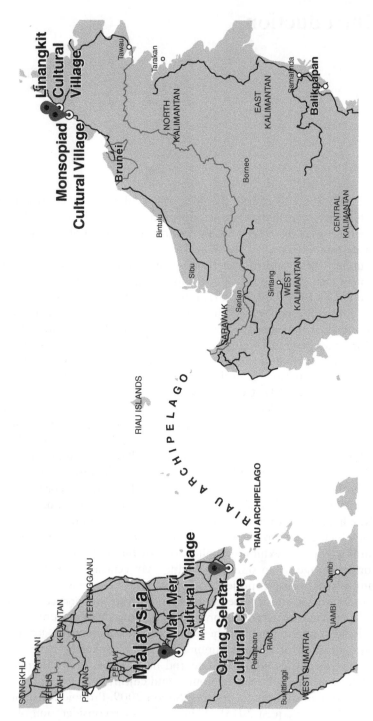

Figure 1.1 Location of case studies in Malaysia.

institutions, without reproducing the cultures of dependency that lead to the continued or further marginalisation of their intended beneficiaries.

Comparative case studies from both East and Peninsular Malaysia are selected, as I seek to consider the very different political contexts faced by Indigenous people in Malaysia. In Peninsular Malaysia, the Indigenous people, collectively known as the Orang Asli, constitute less than 0.6 per cent of the local population based on the 2010 census (Leonie et al. 2015), and face severe marginalisation and strong pressures to convert to Islam and assimilate into mainstream Malay-Muslim Malaysian society. By comparison, Indigenous people in East Malaysia constitute about 65.5 per cent of the local population based on the 2010 census (Leonie et al. 2015). As a majority, the Indigenous people in East Malaysia enjoy relative political autonomy from the Federal Government and hold significant political influence within the state, as compared to their counterparts in Peninsular Malaysia. In addition, the Indigenous people of East and Peninsular Malaysia are subjected to different transnational imaginaries. While the Indigenous people in East Malaysia are stereotyped in early Western travel literature as the 'fearless head-hunters of Borneo', known for carrying out cannibalism (Bock 1881; Furness 1902; Krohn 1927; Wyn 1974), the Indigenous people in Peninsular Malaysia are faced with enslavement by the Malays and the Bataks in the region (Dentan et al. 1997).

Grounded in critical museology, this book contributes to the growing body of literature aimed at decolonising Eurocentric perspectives on museology by exploring a museological phenomenon in Southeast Asia, an under-researched geographical region in the field of museum studies. The 'critical museology' movement emerged in the 1980s, borne out of a period of intensive reflection and self-critique about the hegemonic discourse and practice of museology. There is growing recognition that museums are not merely passive storehouses of objects but are actively embroiled in the production of certain knowledge structures, and intricately bounded by the historical, political, social, and cultural politics of the wider society in which they are embedded. As a broad term, critical museology encompasses a boundless plethora of diverse strands of rethinking about the epistemological positions and the methodological intersections of museum discourse and practice (Shelton 2013). This movement has led to a number of interventions in the conceptualisation and understanding of museum objects, meanings, curation, discourses, politics, processes, and audiences (Lumley 1988; Vergo 1989; MacDonald and Fyfe 1996; Luke 2002; Macdonald 2006a; Dewdney et al. 2013; Marstine 2016; Hohenstein and Moussouri 2018).

A prominent development of 'critical museology' is an emerging interest in the representational critique of museums: how inequalities of class, ethnicity, and gender are reproduced through and by museums. Museums have been called upon to reconsider their relationships with their diverse communities and to engage with source communities. This is especially true for ethnographic museums whose colonial narratives are increasingly out-of-step with post-colonial politics of representation. This interest in identity politics has given rise to a rich body of museological writing (Karp et al. 1992; Kaplan

1994; Witcomb 2003; Lonetree 2012; Golding and Modest 2015; Onciul 2015). Whilst museums have made attempts to engender more equal partnerships with the objects that are sourced, the nature of engagement between museums and their communities remains fraught with challenges due to issues relating to power relations – over identity and representation – and contestations arising from politics of inclusion and exclusion (Peers and Brown 2003; Watson 2007; Crooke 2008; Golding and Modest 2015). This book seeks to address the identity politics concerning an Indigenous museological form in Southeast Asia, a region which has undergone decolonisation from their European colonial rulers since the 1960s and 1970s.

This book responds to the calls for the decolonisation of museums by conceptualising and advocating forms of non-Western and Indigenous museology. It seeks to 'decolonise' Eurocentric perspectives on museology and promote mutual respect for non-Western cultures and museum practices based on an ethos of cultural relativism. Christina Kreps, in her 2003 seminal work *Liberating Cultures*, proposes that the hegemony of a Eurocentric museology conceals different approaches to museology and undermines the abilities and capabilities of local communities to exercise management and control over their own cultural heritage. Drawing on non-Western models of museums and curatorial practices in Indonesia and North America, Kreps (2003) calls for a liberation of thinking away from Eurocentric notions of what constitutes museums and their practice to recognise other museological manifestations.

Since then, there has been a growing interest on non-Western museum models and Indigenous curatorial practices aimed at reclaiming native heritage and museologies. In the settler-colonial contexts of United States, Canada, Australia, and New Zealand, museums are beginning to collaborate with Indigenous communities to integrate their perspectives on museum narratives and practices in collection preservation and management (Hendry 2002, 2005; McCarthy 2007; Peers 2007; Stanley 2007; Sleeper-Smith 2009; Lonetree 2012; Onciul 2015). There is also growing recognition that Indigenous people have agency over the brokering of access to their cultural objects and knowledge, and are actively mobilising this access to negotiate their place and position within the museum (Thomas 1991; Welsch 2000; McCarthy 2007; Torrence and Clarke 2011, 2016).

Elsewhere in the Pacific, a number of scholars have observed the emergence of Indigenous museums grounded in local museological forms and practices (Mead 1983; Eoe and Swadling 1991; Simpson 1996; Stanley 2007). Much of these works paint a highly positive rhetoric on Indigenous museums that resonates with the 'culture for development' discourse. For example, in his edited book on *The Future of Indigenous Museums*, Nick Stanley (2007) envisages that Indigenous museums can help Indigenous people cope with the rapidly changing world, and argues that an Indigenous museum needs to have agency over the management of Indigenous cultural heritage and the support of the Indigenous people it represents. Drawing on Indigenous museums in the Southwest Pacific as exemplars of culturally appropriate, community-based approaches to socio-economic development, Stanley (2007: 16) suggests that the concept of 'Indigenous museums' remains a meaningful and significant subject of enquiry 'as long as the term "Indigenous" itself continues to represent a source of authority and power'.

While there has been a greater recognition of alternative, Indigenous models of museums and curatorial practices in the 'developing' worlds of Asia, Africa, and Pacific, scant attention has been paid to Indigenous museums outside the Pacific.[2] This book adds to the extant literature on Indigenous museums, particularly from a Southeast Asian perspective, where settler colonialism takes shape in the context of a lack of first contact narratives, and intersects with majority settlers' post-colonial nation-building projects. Set within Malaysia's highly heterogeneous ethnic, linguistic, and religious context, this research can shed light on how Indigenous museology and the 'culture for development' discourse play out amidst the complex politics between different ethnic groups, as the post-colonial state reconfigures its relationship with its Indigenous minorities, which has relevance for the wider 'developing' world, especially in Asia or in countries that have undergone decolonisation from the European colonial powers since the 1960s and 1970s.

My observation of the Indigenous cultural villages in Malaysia complicates Stanley's (2007) positive rhetoric of Indigenous museums in the Southwest Pacific. I suggest that Indigenous museums may be better understood as sites of negotiation and contestation, where complex dynamics concerning representation, identity, self-determination, and resource access are played out among different stakeholders with different objectives and agendas, producing variegated outcomes for the Indigenous people that the museums purport to represent. It is the brokers who control and manipulate these museums that benefit economically and socially from them, rendering the Indigenous people to a subordinate position through perpetuating a culture of dependency. Indigenous museums thus become sites of contestation and negotiation where incompatible motivations and interests, as well as unequal power dynamics, are played out among the different stakeholders who seek to advance their own agendas and objectives.

The Indigenous communities of Malaysia also do not constitute homogeneous and unified wholes; rather, they constitute Indigenous individuals with different agendas and allegiances, which may or may not align with one another. The notion of 'community' as an organic 'wholeness' with clear boundaries has been widely critiqued (Bauman 1996; Dwyer 1999; Amit and Rapport 2002; Crooke 2008; Golding and Modest 2015). On the relationship between Indigenous museums and their communities, Stanley (2007: 9) acknowledges that the idea of a 'settled and unambiguous community' with a clear position on the management of their Indigenous cultural heritage is flawed, as the notion of 'Indigenous culture' is a social and ideological construct that is open to manipulation by powerful actors (Linnekin 1992). As Amit and Rapport (2002) put it, what is deemed the collective community is made up of different groups of social networks that cut across different situations, categories, and allegiances, each existing in its own right and operating in a distinctive manner.

Scholars have attempted to reconceptualise previous imaginations of community to forge a sense of it across differences rather than to deny or subsume them (Massey 1994; Hall 1996; Dwyer 1999). This may involve reconstituting 'new ethnicities' based on the recognition of differences (Hall 1996), or reimagining localised, place-based communities as having linkages with globalised webs of connections to forge a 'global sense of place' (Massey 1994). Dwyer (1999) argues that the notion of 'ethnic communities' or 'cultural communities' may be better conceptualised as 'imagined communities' (Anderson 1991), where a strong shared imaginary transcends differences and produces a sense of collective identity, possibly forged through contestation and negotiation among different stakeholders. The notion of community is thus a 'collectivity which is actively struggled over rather than passively received' (Dwyer 1999: 54). This book seeks to understand how the concept of 'Indigenous community' is constructed and imagined historically, and how it continues to be actively forged, struggled over, and negotiated in contemporary Malaysia.

Rethinking culture and brokerage in developmental studies

Situated at the nexus of developmental studies and museum anthropology, my case studies of the four Indigenous cultural villages in Malaysia explore how Indigenous museums and the notion of 'culture for development', widely promoted by UNESCO, often lead to the marginalisation of the intended beneficiary communities, due to the politics of brokerage and representation that cultivate and perpetuate a culture of dependency. Importantly, it demonstrates that the decentralisation of developmental aid provision through brokers such as intermediary agencies and entrepreneurs, a trend popular in the current neoliberalist age, is futile in addressing the developmental needs of the intended beneficiaries.

The notion that culture can contribute to sustainable development stems from the rise of global tourism, which brings to the fore tensions between cultural heritage and tourism (Labadi and Gould 2015). Community-based approaches to tourism, including Indigenous cultural tourism, are perceived as a more socially and culturally sustainable form of tourism development that can neutralise conflicts between cultural heritage and tourism and minimise the disruption caused by tourism to local communities and their cultural heritage (Pearce 1992; Sofield 1993; Low 2003; Landorf 2009; Weaver 2010; Labadi 2013). Nonetheless, there are criticisms that community-based cultural tourism is undermining the existing social structures and well-being of local communities by cynically rationalising a consumerism advanced by national governments and big corporations (Mowforth and Munt 2009; Salazar 2009, 2012).

The relationship between culture and development has been perceived as a 'paired opposite', with culture being framed as a barrier to development (Crewe and Harrison 1998; Yarrow 2008; Basu and Modest 2015), with some attributing the failure of countries to achieve development breakthroughs to cultural factors (Harrison and Huntington 2000). UNESCO's rhetoric on 'culture for development' highlights the incongruence between universal cultural rights, grounded in universal standards of human behaviour, and relative rights based on different standards imposed by individual cultural groups (Niezen 2003). Relatedly, the positive rhetoric of Indigenous museums as exemplars of non-Western museology downplays a fundamental conflict between the idea of open access purported by Western museology under the banner of inclusivity and that of selective access to sacred or secret materials prescribed by Indigenous belief systems (Stanley 2007).

Within the anthropology of development, there has been much discussion about the notion of 'development' as a Eurocentric construct promoting an evolutionary model of progress based on the Western historical experience (Basu and Modest 2015). Post-development theorists such as Ferguson (1994), Escobar (1995), and Rahnema and Bawtree (1997) have argued that 'development' is a discourse that perpetuates power disparities and social inequalities between the industrialised global North and the impoverished South. Specifically, they argue that the rhetoric adopted by international development agencies such as the World Bank frames the developing South as backward, underdeveloped, and in need of intervention, which perpetuates the power structures that underpin existing global inequalities.

Drawing on his study of the World Bank-sponsored Thaba-Tseka project in Lesotho, Ferguson (1994) argues that the 'development' apparatus is established not to eliminate poverty, but to deliberately reinforce and expand the exercise of bureaucratic state power. This 'development' apparatus discursively constructs Lesotho as a poor, isolated, and impoverished peasant society to justify development intervention by international institutions based on standardised 'blueprints' that are often ill-suited to the needs of its recipients (Ferguson 1994). Based on his study of externally sponsored developmental projects in Latin America in the 1970s and 1980s, Escobar (1995) argues that 'development' is discursively constructed through a corpus of rational techniques and institutional practices that organise forms of knowledge and the exercise of power to promote an oversimplified myth of the underdeveloped Third World that perpetuates the dominance of the First World. In this regard, Escobar (1995: 62) suggests that the economic models and rhetoric for development ought to be read as a cultural discourse: a 'construction of the world and not [unquestionably accepted as] an indisputable, objective truth'.

The discursive construction of 'development' as critiqued by Ferguson (1994) and Escobar (1995) finds its parallel in the universal UNESCO discourse that promotes the rhetoric of culture for development. As with the discussion on the discursive notion of 'development', there have been calls to critically interrogate this narrative, in order to uncover its inherent agendas and implications. There is also a growing recognition of a need for more nuanced analyses of the impact of culture on development practices and encounters (Altbach and Hassen 1996; Crewe and Harrison 1998; Schech and Haggis 2000; Radcliffe 2006; Basu and Modest 2015; Labadi 2019).

Engaging with these debates, Basu and Modest (2015: 26, original emphasis) suggest that 'the true power of culture as *a force acting in relation to development* has yet to be fully explored and understood'. They argue that there is a need to 'look beyond both the economic and instrumental value of cultural heritage *for* development, and to explore its intrinsic value in reimagining development *as* a cultural project, and particularly as a culturally context-specific project' (Basu and Modest 2015: 26, original emphasis).

The need to address the culturally specific contexts of cross-cultural collaborations is underscored by Kreps (2008: 27), who suggests that

> the outright transfer of Western models of development to so-called developing areas, including the transfer of technology and scientific know-how … [has] worked to undermine other cultures' technologies, knowledge systems, and institutions, as well as their value and sense of identity.

In the realm of political ecology, prototype solutions to environmental problems are often ill-suited to local contexts, and work to restrict local practices and undermine Indigenous knowledge (Jones 2008). In overcoming these culture-oriented issues, Kreps (2008: 26) extends the concept of 'appropriate technology' to museums: 'an approach to museum development and training that adapts museum practices and strategies for cultural heritage preservation to local cultural contexts and socioeconomic conditions'. She sees appropriate technology as a bottom-up, community-based, participatory approach that can provide a means of empowerment for local people by valuing their existing skills and knowledges, thereby contributing to a more sustainable form of development (Kreps 2008). This book engages with these ideas within the context of Indigenous cultural villages in Malaysia.

My research also expands on the literature on brokerage in developmental work by critically examining the roles that brokers play in bridging differences between the various stakeholders in Indigenous activism and cultural preservation. Heritage brokers seem to take centre-stage in the complex interplays of power relations among the different stakeholders at the Indigenous cultural villages. Rather than translating and mediating between different worlds for the benefit of the Indigenous people, these brokers often strategically mobilise UNESCO's 'culture for development' rhetoric and the discourses on community-based Indigenous museums for their personal agendas and self-interests. The process of brokerage can be broadly defined as 'the process of connecting actors in systems of social, economic, or political relations in order to facilitate access to valued resources' (Stovel and Shaw 2012: 141). Kurin's (1997: 19) seminal book, *Reflections of a Culture Broker*, explores how the Smithsonian Institution engages in brokering culture by studying, understanding, and representing other cultures through its museum exhibitions and programmes. He recognises that the resultant representations 'are to some degree negotiated, dialogical, and driven by a variety of interests on behalf of the involved parties'.

Brokers play a key role in the instrumentalisation of culture, heritage, and tradition by bridging gaps in social structures through facilitating the flow of information, goods, and knowledge (Stovel and Shaw 2012). As intermediaries, mediators, interpreters, or translators, their role involves the selection and interpretation of a message that is 'calculatingly engineered, carefully fabricated' (Peace 1998: 279) for a particular clientele. They are active agents, involved in translating and mediating between different worlds, often exploiting opportunities to make gains from the mediation of valuable resources over which they do not have direct control (Simon 2009; Probojo 2010; Lindquist 2015). Brokers not only facilitate communication and transactions by interpreting diplomatic, political, religious, and social concepts across cultures, they can also cross from their own cultural realm to another, thus becoming symbols in their own right by taking on meanings ascribed by members of another cultural realm (Hinderaker 1996; Deloria 1998; Hinderaker 2002).

There is a dual dimension to brokerage: a broker may strengthen group solidarity, ease social interaction, encourage trade activities, and promote development by mediating across different worlds or take advantage of conflicts and tensions between different groups, exploiting such dynamics and thereby making worse existing inequalities (Stovel and Shaw 2012). The brokerage process is thus not homogeneous, but can take different forms, depending on the configuration of information flow and the relational closeness between actors, which, in turn, has an impact on the direction, effectiveness outcome of the brokerage (Gould and Fernandez 1989; Hinderaker 2002; Stovel and Shaw 2012). Brokers are often caught in an uncomfortable position, having to manage different and sometimes conflicting roles. While they need to establish the trust of their clients by proving their integrity and credibility, they are also compromised by their own agendas, allegiances, and dependencies (Szasz 2001; Merrell 1997; Hinderaker 2002).

Despite the critical roles that these broker figures play in determining the outcomes of these community-based cultural projects, including how they are instrumentalised in relation to UNESCO's 'culture for development' rhetoric, the concept of brokerage is rarely discussed in museological and heritage studies literature. Much of the current discussion on brokerage is taking place within the domain of developmental anthropology (Feldman-Bianco 1999; Szasz 2001; Baud and Rutten 2004; Gershon 2006; Lewis and Mosse 2006; Stahler-Sholk 2007; Simon 2009; Urteaga-Crovetto 2012) and tourism studies (Adams 1984; Smith 1989; Koh and Hatten 2002; Glass 2006; Macdonald 2006b; Salazar 2007; Brulotte 2012; Fonneland 2013; Yang et al. 2014; Osorio and Best 2015). This book seeks to address this lacunae by focusing on the roles of brokers in the mediation and translation of cultural heritage in such community-based projects, as well as the impacts of their brokerage on the cultural heritage, identity, and empowerment of local people, based on a comparative study of four Indigenous cultural villages in Malaysia.

Situating critical museology within the Indigenous discourse

This book seeks to situate critical museology and heritage studies within the Indigenous discourse by examining the phenomenon of Indigenous museums in the context of Indigenous self-determination and the transnational Indigenous rights movement. The current widespread positive perceptions associated with Indigeneity, and the equally positive rhetoric about Indigenous museums, can be traced to the rise of the international Indigenous rights movement in the 1980s and 1990s. The movement reached its zenith in the mid-1990s, when the United Nations declared the decade from 1994 to 2003 as the International Decade for the World's Indigenous People (Kingsbury 1998; Niezen 2003). The movement, which garners much support among activists and academics alike, has its roots in the historicity of colonial politics, racial discrimination, and material dispossession, and motivates Indigenous people to come together to articulate and forge a collective identity and common purpose based on their historical marginalisation (Rata 2002; Karlsson 2003; Hodgson 2009; Zenker 2011). Its later internationalisation can be attributed to the prevailing neoliberalist political climate, which has created the conditions for a range of marginalised and disadvantaged actors to reach out to supra-national organisations in order to politicise their struggles by essentialising the representation of Indigenous people and making claims based on social justice (de Costa 2006; Hale 2006; Merlan 2009; McCormack 2011).

Niezen (2003: 40–42) has outlined four conditions responsible for the rise of international Indigenisms in the late twentieth century: first, the struggle against fascism increased the receptiveness of international authorities with respect to the protection of minorities; second, the decolonisation process brought greater awareness of the cultural suppression of minorities caused by European colonialism, which provided a climate of liberation for the pursuit of self-determination among Indigenous people; third, the failure of assimilation and integration policies contributed to the growth of intertribal identity and greater political unity among educated Indigenous elites in the fight against institutionalised marginalisation; and finally, the growth of NGOs promoting international Indigenous activism provided a catalyst for the worldwide movement. The rise of the transnational Indigenous movement also led to the global circulation of ideas and practices of human rights through policy documents, legal precedents, and the work of activists (Merry 2006).

The term 'Indigeneity' is a social and ideological construct that is constantly being contested and negotiated by different stakeholders. As such, it carries different connotations at different points in time, depending on prevailing social and cultural circumstances. The most widely cited working definition of Indigeneity comes from the Office of the United Nations High Commissioner for Human Rights (OHCHR 2013: 6), which states that:

> Indigenous communities, peoples and nations are those which, having a historical continuity with pre-invasion and pre-colonial societies that

developed on their territories, consider themselves distinct from other sectors of the societies now prevailing on those territories, or parts of them. They form at present non-dominant sectors of society and are determined to preserve, develop and transmit to future generations their ancestral territories, and their ethnic identity, as the basis of their continued existence as peoples, in accordance with their own cultural patterns, social institutions and legal system.

This definition, however, has not been officially adopted, as Indigenous participants of the Working Group of Indigenous Peoples (WGIP) under the OHCHR have insisted on an unrestricted self-identification policy (Corntassel 2003). The term 'Indigenous communities, peoples and nations' has come to replace earlier iterations such as 'tribal people', 'semi-tribal people', 'tribes', 'aboriginals', *'sakai'*, 'wild men', 'noble savages', 'primitives', and 'natives', most of which carry negative connotations of backwardness, underdevelopment, and uncivility. Today, the term has 'become a marker of global identity, associated with mainly positive ideas about cultural wisdom and integrity and with politically significant claims to self-determination' (Niezen 2003: 217). Nonetheless, defining the concept of Indigeneity remains fraught with challenges, because 'any definition of Indigenous peoples runs the risk of being incomplete historically, culturally, politically and economically while reifying native peoples in a "continued subordination of differences to identity"' (Corntassel 2003: 90).

Key debates surrounding discourses of Indigeneity were provoked by a controversial 2003 article by Adam Kuper, in the journal *Cultural Anthropology*, entitled 'The Return of the Native', in which Kuper criticises the concept of Indigeneity as being essentialist on three accounts: first, contemporary anthropological and archaeological knowledge has negated the long-held view that Indigenous people are primitive and therefore deserve a right to resources by their status as primitive people; second, the Nuremberg principle of descent is applied even though culture is now conceptualised as dynamic and fluid; and third, it creates fissures in liberal-democratic states by evoking individual rights of citizens. Kuper's article sparked much discussion within anthropological circles, with some anthropologists seeing it as a welcome contribution in addressing the incongruence between the Indigenous rights doctrine and contemporary anthropological thinking (Omura 2003; Suzman 2003), while others argued that such an approach masked the historical factors that gave rise to the Indigenous rights movement, and did not give sufficient credit to the agency of Indigenous activism (Ramos 2003; Robins 2003; Asch and Samson 2004; Heinen 2004; Kenrick and Lewis 2004a, b; Saugestad 2004; Turner 2004). Commenting on this debate, Barnard (2006: 7) suggests that whilst Indigeneity 'is an ideological and social construct recognised by those who claim the status, by anthropologists who support their cause and no doubt by the educated public at large', there is nonetheless consensus in international discourses to recognise a polythetic definition of Indigeneity based on four criteria:

'first-come, non-dominance, cultural difference, and self-ascription' (Saugestad 2001: 43), so that it can be mobilised as a 'useful tool for political persuasion' (Barnard 2006: 7).

Kuper's article and the ensuing debates surrounding the politics of Indigeneity constitute the emerging field of 'critical Indigeneity', which calls for attention to be given to the embodiments, positionalities, and subjectivities of Indigeneity within the broader power dynamics of colonial histories, nationalistic formations, capital expansion, and Indigenous resistance (Perley 2014; Radcliffe 2017, 2018). Indigeneity, like cartography, serves to represent the outcomes of certain historical and geographical processes as they are, naturalising the unequal power relations on Indigenous subjects from the colonial experience through an essentialist focus on the connection between place and autochthonism (Bryan 2009; Radcliffe 2017). There is an emerging call under the rubric of 'critical Indigeneity' to think about Indigeneity as a selective articulation, and how Indigeneity is being actively constructed and produced in relation to non-Indigenous subjects, institutions, and ontologies, giving attention to the forms that power interplays take, under the prevailing economic, political, and social circumstances (Radcliffe 2017).

Drawing upon Massey's (1994) re-imagination of a 'global sense of place', there has been a reformulation of Indigeneity as a concept that is simultaneously grounded in roots and locality, as well as subjected to modernisation and globalisation. Processes of globalisation in the 1980s and 1990s have led to the formation of a transnational solidarity and an international Indigenous rights discourse extending beyond nation-states and embodying a cosmopolitan outlook (Merlan 2009; Blaser et al. 2010; Forte 2010) This contradicts the dominant notion of Indigeneity as meaning 'racially unmixed, culturally undiluted, geographically remote, and materially impoverished' (Forte 2010: 1). In this vein, the Indigenous people of Africa, Latin America, and Southeast Asia have been able to draw upon international networks of Indigenisms to engage in a complex politics of alliance and competition, though not without challenges, to advance their economic and political agendas (Jung 2003; Kirsch 2007; Schiller 2007; Zips and Zips-Mairitsch 2007; Hodgson 2009; Bertrand 2011; Lynch 2011).

In the articulation of Indigeneity, history has been selectively remembered and heritage has been refashioned to respond to changing political contexts and the forces of globalisation (Clifford 2001; Mason 2010; Clifford 2013). As an articulation, Indigeneity is open to instrumentalisation by 'the *diversity* of cultures and histories that currently make claims under this banner' (Clifford 2013: 54, original emphasis). Heritage has been used to mobilise spatial and temporal orders to construct and legitimise Indigenous identities and social order for communal activism (Clifford 2001; Mason 2010; Clifford 2013; Bennett et al. 2017). This has led to what Panelli (2008) terms as a worldwide 'Indigenous cultural renaissance'. Yet, the strategic essentialism of Indigeneity based on a pre-contact notion of authenticity and produced through material expressions of Indigenous cultural heritage can often confine Indigenous politics, as it not only forecloses opportunities for Indigenous people to connect their pasts with their presents (Mandelman 2014) but also enmeshes them in 'intractable double binds [from] an assumed contradiction between material wealth and cultural authenticity' (Clifford 2013: 17).

As a liberal government technology, Indigenous culture also imposes certain limitations on economic, political, and social development, as settler colonialism is predicated upon the 'governance of the prior', where the settler governing logic still prevails against that of the 'prior' subjects (Povinelli 2011; Bennett et al. 2017). Moving away from these double binds, Native American scholars and academics have attempted to draw on the concept of 'survivance' (Vizenor 1999) to express the continuity of the past with the present and emphasise the living vibrancy of Indigenous culture in contemporary societies. As Vizenor (1999: vii) notes, 'survivance is an active sense of presence, the continuance of native stories, not a mere reaction, or a survivable name'. From the survivance point of view, Indigenous culture should be actively refashioned for the present, and not passively inherited for subsistence (Vizenor 1999, 2007).

A critical approach to heritage instrumentalisation

I seek to develop a critical perspective on the concept of the instrumentalisation of cultural heritage, by investigating how cultural heritage is produced and interwoven with the power relations that reify it, as well as the political, economic, social, and cultural implications of this instrumentalisation (Baird 2013; Winter 2013). In so doing, I seek to fill a lacuna in the literature relating to the instrumentalisation of culture, which has so far focused on the instrumental value of culture for social and economic objectives, as well as the mobilisation of cultural differences to achieve instrumentalisation. To illuminate the complex social, political, and economic power dynamics surrounding the heritage-making process, I draw on the politics of heritage instrumentalisation as a conceptual framework, extending it to incorporate other processes relating to brokerage, staging, and representation.

Since the 1970s, there has been a gradual shift towards a constructivist perspective on culture, in which it is perceived as a social construction, actively produced, maintained, and mediated by different agencies. Wagner's (1981) seminal work *The Invention of Culture* questions the ontology of culture, proposing that it is an invention and constructed through the objectification of other cultures by anthropologists, mainly to add to a body of knowledge called 'anthropological literature'. Wagner (1981) argues that the body of anthropological literature, which is discursively produced using the anthropologists' own languages and terminologies, is a kind of invention and constitutes a form of culture. In another work, *The Invention of Tradition*, Hobsbawm and Ranger (1983: 1) suggest that many traditions and rituals that are believed to have existed for centuries are 'actually invented, constructed and formally instituted [through] repetition, which automatically implies continuity with the past'.

The shift towards a constructivist perspective on culture and tradition coincides with a period of burgeoning public funding for cultural development, especially in Europe. This was in recognition of the wider economic, political, social, and urban impacts of culture (Gibson and Pendlebury 2009; Calligaro 2013). Since the 1980s, cultural strategies, especially cultural institutions, have gradually been incorporated into urban-economic regeneration plans aimed at rejuvenating cities' post-industrial decline (Zukin 1988, 1995; Vaughan and Booth 1989; Bianchini 1991; Wynne 1992; Bassett 1993; Bianchini and Parkinson, 1993; Hudson 1995; Graham et al. 2000; Hall and Robertson 2001; Heibrum and Gray 2001). Culture came to be enlisted as a tool for government policy, strategically instrumentalised by government agencies to fulfil government policies and objectives (Holden 2004; Gray 2007; Gibson and Pendlebury 2009; Calligaro 2013).

The instrumental value of culture, which Holden (2006: 16) considers to be 'the ancillary effects of culture, where culture is used to achieve a social or economic purpose', has been well-documented in research looking into the impact of arts and culture on people and society (Holden 2004, 2006; Carnwath and Brown 2014; Crossick and Kaszynska 2016). The instrumental value of culture – as a means to achieve economic or social ends – is often perceived as a 'paired opposite' to the intrinsic value of culture, where it is valued for its own sake as an end in itself (Weber 1978; Holden 2004, 2006; Bunting 2008). That said, there is increasing recognition that both the instrumental and intrinsic values of culture are integrally intertwined (McCarthy et al. 2004; Coles 2008; Knell and Taylor 2011).

The instrumentality of culture is expounded by Appadurai (1996: 14), who states that

> the idea of culture as involving the naturalised organisation of certain differences in the interests of group identity, through and in the historical process, and through and in the tensions between agents and structures, comes closer to what has been called the instrumental conception of ethnicity, as opposed to the primordial one.

Indigenous movements, whether local, national, or transnational, can be considered to be culturalist movements, which, Appadurai (1996: 15) suggests, involve the 'deliberate, strategic, and populist mobilisation of cultural material that justifies calling such movements culturalist, though they may vary in many ways'. In other words, culture can be mobilised through the construction and rectification of cultural differences, which are, in turn, 'fabricated with an eye politic to the present situation' (Sahlins 1999: 402) based on the needs and interests of the local circumstances. As Sahlins (1999: 403) puts it, 'what is called culture or tradition is strategically adaptable to the pragmatic situation ... an ideological smokescreen of more fundamental interests, principally power and greed'.

Expressing similar sentiments, Mitchell (1995: 102) declares that 'there's no such thing as culture', proposing a re-conceptualisation of culture in the discipline of geography: to conceive of 'the idea of culture as a means of ordering and defining the world' (Mitchell 1995: 112). A possible agenda for this, Mitchell (1995: 113) suggests, is to understand 'how powerful groups have historically operationalised the notion of culture'. He proposes a series of questions one can ask to uncover the intricate of culture:

> We can begin to ask the important questions: who reifies? In whose interest is the idea of culture deployed? What relations of power are maintained by invoking this idea? How does the idea of culture become operationalised and made real through the ability of social actors to halt its infinite regress externally? In short, I suggest that we can begin to see purposefulness and intentionality behind the deployment of ideas that seem so common-sensical.
>
> (Mitchell 1995: 110)

While culture is the composite form of knowledge and a way of life that is socially constructed and acquired by its cultural groups through their everyday lived experiences, heritage is a legacy of the past that is inherited from previous generations (Graham et al. 2000). The manifestations of culture, in the form of cultural practices and beliefs, are transformed into heritage by inheritance, where a legacy of the past is handed down from the past to the present. Heritage is 'culturally ascribed' (Harrison 2010: 26), rather than being inherent and intrinsic. It is a value-laden, loaded, and ambiguous concept, broadly defined as a perception of the past in the present, shaped by power relations and embroiled in questions of who it belongs to, who has the right to represent it, and for whom it is represented (Lowenthal 1998; Hall 1999; Graham et al. 2000; Harrison 2013).

An official representation of heritage is often promoted, privileged, and normalised by the state and other establishments of power, in the form of an authorised (or authorising) heritage discourse, that contests and marginalises alternative perspectives of heritage. This can lead to heritage dissonance (Tunbridge and Ashworth 1996; Smith 2006; Harrison 2010). Heritage can thus be viewed as a kind of persuasion or rhetoric that has been 'mobilised creatively within a wide array of social, political, economic, and moral contexts where it gives persuasive force to particular standpoints, perspectives, and claims' (Samuels 2015: 4). Heritage provides a catalyst for changes and actions. As Hafstein (quoted in Samuels 2015: 6–7) argues, 'the major use of heritage is to mobilise people and resources, to reform discourses, and to transform practices ... Don't be fooled by the talk of preservation: all heritage is change'.

Tradition, like heritage, is a representation of the customary past, which is handed down from one generation to another (Linnekin 1992). It is a symbolic construction, comprising 'a selective representation of the past, fashioned in the present, responsive to contemporary priorities and agendas, and politically instrumental' (Linnekin 1992: 251). What is deemed tradition is therefore shaped by complex power dynamics among the different stakeholders over who the tradition belongs to, who has the power to define it, and for whom is it being defined, rather than 'a passively and unreflectively uninherited legacy' (Linnekin 1992: 251). As Linnekin (1983: 241) puts it, 'the selection of what constitutes tradition is always made in the present; the content of the past is modified and redefined according to a modern significance'. As ideological and social constructs, the concepts of 'culture', 'heritage', and 'tradition' are fluid, nebulous, and ambiguous, rendering them susceptible to instrumentalisation, manipulation, and mobilisation by different stakeholders to serve different interests and agendas.

Staging Indigenous heritage in Malaysia

While the prevailing literature has painted a largely positive rhetoric about the 'culture for development' discourse and the roles of Indigenous museums, the situation in Malaysia is more ambiguous and complex. The predominant rhetoric of international agencies such as UNESCO and much of the museological literature has paid inadequate attention to the complex motivations and uneven power relations evident in these museums. My observations at the four Indigenous cultural villages reveal that Indigenous people in Malaysia do not have full agency over how their cultural heritage[3] is represented or how it is employed to serve contemporary agendas that they themselves determine. Neither do the Indigenous people whose cultural heritage is represented at the different Indigenous cultural villages constitute a homogeneous community; rather, they are made up of social networks that cut across different situations, categories, and allegiances that complicate the workings of these cultural villages (Amit and Rapport 2002).[4] As much as UNESCO's rhetoric has emphasised the positive values of culture in promoting economic development and social cohesion, it is often broker figures who benefit financially and sometimes socially from the cultural villages, more so than the Indigenous people that these cultural villages purport to represent. These brokers, who may or may not be ethnic outsiders, do so by controlling and manipulating the operation of these sites, as well as interactions between the Indigenous people and other stakeholders of the cultural villages.

For example, at the Mah Meri Cultural Village on Carey Island, which exhibits Mah Meri cultural practices, there is a tense relationship between the non-Indigenous, ethnic Malay manager who is responsible for the cultural village and the local Mah Meri villagers whose cultural heritage is being represented. At its establishment in 2011, which was funded by the Malaysian Ministry of Tourism, Arts and Culture (MOTAC), it was intended that the manager would oversee the cultural village for a period of three years, after which it would be handed over to the local Mah Meri villagers to be run as a community-owned project. During the initial three years, the manager was expected to train the villagers to prepare them to manage the cultural village on their own. However, the handover did not happen, and the cultural village remains under the control of the manager up until 2020. The villagers feel sidelined by the manager, as they are not given the authority to run the operation and to represent their own cultural heritage in their own cultural village. While the manager appears to draw a decent income from the operation of the Mah Meri Cultural Village, most of the Mah Meri villagers employed at the site are casual workers and are allocated work and paid only when their labour is needed. The Mah Meri Cultural Village also cultivates a culture of dependency between the manager and the Indigenous Mah Meri people, based on a form of 'patron-client' relationship that existed historically, propagating the existing inequalities rather than alleviating local poverty. What is promoted as community-based capacity-building for the Indigenous people at the Mah Meri Cultural Village appear to resonate with the colonial civilising mission of the twentieth century, rooted in the historic 'patron-client' relationship that conceptualises Indigenous people as backward, uncivilised and inferior, relative to other non-Indigenous groups, and therefore, in need of external assistance to achieve a higher rung on the evolutionary hierarchy.

The Orang Seletar Cultural Centre, which presents the cultural heritage of the Orang Seletar people, is situated in the Indigenous village of Kampung Sungai Temon at Johor Bahru. Both the cultural centre and the village as a whole are under threat of eviction, as the villagers do not possess the legal land titles to the village. Established in 2011 by an external ethnic Chinese broker with funding from an international NGO, the cultural centre was handed over to the local Orang Seletar villagers after its completion and is now managed by the Village Headman's second son with participation from local villagers. Through the brokerage of the owner of an eco-tourism business, the Orang Seletar Cultural Centre now serves as an alternative means of livelihood for the villagers, reducing their dependency on fishing – their customary livelihood – as fish stocks are depleting at a rapid rate due to urban development and severe pollution in the area. The villagers are able to draw on their cultural heritage and tacit knowledge of the sea and surrounding environment to offer mangrove walks, bird watching, fishing, and shell harvesting tours, as part of the eco-tourism initiative alongside the cultural centre. Here, I demonstrate how cultural projects, including those owned and managed by the local communities themselves, can still cultivate a culture of dependency between the external brokers and the Indigenous beneficiaries. Since 2012, the villagers have been involved in a court case to claim their native rights to their ancestral lands, territories, and resources, and protect them from encroachment. The lands on which their village sits were sold by the Malaysian government to private landowners and property developers for a waterfront redevelopment project without the villagers' knowledge or consent. During the court case, the judge was invited on a tour of the Orang Seletar Cultural Centre to learn about the villagers' Indigenous cultural heritage through the brokerage of Indigenous rights activists. Although the future of the cultural centre remains in limbo pending the outcome of their appeal against the court's judgement for them to move out of their village in return for a monetary compensation, it has played a useful role in the Orang Seletar villagers' assertion of their native customary rights.

The Monsopiad Cultural Village in Sabah portrays the history of a local warrior, Monsopiad, who lived in the village some 300 years ago, as well as a collection of 42 human skulls captured by Monsopiad. There is a loss of trust between the founders of the cultural village (a British businessman and his Malaysian wife, who is a distant descendent of Monsopiad), the direct descendants of Monsopiad who own the lands and artefacts on which the cultural village is based, and the Indigenous workers at the cultural village. It also complicates the insider-outsider divide, as the Indigenous founders and owners of the Monsopiad Cultural Village do not act in the interests of the Indigenous workers, but rather exploit these Indigenous workers for their own benefits, entrenching a culture of dependency on the brokers that leads to the marginalisation of these Indigenous workers. While the Monsopiad Cultural Village has brought significant government investment in the form of infrastructural developments to the village within which it is located, the workers are frequently not paid, as the cultural village is not financially sustainable. The direct descendants of Monsopiad have also been owed rental income by the founders for the lease of the lands on which the cultural village sits, and the loan of artefacts relating to Monsopiad. In addition, the founders have created a fictitious narrative for a menhir, a large standing rock located within the cultural village. This is intended to enhance its seeming authenticity and hence the appeal of the cultural village to visitors but was created without the awareness and consent of the direct descendants of Monsopiad.

At the Linangkit Cultural Village in Sabah, which exhibits the cultural heritage of the Indigenous Lotud people, there are different motives for the establishment of the cultural village and the performance of rituals at the site. The founder of the cultural village is a prominent Lotud leader who no longer believes in these ritual practices due to his Christian faith, whereas the elderly Lotud villagers are still steeped in their ritual beliefs. The cultural village, which has benefitted from the Sabah State Government's investment of RM 1.5 million (£283,000) in 2013 for the construction of a community hall, may have served as a mechanism for facilitating the channelling of government funds to reward political allies, a form of money politics widely practised in Sabah's political arena (Reid 2007; Straumann 2014). This points to the co-existence of multiple interests and agendas of different stakeholders within the cultural village, which may or may not coalign. The cultural village sadly fell into disarray shortly after the unexpected demise of its founder, highlighting the fragility of such a structure and the crucial role the broker play in sustaining the project.

At these four Indigenous cultural villages, there has been a deliberate transformation of some Indigenous cultural practices – mediated by different stakeholders including the self-representations of Indigenous people themselves – into commodified cultural heritage practices for the 'tourist gaze' (Urry 1990). These sites thus become staged arenas where certain aspects of Indigenous cultural practice are constructed and represented by the different stakeholders for tourists' consumption to conform with tourists' imaginings of the exotic Indigenous people of Southeast Asia, in turn, shaped by historically inherited stereotypes (Salazar and Graburn 2015). The process of staging involves the 'displacement of cultural practices from one place to another and their modification to fit new conditions of time and space' (Chhabra et al. 2003: 715). Through the course of staging, Indigenous cultural practices are re-appropriated and translated through a dialogic process of heritage production and framing by multiple stakeholders, including tourists, tourism operators, Indigenous people themselves, and other intermediaries. What results is a commodified performance of Indigenous cultural heritage on display (Harkin 2003). This staged representation of Indigenous cultural heritage also involves the selection of certain Indigenous attributes and cultural practices as well as the mobilisation of time and space to articulate an essentialised historical identity grounded in the exotic and primitive Other (Fabian 1983; Urry 1996; Crang 1999; Johnson 1999; Salazar 2013).

The concept of staging, specifically 'staged authenticity', was first suggested by MacCannell (1973) in the context of ethnic tourism, to explain how tourists seeking authenticity in a tourist setting are instead offered up a form of 'staged authenticity' by tourism operators. MacCannell (1973: 595) further elaborates that the 'staged quality [of cultural practices] lends to them an aura of superficiality, albeit a superficiality that is not always perceived as such by the tourist, who is usually forgiving about these matters'. Drawing on Goffman's (1959) approach to dramaturgical analysis, MacCannell (1973) suggests that the process of staging produces a 'front stage' where cultural practices are re-enacted, offering a kind of staged intimacy for tourist consumption, against a 'back stage' of living vernacular cultural practices, which take place out of the tourists' sight and can be starkly different from the tourist performances on the 'front stage'. In MacCannell's (1973) view, the tourist experience is staged and therefore inauthentic, although tourists themselves may perceive the experience as authentic. In this regard, Chhabra et al. (2003) have demonstrated that staging does not preclude authenticity, by establishing that tourists can still perceive of events that are staged in a location far away from the original source of the cultural practice as highly authentic.

Tilley (1997: 86) argues that the concept of authenticity is neither useful nor relevant in understanding the performance of culture in a tourist setting. Rather, it is more useful to understand this tourist setting as 'an interposed "liminal" structure of communication', where local people are reinventing their cultural practices to adapt to the conditions of global modernity. As MacCannell (1992: 19) puts it:

The image of the savage that emerges from these primitive performances completes the postmodern fantasy of 'authentic alterity' which is ideologically necessary in the promotion and development of global monoculture. The 'primitivistic' performance is our funerary marking of the passage of savagery. In the presence of these displays, there is only one thing we can know with certainty: we have witnessed the demise of the original form of humanity.

Local people are, therefore, actively producing a vanished way of life by becoming a representation of the 'lost' culture. It is always historically constituted, with the tourist setting becoming an 'arena for the exercise of conscious choice, contextualising practices, modes of representation, rationalisation and justification' (Tilley 1997: 87).

Alluding to the various works espousing the invented nature of culture and tradition (Wagner 1981; Hobsbawm and Ranger 1983), Crick (1989: 65) argues that 'cultures are invented, remade and the elements reorganised'. Authenticity, from a constructionist perspective, is a mediated experience between different stakeholders, signs, and symbols, as well as prevailing governmental and social discourses. It can be mutually constructed and customised to suit guests and hosts expectations as 'customised authenticity' (Wang 2007) or constituted through the acts of ritual performance as 'performative authenticity' (Zhu 2012). These invented cultural practices can also be developed over time and embedded as important traditions with mythologised origins, a notion that finds its parallel in Cohen's (1988: 379) concept of 'emergent authenticity'. Here, he suggests that:

> Since authenticity is not a primitive given, but negotiable, one has to allow for the possibility of its gradual emergence in the eyes of visitors to the host culture. In other words, a cultural product, or a trait thereof, which is at one point generally judged as contrived or inauthentic may, in the course of time, become generally recognised as authentic, even by experts.

When these Indigenous cultural practices are staged for tourist consumption, they undergo a process of de-contextualisation and 'sanitisation', during which the original meanings and values attached to them are lost. It appears that the Indigenous people have come to internalise these exotic representations of their own cultural heritage. They draw upon these representations to express their own self-identity in a process of what Foster (2001) terms as 'auto-exoticism'. In turn, this leads to the loss of belief, as these cultural practices are no longer perceived of as being convincing and effective for their ritual purposes (Stanley 2007). The risk of alienation can also occur, when negative aspects of cultural practices and histories are erased to conform to a sanitised script 'neatly package[ed] so as neither to offend or overload the visitor with overwhelming amounts of information' (Bunten 2008: 386). When cultural practices previously held in the private domain are made public through staged performances, there is a problem of cultural theft or appropriation of Indigenous intellectual property by external parties (Geismar 2005, 2013; Stanley 2007).

However, at the same time, the tourist encounter may offer Indigenous people opportunities to rediscover and reflect on their identity and cultural practice (Abram et al. 1997; Theodossopoulos 2015). These practices may even acquire new meanings by becoming symbolic of self-representation and self-identity for Indigenous people, leading to an 'emergent authenticity' (Cohen 1988). Indigenous cultural villages can offer a source of economic livelihood for Indigenous people and serve as a means of reasserting their identities in the face of social and cultural marginalisation (Gingging 2007; Fiskesjo 2015), and facilitate the reinvention of cultural products as tourist art (Glass 2006; Brulotte 2012).

Tourism can also lend political and economic legitimacy to Indigenous cultural practices, thus pressuring national governments to take Indigenous people seriously (Canessa 2012). McKean (1976) shows how in Bali, Indonesia, cultural performances for tourists have provided economic assets to enhance the elegance and scale of the cultural performances for the community's own rituals and celebrations, thus facilitating the preservation of their cultural heritage. In this sense, tourism can offer an avenue for sustaining cultural practices or cultural goods, which may otherwise be lost in the age of modernity and mass production (Cohen 1988).

Yet at other times, Indigenous people 'held back' their cultural practices or return to cultural beliefs at times of calamity, alluding to a more nuanced interpretation of the complexities surrounding the heritage-making process. In the case of Malaysia, there are activists who champion for the empowerment of Indigenous people, motivated by a personal sense of social justice; Indigenous people who adhere to cultural taboos and ritual prohibitions by practising abstinence; and Indigenous ritual specialists who perform rituals to neutralise calamities and restore the balance between the natural and spiritual worlds. Here are instances where Indigenous people demonstrate a deep-seated conviction in the efficacy of ritual practice and cultural belief. Indigenous people still have control and agency over their cultural heritage, even as they negotiate the contemporary realities of modernisation and urbanisation.

The representation of Indigenous cultural heritage within these sites in Malaysia is not a straightforward process, as what is being commodified and made cultural heritage for the consumption of tourists, and what is not, often involves complex negotiations and renegotiations between different stakeholders based on their individual self-interests and beliefs. Hall (1996) argues that representations, which are constructed and reified through the production of differences, are rooted in cultural politics, and hence, they are best conceived as 'a politics of representation'. The politics of representation is, in turn, bound up with 'analyses of ethnicities, identities, and the constitution of subjectivities' (Bottomley 1991: 309). These constant negotiations and renegotiations by different stakeholders lead to the articulation of a 'regime of representation' (Li 2000: 154). Representations are thus formative and actively struggled over, rather than passively received. Hence, 'how things are represented and the "machineries" and regimes of representation in a culture ... play a constitutive, and not merely a reflexive, after-the-event, role' (Hall 1996: 443, original emphasis). The representations of Indigenous cultural heritage within Indigenous cultural villages have the real effect of reproducing and reifying the cultural differences that underlie these representations.

The politics of representation is discursively tied to the production of essentialist discourses, which are actively contested and negotiated by alternative claims to these discourses, thus producing multiple interpretations (Hall 1996). It is also intricately bound up with the process of commodification, as cultural differences can be actively constituted through the commodification process by justifying the production and consumption of cultural differences (Dwyer and Jackson 2003). The staged representation of Indigenous people at Indigenous cultural villages is shaped by their discursive representation as 'exotic noble savages', dating from early colonial literature, which actively constructs and perpetuates the idea of Indigenous people as 'primitive people' living in harmony with nature in a state of primordial innocence (Conklin and Graham 1995; Ellingson 2001). This also aligns with tourists' desires for the idealised 'vanishing savage' (Theodossopoulos 2015).

The commodification of Indigenous cultural heritage through tourism has the effect of perpetuating the historical construction of Indigenous people as 'noble savages' in modern tourism imaginaries, as tourism operators, tourists, and Indigenous people mobilise these discursive narratives in tourism advertising, guidebooks, travel blogs, and through the narratives of tour guides, to capitalise on the benefits of Indigenous cultural tourism (Adams 1997; Salazar 2005, 2007, 2009, 2010, 2013; Bergmeister 2015). As such, the historical essentialisation of Indigenous people as 'primitive people' and 'noble savages', in contrast with 'more civilised' white Europeans, is still actively being produced and consumed through contemporary tourism imaginaries of Indigenous people. As representations of 'culture', 'heritage', and 'Indigeneity' are subjective social and cultural constructs, dominant representations of Indigenous cultural heritage are often contested and negotiated by alternative claims to heritage (Yelvington et al. 2002; Crampton 2003), as well as by visitors who renegotiate the intended narratives (Fyfe and Ross 1996; Adams 2003).

Representations constitute a form of 'imaginaries', which Salazar and Graburn (2015: 1) conceptualise as 'socially transmitted representational assemblages that interact with people's personal imaginings and that are used as meaning-making and world-shaping devices'. These tourism imaginaries are socially and culturally constructed, forged through the contestation and negotiation of different stakeholders and the mediation of different influences such as tourists' imaginaries of Indigenous people as the exotic and primitive Other, tourism operators' perceptions of Indigenous people, and Indigenous people's imaginaries of themselves. These are, in turn, embedded within wider issues of identity politics and institutions of power (Salazar 2010; Salazar and Graburn 2015). The tourism imaginaries are not homogeneous across and within different groups of stakeholders and actors. For example, different tourists may bring with them diverse expectations about authenticity, which are influenced by their personal experiences of travel. Hence, some tourists may expect the commodified performances of Indigenous cultural heritage to be inauthentic, whereas others still expect these performances to be authentic (Theodossopoulos 2013).

Theodossopoulos (2011) argues that these various imaginaries launch a complex 'negotiation of expectations' among different actors and stakeholders, who bring with them their own diverse expectations of what constitutes authentic cultural practice in tourist settings. These tourism imaginaries are hence not innocent, but 'often shrewdly exaggerate the power of difference while neglecting and obfuscating the power of commonality' (Salazar and Graburn 2015: 15). For example, they accentuate the exoticness of Indigenous people to conform with tourists' desires and expectations about the primitive Other. The power dynamics between the different actors within these tourism imaginaries are also unequal, often tipping in favour of tourists, who are the target audience of heritage tourism initiatives (Porter and Salazar 2005; Salazar and Zhu 2015).

Apparent at each of the Indigenous cultural villages I investigated was a specific set of negotiations between the different stakeholders around the processes involved in transforming Indigenous cultural practices into forms of Indigenous cultural heritage for tourists' consumption. I follow Kirshenblatt-Gimblett (2004) in understanding this re-presentation of 'culture' as 'heritage', and as the production of something new, forged, in this case, through processes of instrumentalisation, brokerage, and staging. Each of these representations is embedded within its own interplay of power relations and wider negotiation over the 'ownership' of the heritage performed, who has the right to represent this heritage, and for whom the heritage is being represented (Graham et al. 2000; Harrison 2013). This also speaks to Vizenor's (1999) notion of 'survivance', which emphasises the active refashioning of Indigenous culture for contemporary times as a means to Indigenous self-determination and mobilisation. The representation and performance of Indigenous cultural heritage at the Indigenous cultural villages in Malaysia are also, in turn, 'embedded within local, regional, and global institutions of power' (Salazar and Graburn 2015: 17) that have an influence on which aspects of Indigenous cultural practices are commodified for tourist consumption and which aspects are not commodified.

Building upon these lines of enquiry, this book seeks to explore the political, social, economic, and cultural dynamics surrounding the process of heritage-making at four Indigenous cultural villages in Malaysia. First, I explore how and why certain (and not other) Indigenous cultural practices are commodified and staged for tourists' consumption at Indigenous cultural villages by examining the roles and motivations of different brokers in this process of heritage-making. I explore the processes at play in the transformation of these cultural practices into forms of cultural heritage, as well as the tensions and contradictions between different stakeholders at the four Indigenous cultural villages. In addition, I examine the impacts of this heritage-making process on Indigenous identity and cultural practice and ask whether these Indigenous cultural villages contribute to greater empowerment and sustainable development among the Indigenous people in Malaysia or whether they perpetuate historical cultures of dependency and patron-client relationships between brokers and Indigenous people. Finally, I consider the implications of this process of heritage-making at the Indigenous cultural villages for wider discourses on Indigeneity, culture for development, community engagement, and non-Western museology.

In the next chapter, I provide a historiographical account of Indigeneity in Malaysia to examine how historical stereotypes of Indigenous people, discursively constructed through colonial ethnographic accounts and census, continue to influence how they are perceived and treated in contemporary Malaysia. I then individually analyse the four case studies for this book: the Mah Meri Cultural Village, the Orang Seletar Cultural Centre, the Monsopiad Cultural Village, and the Linangkit Cultural Village. Finally, I conclude the book with a summary of my findings in this research, and recommendations for the development of community-based cultural projects.

Notes

1 The term 'Indigenous' is capitalised throughout this book, in line with the nomenclature adopted by other scholars writing on Indigenous museology such as Conal McCarthy, Amy Lonetree, and Christina Kreps.
2 There are some exceptions. A number of scholars such as Su (1995), Su and An (1998), Lu (2013), Denton (2014), Varutti (2014), and Fiskesjo (2015) have applied the concept of eco-museum to analyse the ethnic minority theme parks or folk culture villages in China, while Gingging (2007) has examined the refashioning of the headhunting narrative at the Monsopiad Cultural Village in Malaysia.
3 Although I consider 'culture', 'heritage', and 'tradition' as fluid and socially constructed, I will be providing an essentialised description of each Indigenous group that I work with to offer a context to the Indigenous cultural villages represented in this study.
4 Notwithstanding that 'Indigenous communities' or 'Indigenous people' do not constitute a homogeneous 'community' but comprise different Indigenous individuals with different agendas and allegiances, the terms 'Indigenous communities' and 'Indigenous people' will be used as a shorthand to refer to local Indigenous populations throughout this book.

2 Historicising Indigeneity in Malaysia

Historical conceptualisations of Indigeneity in Malaysia

What we understand today as Indigeneity and Indigenous cultural heritage in Malaysia has taken on different frames of meaning and actions over the past two centuries. These understandings have been contingent on and integral to prevailing events and circumstances at different periods of time. Although the term 'Indigeneity' only gained popularity in the twentieth century (Niezen 2003), the idea of Indigeneity had existed in other semantic iterations in earlier times such as 'tribes', 'aboriginals', 'sakai', 'wild men', 'savages', 'primitives', and 'natives'. Each term carried certain connotations that had real impacts on how Indigenous people were perceived and treated, which continue to influence contemporary conceptualisations of Indigenous people in Malaysia.

As historian Sandra Khor Manickam (2015) has highlighted in her study of the production of racial knowledge about Indigenous people in Peninsular Malaysia from the beginning of the nineteenth century until 1930, the dominant narratives were discursively constructed based on the confluence of global anthropological trends, ideologies underpinning colonial governance, and conceptualisations of local populations. Today, the people who are known as the Indigenous people of Malaysia were not always deemed to be different from or backward and underdeveloped in relation to the Malay population. The sense of difference was actively constructed and perpetuated through early colonial literature and later colonial policies for governance and administration, which, in turn, were influenced by changing anthropological constructions of the colonial subject. Hence, the idea of what constituted Indigeneity was neither homogeneous nor static across time and space, but was rather multiple and fluid, constantly shaped and reshaped by historical processes underpinning the need for colonial governance and prevailing anthropological trends. Collectively, these processes inscribe, produce, and maintain the 'differences' between Indigenous and non-Indigenous people in relation to their physical bodies and social positionings, as well as their entitlements to lands, territories, and resources. This continues to influence how Indigenous people are perceived and treated in contemporary Malaysia.

The contemporary meaning of Indigeneity has roots in older forms of classification and differentiation of human populations. During the European Enlightenment of the eighteenth century, understandings of race promoted the belief that differences in physical appearance and 'civility' resulted from climate or environment, way of life, or other external conditions (Douglas 2008). In the eighteenth century, discourse on human populations also revolved around issues of primordiality and autochthony. This was popularised by the German school of cultural anthropology that proposed the concept of *Volk* or 'spirit' to refer to different groups of people who shared a common descent, language, and communal solidarity (Spencer 1997).

Influenced by these racial discourses, early colonial writers on the Malay Archipelago were preoccupied with questions of 'originality' and 'purity' among local populations and were keen to identify the first group to inhabit the region (Manickam 2015). Among these writers were William Marsden (1754–1836), who worked for the British East Indian Company in Southeast Asia in the late eighteenth century and published *The History of Sumatra* in 1783, and John Leyden (1775–1811), who wrote a significant linguistic work entitled *Dissertation on the Languages and Literature of the Indo-Chinese Nations* in 1805. In their classifications of the local population of the Malay Archipelago, both Marsden and Leyden considered the coastal Malays as 'natives' but deemed that they were non-autochthonous and less original than the inland 'aborigines', who did not speak Malay and had not converted to Islam (Manickam 2015).

The use of 'natives' to describe the Malays suggests that Marsden and Leyden believed that they had lived in the region for a long time, but did not originate from the lands. This was unlike the inland inhabitants, whom they described as 'aborigines', a term that connotes the idea that they existed on the lands as the first or earliest people to inhabit the region. It is also used interchangeably to indicate primordiality and autochthony. According to Lowenthal (1998: 181), claims to priority or being primordial in the Indigenous rhetoric 'traduced [Indigenous people as] inferior and backward "native" [who were] simple savages doomed by civilisation'. These writings, which conferred upon the inland aborigines the status of Indigenous antiquity, set them apart from others, and cast them as inferior and backward in relation to the Malays in the region.

During the nineteenth century, the construction of Indigeneity in the Malay Archipelago was also entangled with the political rivalry between different European powers for colonial domination in the region. In particular, the enslavement of 'aborigines' by other local groups, such as the Malays, was used as a justification for advancing British colonial ambitions in the region. During the period of Anglo-Dutch rivalry for colonial expansion in the region, Stamford Raffles (1781–1826), who published *A History of Java* in 1817, drew attention to the enslavement of the inland aborigines in order to portray the Dutch as inferior colonisers who tolerated the enslavement of the perceived Indigenous population by the Malays.

This was in contrast to the British who promoted the abolition of slavery (Manickam 2015). Raffles considered the aborigines to be more authentically 'original' than the Malays, stating that the Malays only existed as a distinct group after the arrival of the Arab merchants and traders to the region, and were therefore of modern origin, but he did not dismiss the idea that the Malays could have been descendants of the aboriginal population (Manickam 2015). The enslaved condition of the Indigenous population was thus adopted as a criterion for constructing and reifying racial differences between the aborigines and the Malays in the region.

The perceived racial differences later came to be defined and reified in physical terms through the writings of John Crawfurd (1783–1868), who published the *History of the Indian Archipelago* in 1820. In it, Crawfurd advanced a racial theory for the inhabitants of the Malay Archipelago. He proposed the existence of two racial categories, namely the 'negro' and 'brown' races, as he sought to connect the events in the region with the ongoing debate surrounding transatlantic slavery in Europe. He drew parallels between the perceived superiority of the 'white' race over the 'negro' race in Europe, and the superiority of the 'brown' race (the Malays) over the 'negro' race (aborigines) in Asia. Crawfurd's account marked a turning point in the historical conceptualisation of Indigeneity in Southeast Asia. Human differences came to be reified in biological terms, with the aborigines deemed to be different from and inferior relative to the Malays, due to their darker skin colour and enslaved condition.

In North Borneo, the construction of Indigeneity was also influenced by prevailing racial discourses in the eighteenth and nineteenth centuries that classified local populations according to a racist schema that placed Indigenous people at a lower stage of civilisation relative to the higher stage of civilisation enjoyed by 'fairer' Europeans. Henry Ling Roth's (1855–1925) (1896a, b) *The Natives of Sarawak and British North Borneo* offers one of the earliest European accounts of the Indigenous people living in Borneo. As this was a compilation of historical accounts collected during the early Enlightenment, intellectually it reflected the prevailing racial doctrines of the period. Described interchangeably as 'natives' or 'tribes' in Roth's account, the local populations of Borneo were implied to be closely associated with the lands that they inhabited and perceived as distinct groups of people dependent on their lands for their livelihoods. They were often referred to using names derived from the geographical locations where they lived, after their nearest landforms or river systems. The use of 'native' to describe the populations in Borneo implies that it was perceived that they had lived in the region for a long time, while the use of 'tribe' carries connotations of and associations with not only an isolated and self-contained society but also a state of evolution deemed to be less civilised than the Europeans (Beteille 1998).

The conceptualisation of Indigeneity in Borneo has been fluid and sometimes contested. This is evident in problems associated with the naming of Indigenous populations in European colonial ethnographic accounts, in which terminologies of dubious validity were often given to the Indigenous populations by Europeans, and subsequently adopted by the Indigenous populations themselves (Southall 1970). For example, Roth (1896a: 39–43) devoted a chapter to discussing what he considered to be the misuse of the word 'Dyak', revealing the different emic and etic identifications extended to the Indigenous populations of Borneo. He explained how the term 'Dyak' meant different things to different writers. Sir Charles Brooke indicated that many tribes living in the interior of Borneo called themselves 'Dya', which meant 'inland' in several local dialects. Sir James Brooke used the term to refer to a particular group living on parts of the north-western coast and the mountains of the interior of Borneo. The Dutch had described all inland tribes as 'Dyaks', even though they might be separately known by their own names, such as 'Kayan', 'Pieng', and 'Kiniahs'.

From the late nineteenth century, ethnographic accounts of the region were influenced by evolutionary principles of classification. Culture was not only deemed to be hierarchical, and Indigenous cultures were thought to belong to an earlier stage of human evolution, it was also believed to be biologically determined, hereditary, and innate. The growing use of scientific or pseudoscientific techniques in physical anthropology led to a greater emphasis being placed on obtaining anthropometric measurements for classifying and profiling local populations into different groups according to their perceived stages of evolution, thus producing and naturalising racial differences between them.

Scholars involved in the Cambridge Expedition to the northern Malay States, from 1899 to 1900, were influential in establishing the agenda for and manner of anthropological research on Indigenous populations in the Malay Archipelago (Manickam 2015). One of the most important contributions from this group of scholars was the publication of *Pagan Races of the Malay Peninsula* in 1906, written by two British colonial administrators, Walter William Skeat (1866–1953), who participated in the Cambridge Expedition, and Charles Otto Blagden (1864–1949), a longtime colonial administrator in the Straits Settlements. Drawing connections with the emerging discourses on racial science in India, and building upon an earlier classification schema devised by Swiss anthropologist Rudolf Martin (1864–1925) in 1902, Skeat and Blagden (1906a) proposed a three-category classification of Indigenous people in Peninsular Malaysia, namely Semang, Sakai, and Jakun. These were based primarily on the perceived physical distinctions between these groups:

> At whatever period this was, and in whatever order they may have arrived, we can now recognise with sufficient clearness the Semang, Sakai, and Jakun as three distinct and separate races; the Negritos or Semang, with their woolly hair and round bright eyes, the darkest, the best-developed, and at the same time, the most markedly nomadic of

all the races in the Peninsula; the Sakai, who are the lightest, with their often interesting features, reminiscent may be of their old Dravidian ancestry, though modified by the effect of their somewhat narrow-lidded half-closed eyes, hair of a distinctly wavy character, and their generally somewhat emaciated appearance; and the Jakun or aboriginal Malayans, with their smooth blue-black hair, a race hard to distinguish, because of its admixture with the other two main stock, but who must nevertheless be accepted as a type, if the physical evidence of skull and skull features, skin-colour and hair-character are not to be utterly denied.

(Skeat and Blagden 1906a: 12–13)

The genesis of the names chosen for the tripartite classification is largely unclear, although they alluded to etic identifications of Indigenous people by the Malays and others, with some negative, and even derogatory, connotations. These were different from the emic identifications with which Indigenous people addressed themselves. As Skeat and Blagden (1906a: 22) explained:

The term 'Semang' has never been satisfactorily explained. The term 'Sakai' on the other hand, has (unjustifiably, as I think) explained as meaning 'dog'; a more possible derivation, as Grunwedel points out, being from the Sanskrit 'Sakhi' = 'Friend', in which case its use would be paralleled by the alternative Malay name 'Sahbat' or 'Sabat' (from Arab. 'Sahabat' = 'Friend' or 'Friendly'), though even this is hardly a likely explanation. The word 'Sakai' is also used in Malay (as is 'Semang') in the sense of retainer or follower of a native chief. It is thus more or less analogous to Rayat by the Malays to the Mantra and Besisi; but these last two tribes prefer to speak of themselves as 'Hill Men' (Orang Bukit), or 'Men of the Interior' (Orang Dalam), and 'Men of the Sea' (Orang Laut) respectively, or else simply as 'Jakun'.

Despite its problems, this tripartite classification, largely popularised by Skeat and Blagden, is still used today by the Malaysian Department of Orang Asli Development (JAKOA) to categorise the Indigenous populations in Peninsular Malaysia. This demonstrates how historical classification, however arbitrary, continues to be perpetuated in contemporary conceptualisations of Indigenous populations.

In *Pagan Races of the Malay Peninsula*, Skeat and Blagden (1906a: 10) described the Indigenous people of the region as the 'wild man of the Peninsula'. Skilled in jungle survival, with 'inherent honesty, unselfishness, and single-mindedness' (Skeat and Blagden 1906a: 14), this description alluded to the myth of the 'noble savage', a discourse that was popular in the nineteenth century. The discursive portrayal of Indigenous people as being 'wild' carried many connotations. The description indicated a lack of tameness and civilisation, and implied a state of nature in which a place was left undomesticated and uncultivated (Manickam 2015). Hence, the state of wildness was conceptually separate from a state of civilisation by constructing differing notions of time: being wild and primitive was conceptually the binary opposite of being tame and modern (Fabian 1983; Kuper 1988). In particular, the relationship between colonial writers and Indigenous subjects was not coeval. Instead, the ethnographic subjects were actively produced as 'the Other', through placing them conceptually in a different time and space to metropolitan civilisation (Fabian 1983). Indigenous people were placed at the lower rungs of the comparative taxonomy of civilisation, in contrast to Europeans who occupied the pinnacle. Indigenous people were to be civilised (by Europeans) to attain higher levels of human development. Such a stance set the tone for subsequent paternalistic colonial policies towards Indigenous people in Peninsular Malaysia during the twentieth century.

Colonial censuses, as a central organising instrument to facilitate colonial rule and governance by counting and classifying colonial populations, offered another mechanism for investigating the ideological conceptualisation of Indigeneity in Peninsular Malaysia (Cohn 1996; Anderson 1991). Tracing the classifications of Indigenous populations used in colonial censuses over time, Manickam (2015) argues that the categorisation of Indigenous populations in Peninsular Malaysia was constantly re-organised relative to the Malay category, which was also frequently modified to reflect the shifting geographical boundaries under British colonial rule. In the 1901 Straits Settlement census, Indigenous people were referred to as 'Aboriginal Malays' (Manickam 2015), which not only implied that they were 'underdeveloped' Malays but also suggested that the Malays had progressed up the hierarchy to occupy a more civilised status within the evolutionary schema and hence held the mandate, based on racial superiority, to govern the Indigenous population. A past belonging to the Indigenous subject was thus actively created through an anachronistic process, in which pasts were retrospectively invented for what were perceived to be different groups, to 'explain' these differences in the present. This resulted in a taxonomy of difference based on degrees of primitiveness, reinforcing the prevailing view that the Malays were less primitive than the Indigenous people (Fabian 1983; Skaria 1997). Importantly, this process posited that the Malays had also originated from the lands and, therefore, had an autochthonous claim to them. This influenced the contemporary 'sons of the soil' or *bumiputera* policy in Malaysia that considers both the Malays and the Indigenous people as the original inhabitants of Malaysia, entitling the Malays to special privileges alongside Indigenous people.

The Pagan Tribes of Borneo, written by Charles Hose (1863–1929) and William McDougall (1871–1938) in 1912, offers an in-depth, descriptive account of six 'less known pagan tribes of the interior' (1912a: 30). These were the sea Dyaks or Ibans, Kayans, Punans, Kenyahs, Klemantans

[Kalamantan], and Muruts. Hose was a colonial administrator in Sarawak for over 20 years, while McDougall served as a member of the Cambridge Anthropological Expedition to the Torres Straits (1898–1899), under the leadership of anthropologist A.C. Haddon (1855–1940), during which time some members of the team spent several months in Sarawak, Borneo (Hose and McDougall 1912a). This selection of only six representative pagan tribes out of the many groups in Borneo subscribed to the essentialist conceptualisations of Indigeneity of the time. Indigenous groups that did not conform to the idealised racial or tribal 'types' of pure blood, untainted by other ethnic groups, were excluded from such analyses. Influenced by the racial ideologies in vogue at that time, Hose and McDougall (1912a: 28) argued that other races had

> become blended with the Indigenous populations, and that a considerable proportion of their blood still runs in the veins of some of the tribes ... and it seems probable that some of the elements of their culture have spread widely and been adopted throughout a large part of Borneo.

To explain the different racial categories in Borneo, Hose and McDougall drew on the anthropometric measurements made by Haddon, who identified five main groups of people in Borneo: the Punan, Kalamantan, Kenyah-Kayan, Iban or Sea Dayak, and Malay. These categorisations were based on comparisons to measurements made during Dutch expeditions to Borneo. Although Haddon noted that there were numerous smaller tribes, which were 'frequently difficult or quite impossible to differentiate from one another' (Hose and McDougall 1912b: 314), he explained this away by suggesting a mixing of races. For example, he stated that the Kalamantan

> were originally a dolichocephalic people who mixed first with the Indigenous brachycephals (Punan group) and later with the immigrant brachycephals (Kenyah-Kayan group) or the Kalamantans may have been a mixed people when they first arrived in Borneo and subsequently increased their complexity by mixing with these two groups.
>
> (Hose and McDougall 1912b: 314)

Haddon's account highlights how colonial anthropologists continued to draw upon essentialised notions of Indigeneity based on primordiality, autochthony, and racial purity to justify the classification of Indigenous people in Borneo, despite the difficulties of differentiating one group from another. This demonstrates the enduring influence of prior classificatory conceptualisations of race and Indigeneity in Borneo.

The opening up of the interior areas of the Malay Archipelago to development and urbanisation in the 1930s not only made more information about the Indigenous people living in the interior areas available but also brought about significant changes to their lives and cultural practices, rendering earlier classifications of the Indigenous populations, such as the distinction between 'wild' and 'tame' aborigines, more problematic than before. However, most of twentieth-century colonial writings on the Indigenous people of Malaysia continued to draw on the earlier classification schemas proposed by Skeat and Blagden (1906a, b) to classify Indigenous populations in Peninsular Malaysia and those of Hose and McDougall (1912a, b) to classify Indigenous populations in Borneo. These classifications were made largely on linguistic, behavioural, and cultural attributes, rather than on physical characteristics.

The ethnographic writings of the twentieth century continued to use a highly essentialised notion of Indigenous people in Malaysia, viewing their interactions with foreigners and racial mixing as a threat to their purity and authenticity. These texts point to the enduring influence of earlier racial discourses and reflect the desire of colonial ethnographers to essentialise Indigenous people based on historical stereotypes. One can also detect here the influence of the 'salvage paradigm' in anthropology, a movement borne out of the concern of anthropologists to document what they perceived as endangered cultures to preserve them prior to their inevitable extinction in the face of colonisation and modernisation. The paradigm underpinned the establishment of ethnographic museums as repositories of 'salvaged' materials and knowledges belonging to fast disappearing communities and cultural practices (Gruber 1970). There is also a direct connection between these colonial institutions and alternative forms of museology that have developed in the post-colonial era, including Indigenous cultural villages that are also underpinned by the motivation to preserve endangered Indigenous cultural practices (Cohen 2008).

One ethnographic account that subscribed to the earlier racial discourses on the conceptualisation of Indigeneity in Malaysia was *Among the Forest Dwarfs of Malaya*, published in 1929 by Father Paul Schebesta (1887–1967), a German-trained physical anthropologist. Schebesta observed the Negritos in Peninsular Malaysia, whom he referred to as the 'dwarf tribes, who are at the same time the original occupants of the land' (1929: 13), living among 'this wonderful silence of the primeval forest, in this tangle of thorny undergrowth, liana, and reed, wander[ing] with inaudible tread' (1929: 12). He alluded to the myth of the noble savage in idealising the Negritos as living in perfect harmony with the natural environment, in a state of primordial innocence, untainted by modernity (Conklin and Graham 1995; Ellingson 2001). Schebesta had spent time studying Pygmies[1] in Africa, and upon encountering the dark-skinned Negritos in Peninsular Malaysia, he resurrected the Pan-Negritos theory first proposed by Crawfurd: that all Indigenous people in Malaya had originated from Africa due to their physical similarities with the 'negro' races in Africa (Endicott 2015; Manickam 2015). Schebesta (1929) also alluded to the civilising effect on the Negritos brought about through interactions with the Malays, demonstrating that the racial hierarchy, which conceived of the Negritos as an inferior, backward, and under-developed race, relative to white Europeans and other racial groups in Peninsular Malaysia, still had currency in the early twentieth century.

Several ethnographic accounts about the Indigenous people of Malaysia by colonial ethnographer Ivor H.N. Evans (1886–1957) also subscribed to ear-lier racial ideologies about Indigeneity. A Cambridge-trained anthropologist, Evans spent most of his adult life working for the Federated Malay States Museums in Malaya and wrote extensively on the Indigenous populations of Peninsular Malaysia and North Borneo. He authored several books based on his travels and study of the region as a curator, namely *Among Primitive Peoples in Borneo* (1922); *Studies in Religion, Folklore and Custom in British North Borneo and the Malay Peninsula* (1923); *Papers on the Ethnology and Archaeology of the Malay Peninsula* (1927); *The Negritos of Malaya* (1937); and *The Religion of the Tempasuk Dusuns of North Borneo* (1953).

Like other scholars of the time, Evans was interested in questions of pri-mordiality and autochthony among local populations. He studied 'primi-tive' and 'pagan' people, who were thought to be of pure blood and had retained many of their 'traditional' cultural practices. He attributed the growing complexity he observed among them to racial mixing. In particu-lar, Evans explained that he had focused on the 'pagan tribes' of Peninsular Malaysia, as they were thought to have retained many of their older cul-tural practices, compared with the Malays, whose adoption of Islam 'had sufficient influence partially to destroy the older beliefs and customs' (1923: 136). Similarly, Evans claimed that the Dusuns were the only original in-habitants of Borneo, whereas other groups, such as the Bajaus and Illanuns, came from elsewhere (1923). At the same time, he acknowledged that the

> Dusuns [were] not a single tribe, but an assemblage of tribes, or rather the appellations embrace[d] large numbers of village communities, some of which [could] be grouped together as closely related owing to identity in dialect and minor details of custom, while the whole of them [were] roughly classed together as Orang Dusun, owing to their similarity in language, beliefs and general habits.
>
> (Evans 1922: 35)

Evans' views on primordiality and autochthony among the local popula-tions in Malaysia were not uncontested. Another colonial scholar, Owen Rutter (1889–1944), who published *The Pagans of North Borneo* in 1929, argued that none of the Indigenous groups in Borneo were original inhab-itants of the lands, but had migrated to Borneo from elsewhere in Asia, all except the Negritos, who were native to the Malay Peninsula, but could not be found in Borneo. He also claimed that the Dusuns and Muruts could have come from common stock, but environmental factors had led to the differential rates of social and cultural development: the Dusuns became more civilised than the Muruts due to their interactions with the outside world, facilitated by accessible natural terrain, suggesting that 'geographical formation has influenced ethnography' (Rutter 1929: 22). Although there is no consensus on the naming and origins of the local populations in Malaysia, the Dusuns, Bajaus, and Illanuns in North Borneo, as well as the Malays, Jakuns, Sakais, and Semangs (or Negritos) in Peninsular Malaysia, are officially considered to be the original inhabitants or *bumiputeras*, and hence extended special privileges under Malaysia's 'sons of the soil' policy. This points to the ambiguous reasoning around 'originality' upon which the policy is based. Today, these racial classifications are also drawn upon by different stakeholders in Malaysia, including Indigenous people themselves, for fulfilling different objectives and agendas.

Evans saw the Negritos' interactions with other races in Peninsular Malaysia (1937) and the interactions of 'pagan' tribes with white foreigners in Borneo (1922) as threats to their purity and authenticity, reflecting a nostalgia for the idealised 'vanishing savage' (Theodossopoulos 2015). Evans (1922: 32) attributed the destruction of 'traditional' cultural practices to the civilising mission of foreign missionaries, suggesting that the process of disintegration and decay have often been aided and hastened by the efforts of well-meaning but misguided missionaries and others, who, instead of attempting to arrest the progress of many of the innovations (e.g. the use of clothing), which have been partly responsible for the decay of savage races, have deliberately aided in their adoption, and have done everything in their power to break down old customs, religious or otherwise. He alludes to the idealisation of Indigenous people as noble savages 'living in a pure state of nature – gentle, wise, uncorrupted by the vices of civilisation' (Ellingson 2001: 1), a binary discourse that implies the inferiority, backwardness, and underdeveloped status of Indigenous people relative to the civility and superiority of white Europeans. His critical view of modernisation reflects the desire to preserve the authenticity of a highly essentialised conception of Indigenous people in Malaysia among colonial administrators, a desire that finds its modern equivalent in cultural tourists searching for the authenticity of Indigenous people and their cultural heritage.

Analysing the racial discourses underpinning colonial accounts of Indigenous populations in the Malay Archipelago demonstrates that the differences between Indigenous people and other races in Malaysia are not neutral but are actively produced and reified through discursive strategies, based on racial hierarchies. These racial discourses still underpin the ideological construction of Indigeneity in post-colonial Malaysia and continue to construct and perpetuate structures of domination that marginalise Indigenous people today, even as they are increasingly being challenged. In the last three decades, Indigenous consciousness and activism have emerged and Indigenous people invariably draw on colonial constructions of Indigeneity (the 'noble savage') in asserting their rights to empowerment and self-determination, which includes capitalising on cultural tourism.

The political position of Indigenous populations in Malaysia

While the Indigenous populations of Peninsular Malaysia and East Malaysia were perceived as 'pagan races' or 'tribes' and deemed to be inferior and backward relative to white Europeans, there were regional differences in the way they were treated by British colonial officers. This was due to perceived differences in their degrees of primitivism and relative autochthony, and the different needs of the colonial administration in Peninsular Malaysia and East Malaysia. In Peninsular Malaysia, the Indigenous people, known locally as Orang Asli, were treated as a vulnerable minority due to their historical enslavement by more powerful groups in the region, and hence required the protection of the British (Dentan et al. 1997). In East Malaysia, and particularly in North Borneo, Indigenous people made up the majority and were integrated to varying degrees into the colonial administration via indirect rule, as the British administrators lacked the resources to directly govern these vast territories (Tregonning 1958; Singh 2011).

In Peninsular Malaysia, which was under direct British administration, colonial officers adopted a more paternalistic approach to governing the Orang Asli, who were conceptualised as underdeveloped Malays and Malay subjects with the limited capacity to cope with external pressures. Therefore they needed protection to enable them to continue to lead their distinctive way of life (King and Wilder 2003; Andaya 2008; Idrus 2010). Early efforts to 'protect' the Orang Asli from the influences of the outside world emerged from Herbert Deane Noone's 1939 Aboriginal Tribes Enactment (State of Perak, No. 3), which proposed the establishment of extensive aboriginal forest reservations for the Orang Asli to allow them the freedom to continue their ways of life (Dentan et al. 1997; Nicholas 2000). The safeguarding of Indigenous rights and practices within forestry legislation was an aspect of nineteenth-century colonial custodianship already established in India. It was later extended to other British colonies through legislative migration (Basu and Damodaran 2015). Underlying this ideology was the aforementioned romanticism of Indigenous people as noble savages, perceived to be closer to nature than civilisation (Ellingson 2001). The Enactment also proposed other measures such as banning alcohol in Orang Asli reserves and promoting Orang Asli handicrafts (Carey 1976; Nicholas 2000). Although not all measures were implemented by the colonial government due to the impending threat of Japanese occupation, they set the groundwork for future paternalistic policies towards the Orang Asli.

After the Japanese occupation, the Orang Asli became a focus of policy for the colonial government, who realised that they could play a strategic role in the conflict with Malayan Communist Party (MCP) guerrillas during the Malayan Emergency (1948–1960). The MCP, comprising predominantly ethnic Chinese, had engaged the assistance of some Orang Asli to fight against the British-led security forces (Jones 1968). The Orang Asli were not passive onlookers in this conflict but had strategically aligned themselves with the groups that were deemed most influential in their respective areas (Leary 1995). The events of the Malayan Emergency accelerated the plans of the colonial government to administer the Orang Asli directly. The British administration realised that if it wanted to win the war against the MCP, it would have to gain the support of the Orang Asli in fighting against rather than supporting the insurgency.

An initial effort to control the Orang Asli and curb their involvement with the MCP, some groups were resettled by the British military and police in Pahang, in camps close to jungle areas. However, the forceful and sometimes brutal coercive removal of unwilling Orang Asli by British officers resulted in many deaths from starvation and disease in poorly equipped resettlement camps, further alienating them from the British (Jones 1968; Dentan et al. 1997; Nicholas 2000). Many Orang Asli fled the camps and returned to their villages with stories of brutality and mistreatment. Subsequently, the Orang Asli abandoned their villages and moved deeper into the interior areas, collaborating more closely with the MCP insurgents (Carey 1976; Dentan et al. 1997). The British then adopted an alternative strategy to resettle the Orang Asli in 'jungle forts' close to their villages, with medical facilities and shops, and armed by the Police. Designed to protect the Orang Asli from MCP intimidation, it has been argued that the success of these 'jungle forts' was limited (Dental et al. 1997).

The Malayan Emergency also saw the adoption of the Aboriginal Peoples Ordinance (1954), adapted largely from the 1939 Enactment, to implement 'regulations for the protection and control of the Orang Asli and their traditional territories' (Nicholas 2000: 82). With the introduction of this legislation, the nascent Department of Aborigines, the predecessor of the Department of Orang Asli Affairs (JHEOA), [2] set up in 1947, was expanded to provide 'education, welfare, and medical facilities in Orang Asli areas' (Jones 1968: 298). As the Aboriginal Peoples Ordinance (1954) was conceived during the Malayan Emergency to discourage interactions between the Orang Asli and the MCP insurgents, there were provisions within the legislation to prohibit the entry of non-Orang Asli persons to and the circulation of written materials within Orang Asli areas. Although the legislation offered some recognition of Orang Asli rights with respect to access to education and the right to lead their own lifestyle, and provided for the establishment of Orang Asli areas and reserves, which recognised their customary territories, it also granted the state the authority to demand that Orang Asli leave or remain in an area. Hence the Orang Asli effectively became tenants on their own lands and could be evicted from these lands without notice (Nicholas 2000).

While Carey (1976: 293) has argued that the Aboriginal Peoples Ordinance (1954), which was later amended in 1967 and revised as the Aboriginal Peoples Act in 1974, 'was a milestone in the administration of the Orang Asli, for at long last the government officially admitted its responsibility towards them, as well as the right of the aboriginal tribes to follow their own way of life', the legislation contributed significantly to the marginalisation of the Orang Asli regarding their customary rights to their ancestral lands, territories, and resources. Despite legal challenges to the constitutionality of many provisions within the Ordinance, little has been done to amend the law due to the lack of an explicit decision from the courts, rendering it susceptible to strategic mobilisation by the Malaysian government for its own interests (Nicholas 2000). This was notwithstanding the 1961 Statement of Policy Regarding the Long-Term Administration of the Aboriginal Peoples (JHEOA) stated commitment to 'the special position of the Orang Asli in respect of land usage and [that their] land rights shall be recognised ... (and that they) will not be moved from their traditional areas without their full consent' (JHEOA 1961, quoted in Nicholas 2000: 95).

In East Malaysia, which came under British 'protection' via the British North Borneo Company in Sabah and the Brooke family in Sarawak, the Indigenous populations were treated differently. The nature of British intervention in Borneo was primarily motivated by commercial interests. British involvement in North Borneo was first established by way of separate leases made with the Brunei and Sulu Sultanates by the Overbeck-Dent Association, an association formed by Gustavus Baron von Overbeck (1830–1894) and Alfred Dent (1844–1927) on 27 March 1877, with the purpose of selling these leases for a profit (Tregonning 1958; Singh 2011). However, due to the restrictive conditions imposed on the leases, which impeded their sale, Alfred Dent decided that it would be in their best interests to set up a company to govern the territories and to apply for a Royal Charter from the British government to grant it legitimacy, security, and credibility (Tregonning 1958; Singh 2011). The Royal Charter was eventually granted in 1881 in the name of the British North Borneo Company and, in return for trade monopolies, the Company agreed to abolish slavery and to preserve the religions and customs of the Indigenous populations. The British government was granted a say in the appointment of key officers (Kahin 1947; Tregonning 1958; Singh 2011).

Until this time, most of the territories of North Borneo were under the jurisdiction of the Brunei and Sulu Sultanates (Luping 2009; Singh 2011). The Brunei Sultanate exercised suzerainty over the western coast of Sabah, extending as far as the Kota Belud region, which was administered through a *Jajahan* political framework comprising a hierarchy of officers that corresponded with the division of society into different social classes, and maintained a balance of power between the central polity and its dependencies (Luping 2009; Singh 2011). The Sulu Sultanate exercised control over the eastern coast of Sabah, extending from Sandakan to Lahad Datu and Tawau, which was administered through a *Datu* system or a segmentary state, where the power was largely diffused between the Sultan and the aristocratic overlords, known as the *Datus*, such that the Sultan's influence depended on his wealth and the alliances he could build with the individual aristocratic overlords (Luping 2009; Singh 2011). The interior areas of Sabah remained independent of both Sultanates' control, and the Indigenous populations occupying the region retained their customary social systems (Singh 2011).

Due to a lack of financial and labour resources to directly run this vast territory, the British North Borneo Company adopted indirect rule through native participation, which formed the genesis of Indigenous administration in North Borneo (Tregonning 1958; Singh 2011). The system of British indirect rule over its colonies originated in India and was later applied to other colonies within the British Empire (Dirks 2008; Datla 2015). In North Borneo, this was achieved by establishing the Village Headman, the Native Chiefs, and the Native Court as intermediaries between the Indigenous populations and the British North Borneo Company, to maintain peace and security in their villages, as well as to collect taxes for the Company (Singh 2011). This arrangement was later formalised through the Village Administration Proclamation of 1891, which outlined the roles and authority of native appointees in administering native laws (Wong 2009; Singh 2011).

In the 1910s, the colonial administration strengthened native participation by introducing significant changes that allowed the Company to exert stronger influence and more holistic oversight over the local populations. This was motivated by a desire to address Indigenous discontent arising from the disastrous Rundum Rebellion of 1915, during which the Muruts of Rundum District revolted against the colonial administration (Wong 2009; Singh 2011). First, the Village Administration Ordinance was introduced in 1913 to make it mandatory for Native Courts to be established in every district, allowing the Company to exert administrative supervision over districts that had not previously been under full oversight (Wong 2009; Singh 2011). Second, a state-wide consultative council involving Native Chiefs and the Advisory Council for Native Affairs (ACNA) was established in 1915 as a platform for Native Chiefs to highlight common problems faced by the local populations to the Governor, and to provide an opportunity for colonial officers to seek support and cooperation from Native Chiefs in implementing controversial policies (Wong 2009; Singh 2011).

Third, several schemes were introduced from 1915 to strengthen Indigenous representation in the Civil Service (Tregonning 1958; Singh 2011). Native Chiefs could now aspire to become Deputy Assistant District Officers, posts previously held only by Europeans. The Government Training School for the Sons of Native Chiefs was established in 1915 to train Indigenous elites for positions within the Company's administration, to make them more compliant with the practice of indirect rule, and to achieve 'the full realisation of the British ideal to delegate authority' (Furley 1971: 63). Efforts to train Indigenous people for the Company's administration, however, tended to focus on the Malay-Muslim groups, especially the local chiefs from the more politically and administratively sophisticated Brunei and Sulu Sultanates, as they could more quickly adapt to the Company's complex administrative and juridical systems (Singh 2011). Out of the first batch of nine top-ranking officers appointed on the ACNA in 1915, eight officers were from the Malay-Muslim coastal groups, and one officer was a Kadazandusun from the Papar District (Singh 2011). As it was too expensive to maintain, the training school was closed in 1922 (Singh 2011).

The Chartered Company governed North Borneo from 1881 until the Japanese occupation in 1941. The territory was briefly under an Australian administration from the end of the Japanese occupation in 1945 to early 1946, after which it was handed over to Britain, renamed Sabah, and made a Crown Colony (Luping 2009). Members of Indigenous populations were initiated into the Civil Service to form part of the colonial administration (Luping 2009) and the Colonial Administration of Sabah introduced the Native Tutorial Programme in 1959 to train able Indigenous officers to take on the roles of administrative officers and magistrates within the Civil Service (Luping 2009). A partial representative system, involving the Indigenous population, was adopted for Sabah's governance. Native Courts, administered by Local District Officers and Native Chiefs, were established in various districts around Sabah to handle the domestic affairs of the people (Luping 2009). These political structures, headed by local Indigenous elites, remained largely intact into the post-colonial period, and form the basis of Sabah's governance in contemporary Malaysia.

On 31 August 1957, the Federation of Malaya, comprising Peninsular Malaysia, was granted independence within the British Commonwealth. The Federation of Malaysia was formed on 16 September 1963 from the merger of the Federation of Malaya, Singapore, and the states of Sabah and Sarawak.[3] After Malaysia gained independence, the status of Indigenous people in Malaysia deteriorated significantly. A key reason for this was the introduction of the New Economic Policy (NEP), also known as the *bumiputera* or 'sons of the soil' policy. Conceived in 1969 following racial riots between Chinese and Malay populations over economic disparities in Malaysia, and officially implemented in 1971 (Andaya and Andaya 2001), the NEP regards both Malay-Muslims and the Indigenous population as 'sons of the soil' and extends wide-ranging preferential policies to both groups such as university admissions and access to Civil Service jobs. The NEP was conceived mainly to counter the economic dominance of the Chinese and Indian populations (*The Economist* 2013). However, as they are not Malay-Muslims, Indigenous people are considered second-class *bumiputeras*, and they continue to be marginalised by Malay-Muslims regarding access to economic and social privileges under the NEP.

After independence, the Orang Asli became a target of the Malaysian government's integration policy. In 1961, the Malaysian government issued the 'Statement of Policy Regarding the Long-Term Administration of the Aboriginal Peoples', which aimed to 'adopt suitable measures designed for their protection and advancement with a view to their ultimate integration with the Malay section of the community' (JHEOA 1961: 2, cited in Nicholas 2000: 94). The early leadership of the JHEOA, however, focused on their socio-economic development (Nicholas 2000), as full integration with the Malay population through religious conversion to Islam was highly unpopular among the Orang Asli. It was only from the 1980s, when threat of MCP's resurgence grew, that JHEOA began to actively pursue the objective of integrating the Orang Asli into the mainstream Malay population (Nicholas 2000).

In 1979, the resurgence of the MCP after their retreat and retraining at the Malaysian-Thai border, following the end of the Malayan Emergency in 1960, prompted the Malaysian government, through JHEOA, to implement 're-groupment schemes'. The Orang Asli were resettled in wooden stilt houses with modern amenities that were close to their native customary homelands. Here, they were provided the opportunity to participate in waged labour in nearby plantations (Denton et al. 1997; Nicholas 2000). There was also active Islamisation of the Orang Asli during this time, with the implementation of the *dakwah* programme involving positive discrimination towards Orang Asli who converted to Islam. Incentives such as cash payments and the promise of development projects to improve their lives were provided (Dentan et al. 1997; Nicholas 2000). The missionary arms of Islamic religious councils in Malaysia regularly carried out home visits, organised religious celebratory programmes during fasting periods, and built mosques and prayer rooms in Orang Asli villages (Dentan et al. 1997; Nicholas 2000; Toshihiro 2009). Like the British colonial mission before it, the Malaysian government sought to civilise and integrate the Orang Asli through Islamisation, which would, in turn, legitimise the Malay-Muslims, alongside the Orang Asli, as the 'sons of the soil' under the NEP.

Since the 1990s, JHEOA has appeared to have abandoned its integration policy, replacing it with a 10-pronged strategy aimed at placing 'the Orang Asli firmly on the path of development in a way that is non-compulsory in nature and allows them to set their own pace' (JHEOA 1993, cited in Nicholas 2000: 96). This was a result of changing governmental attitudes towards Orang Asli following the emergence of Indigenous consciousness and activism in Malaysia from the 1980s. In 2010, JHEOA was renamed the Department of Orang Asli Development (JAKOA) to better reflect its new remit, which is to promote the development of Orang Asli. The current strategy, outlined by JAKOA (2016) in its 2016 to 2020 Strategic Plan, states the objectives of the government department as being to:

a   Improve the administration of Orang Asli Customary Lands.
b   Improve facilities and amenities in Orang Asli villages.
c   Develop human capital and provide skills training for Orang Asli, especially Orang Asli youths.
d   Support Orang Asli in the development of economically sustainable projects.
e   Preserve and promote the art, culture, and heritage of Orang Asli.

f   Strengthen welfare and societal support networks for Orang Asli.

g   Improve service delivery of JAKOA through organisational development.

While JHEOA's policies and programmes have brought about improvements in the economic and material well-being of the Orang Asli, several critics (Dentan et al. 1997; Nicholas 2000; Toshihiro 2009; Subramaniam 2011) argue that JHEOA's policies and programmes are intended to serve the ideological objective of controlling the Orang Asli – by destroying their political autonomy and engendering dependency on the government through resettlement, legislative fiat, and administrative intervention and de-culturalisation – so as to control their lands, territories, and resources. Similar to the colonial civilising mission, while the developmental programmes imposed on the Orang Asli by JHEOA serve to minimise the differences between the Orang Asli and Malays, they also consciously maintain the construct of the Orang Asli as not quite/not Malay (Nah 2003), thus accentuating the inferiority of the Orang Asli relative to Malays. The Aboriginal Peoples Act (1974) confers the minister in charge of Orang Asli Affairs the powers to decide on a wide range of Orang Asli matters such as

> the creation and regulation of Orang Asli settlements, control of entry into Orang Asli abodes, appointment and removal of Orang Asli headmen, prohibition of the planting of any specified plant in Orang Asli settlements, [and] permitting and regulating the taking of forest produce, birds and animals from Orang Asli areas (Nicholas 2000: 108).

The responsibilities of administering all Orang Asli matters are also entrusted upon JHEOA, with decision-making powers lying with Malays, since representatives of the Orang Asli hold only low-level positions within the agency (Nicholas 2000).

At the negotiation for Sabah's admission into the Federation of Malaysia on 16 September 1963, a list of terms and conditions, known as the 20-point Treaty, was agreed upon in order to safeguard the interests of the people of Sabah and lay the foundation for its post-merger self-governance, with the content of the Treaty integrated, in varying degrees, into the Constitution of Malaysia. Today, Sabah has its own State Parliament and elects its own Chief Minister, who oversees the administration and governance of the state (Luping 2009). The state administration of Sabah comprises local Indigenous elites, although this is increasingly undermined by the predominantly Malay-Muslim Federal Government based in Kuala Lumpur.

Despite the integration of Indigenous people into Sabah's state administration, post-independence power struggles among the major ethnic-backed political parties in Sabah, coupled with significant pressures from the Federal Government which favoured a Muslim Chief Minister to lead Sabah, led to the short-lived appointments of the first two non-Muslim Chief Ministers from 1963 to 1967. It was only in 1967, with the appointment of a Suluk

Muslim – Tun Mustapha – who had the backing of the Federal Government and served as the Third Chief Minister of Sabah from 1967 to 1975, that the state achieved greater political stability. Donald Stephens, an ethnic Kadazan leader, who served as the first Chief Minister of Sabah from 1963 to 1964, appealed to his fellow Kadazan people to accept that the *bumiputeras* of Malaysia, including the non-Muslim Indigenous people of Sabah, should unite behind the Malay-Muslim leadership of Malaysia (Reid 2009). This was a major turning point, which led to the significant erosion of influence and rights for non-Muslim Indigenous people in Sabah. In an address to his party's National Council in December 1967, he reportedly said: 'The Kadazans, in order to be saved, must lose our sense of racialism or rather tribalism and not only accept all *bumiputeras* as one but we must also learn to feel one' (Luping 1994: 240–241, cited in Reid 2009: 197). This severely undermined the position of the non-Malay-Muslim Indigenous people in Sabah in the early period of Malaysia's independence, and set the climate for their subservient position in Sabah's state policies and politics in the following decades.

In the quest to forge a united identity among the Sabah people, Tun Mustapha promoted a 'one language, one culture and one religion' national unity policy, which promoted the supremacy of the Malay language, Muslim culture, and Islamic religion (Reid 2009). The Kadazan language was removed from the school curriculum in the late 1960s, and all other languages, except Malay and English, were banned in radio broadcasts from 1974 (Reid 2009). Islam was declared the state religion in 1973, against the spirit of the 20-point Treaty, and the state devised several ways to encourage active conversion of the Sabah people to Islam (Reid 2009). The colonial conceptualisation of the Indigenous people of Borneo as a separate racial category, less cultured and civilised than the Malays, continues to feed into local policies and politics in Sabah, relegating these non-Malay Indigenous people to the position of inferior races to be civilised and integrated into mainstream Malay-Muslim society. The adoption of policies aimed at suppressing political and cultural expressions of non-Malay Indigenous identities in Sabah led to the perpetuation of Malay-Muslim dominance, severely undermining their political, social, and cultural status in present-day Malaysia.

The rise of Indigenous consciousness and activism in Malaysia

The fragile economic and social realities of Malaysia in the late 1960s and 1970s, and the perceived social injustices of the NEP associated with extending preferential policies to the Malay-Muslims, motivated the emergence of a nascent Indigenous consciousness movement in the 1980s. This emerging political consciousness also corresponded with a period of increased encroachment onto Indigenous people's customary territories by government agencies and private companies. In addition, the government actively promoted policies aimed at integrating them into the mainstream Malay-Muslim population, against which they were powerless due to their weak political status (Nicholas 2000; Reid 2009; Aiken and Leigh 2011a). The prevailing political and economic climate in Malaysia, coupled with the rise of the global transnational Indigenous rights movement, provided the impetus for the development of a shared consciousness forged around Indigenous identity, which various Indigenous groups in Malaysia could mobilise and unite around for the assertion of their rights and to redress the injustices they had experienced.

In Peninsular Malaysia, early efforts to mobilise Indigenous people could be traced to the formation of the 'Peninsular Malaysia Orang Asli Association' (POASM) in 1976, an association borne out of early efforts by educated Orang Asli to resist the government's intention in 1973 to re-classify the Orang Asli as 'Putra Asli', translated as 'native son' (Nicholas 2000). POASM remained dormant thereafter, until it was revived in 1987 by Anthony Williams-Hunt (Bah Tony) – a Malaysian with Orang Asli ancestry, the son of a prominent British colonial administrator P.D.R. Williams-Hunt, who headed JHEOA from 1947 to 1953, and his Orang Asli wife – in partnership with Colin Nicholas, a Malaysian Orang Asli activist of Eurasian ancestry (Nicholas 2000; Moore 2010). Both Anthony Williams-Hunt and Colin Nicholas embarked on a series of radical reforms that challenged JHEOA's paternalistic approach towards the Orang Asli, leading to heightened tensions between the leadership of POASM and JHEOA (Jumper 1999). They embarked on aggressive media lobbying to bring Orang Asli issues to the mainstream media, conducted active membership campaigns for POASM to reach out to new bases of Orang Asli, and broadened their engagement by collaborating with Malaysian and international organisations to bring Orang Asli agendas to the fore (Jumper 1999; Nicholas 2000). Their efforts paid off, and POASM membership among the Orang Asli increased from a mere 250 in 1976 to over 10,000 in 1991 (Nicholas 2000).

The revival of POASM in the late 1980s occurred at an embryonic period of a nation-wide Indigenous consciousness in Malaysia that was taking shape on the campus of the National University of Malaysia [Universiti Kebangsaan Malaysia] (UKM). A group of students from the Catholics Student Society and Sabah Students Association Group at the University were greatly inspired by the Christian social justice movement that was gaining popularity at that time. Concerned with the social injustices that they witnessed, especially in Sabah, they established a small project under the Sabah Christian Movement known as 'Projects for Awareness and Community Organisations in Sabah' (PACOS) in 1987 to bring awareness to the rights of the Indigenous people in the state (Nicholas 2000). Among the founders of PACOS were Jannie Lasimbang from the influential Lasimbang family (see Chapter 5), and Colin Nicholas, who lobbied for POASM. Colin

Nicholas left PACOS in 1990. Jannie Lasimbang later worked with her elder sister, Anne Lasimbang to convert PACOS into a trust, and renamed the new organisation PACOS Trust, with Anne Lasimbang leading the organisation as its Executive Director.

The formation of PACOS Trust coincided with a period of unrestrained timber logging in the 1970s and 1980s in the interior areas of Sabah. Timber logging was embroiled in Sabah's money politics: the Forest Enactment (1968), and its related set of regulations, the Forest Rules (1969), extended to the Chief Minister's exclusive discretion over the issue of logging concessions, which were often given to reward political allies (Reid 2009). By the late 1980s, disputes over logging on Indigenous lands in the East Malaysian states of Sarawak and Sabah had reached acrimonious levels. Roadblocks set up by Indigenous people were gaining international media attention (Inguanzo and Wright 2016). Of these, the Penan issue in Sarawak was the most prominent and visible act of resistance by an Indigenous group in Malaysia.[4] This media visibility attracted the interest of international NGOs such as the World Wide Fund for Nature (WWF) and others, which launched international campaigns against indiscriminate and illegal timber logging, and also contributed to heightened interest in Indigenous issues in Sabah and the neighbouring state of Sarawak (Inguanzo and Wright 2016).

PACOS Trust's early efforts were centred on raising awareness among Indigenous people of their rights. Their activists conducted regular visits into the remote regions of Sabah, to meet and share with Indigenous people the concept of human rights through talks, posters, and exhibitions, as well as provide aid and advice on problems faced by community members. Over time, PACOS Trust forged a rapport with the Indigenous people and became a trusted NGO that people could consult for assistance and advice on environmental, social, and economic problems that they faced with the increasing incidences of encroachment on their native customary lands. In 2003, PACOS Trust was renamed 'Partners of Community Organisations, Sabah' to better reflect its role, which had shifted from a project-oriented to an advocacy focus, although the acronym 'PACOS Trust' was retained for brand awareness (PACOS Trust n.d.). PACOS Trust currently brings together a network of community organisations around Sabah, set up by Indigenous people themselves, to promote projects supporting education, socio-economic development, resource management, cultural mapping, and heritage preservation in these areas (PACOS Trust n.d.).

Concerned with the marginalisation suffered by the Orang Asli in Peninsular Malaysia, and the lack of a rallying voice on their behalf, in 1989, Colin Nicholas returned to Kuala Lumpur from Sabah to establish the Center for Orang Asli Concerns (COAC), a research and advocacy centre. In Peninsular Malaysia, there was a growth of Indigenous-based organisations seeking to assert and reclaim Orang Asli identity and representation, as well as Orang Asli businesses seeking to exploit natural resources in native customary areas claimed by the Orang Asli, which invariably led to the exploitation of Orang Asli by themselves through the unethical practices of some Orang Asli organisations and businesses (Nicholas 2000).

At the height of the Indigenous movement in Malaysia, when Penan resistance to rainforest clearance in Sarawak was brought to international attention at the Earth Summit in 1992, the then Prime Minister of Malaysia, Mahathir Muhammad, criticised the activists: 'They want to preserve the Penans as jungle inhabitants who do not need care and supervision. They wish to see the Penans remain as museum pieces and as remnants of the cavemen for them to gawk at' (Merry 1991: 11). The Malaysian government also criticised the alliance between the Indigenous Penan and the international activist groups as being 'a reflection of condescension and patronage' (Merry 1991: 11), drawing upon the imaginary of the idealised noble savage, while playing scant attention to contemporary issues facing Indigenous people. The episode reflected the incompatible agendas arising from such alliances between Indigenous people and environmental conservation groups, which drew upon an essentialised and idealised portrayal of Indigenous people as leading a simple way of life, close to nature, and as de facto nature conservationists. The historical construction of Indigenous people as noble savages was thus strategically mobilised by Indigenous people and environmental conservation groups to advance their respective agendas. However, this presented a risk, as the Indigenous people had to position themselves as anti-development in order to conform to this image of the 'ecological noble savage' (Redford 1990). This had the unintended consequences of misrepresenting their priorities and compromising Indigenous self-determination and agency (Conklin and Graham 1995; Kirsch 2007).

In 1995, the leaders of PACOS Trust initiated the formation of the Jaringan Orang Asal SeMalaysia [Indigenous Peoples Network of Malaysia] (JOAS), an umbrella network for Indigenous grassroots organisations across Sabah, Sarawak, and Peninsular Malaysia. The network was mainly intended to represent Malaysia's Indigenous people at national, regional, and international levels (JOAS n.d.). By this time, many international and national Indigenous-based organisations had been established in Malaysia to capitalise on the emerging sense of Indigenous consciousness and activism. Since its formation, JOAS has organised the annual national Indigenous Peoples' Day celebrations on a rotational basis in Peninsular Malaysia, Sarawak, and Sabah. These events incorporate national workshops that also serve as forums for dialogue and exchange between representatives of Indigenous people from across Malaysia on Indigenous rights and concerns (Nicholas 2000). JOAS currently represents Malaysia on various regional and international alliances of Indigenous people, such as the Asian Indigenous Peoples Pact (AIPP), a regional organisation of Asian Indigenous movements founded in 1988 in Thailand for the promotion and defence of Indigenous rights, and the articulation of Indigenous concerns for Indigenous people in Asia (AIPP 2016).

A significant chapter in Malaysia's history of Indigenous activism was the Malaysian government's adoption of the United Nations Declaration on the Rights of Indigenous Peoples (UNDRIP) in 2007, which reaffirmed the 'urgent need to respect and promote the inherent rights of Indigenous people which derive from their political, economic and social structures and from their cultures, spiritual traditions, histories and philosophies, especially their rights to their lands, territories and resources' (UNDRIP 2007: 2). The UNDRIP serves as an important document for providing a basis for Indigenous recognition and assertion of Indigenous rights in Malaysia. PACOS Trust took the lead in translating and interpreting the UNDRIP Convention into the Malay language for wider dissemination, as well as by organising workshops and meetings to educate Indigenous people in Malaysia about the ethos of the UNDRIP Convention. Malaysia also has a representation through JOAS on the United Nations Permanent Forum on Indigenous Issues (UNPFII), the UN's central coordinating body on the concerns of Indigenous people worldwide. Although Malaysia is a signatory to the UNDRIP Convention, there has been no abatement in the Malaysian government's efforts to commandeer Indigenous lands for development without proper compensation and in its assimilation policies targeted at Indigenous people (Aiken and Leigh 2011a). The UNPFII thus provides an important avenue for Indigenous organisations in Malaysia to obtain expert advice and access to international funding for Indigenous-related programmes, while also offering an international platform for voicing the concerns of the Indigenous people in Malaysia, which, in turn, adds pressure on the Malaysian authorities.

Since the late 1990s, Indigenous people in Malaysia have started to turn to the courts to address alleged breaches of their land and resource rights. This has been motivated by increased awareness among Indigenous people of their rights, the exhaustion of other avenues such as dialogue and negotiation for making their concerns heard, and the successes of Indigenous people in seeking compensation for infringement of their native rights through legal jurisprudence elsewhere (Nicholas 2000; Idrus 2010; Aiken and Leigh 2011a). A landmark judgement in 1996 (Adong bin Kuwau & Ors v Kerajaan Negeri Johor & Anor, 1997), in which the Indigenous Jakun people of Johor won a case against the Johor State Government for preventing them from foraging on their ancestral lands that had been set aside as a reservoir to supply water to Singapore, demonstrated that native title could be accommodated within common law (Aiken and Leigh 2011a). This also implies that the Indigenous people in Malaysia can claim native titles on their ancestral lands, territories, and resources by articulating their *adat* (customs): the 'accepted norms and customs that govern the lives of Indigenous communities, which include their way of life, basic values, systems of belief, codes of conduct, manners, conventions, agricultural and cultural practices according to which Indigenous societies are ordered' (Malaysian Forestry Department 2015: 30).

In 2010, the Malaysian Bar Council established the Committee on Orang Asli Rights to focus exclusively on providing pro-bono legal assistance to Orang Asli involved in legal disputes in the Malaysian courts relating to their lands and resource rights. The COAC, principally represented by Colin Nicholas, has provided research assistance and served as an expert witness on the historical and anthropological aspects of Orang Asli cultural heritage in these legal disputes, often drawing upon an essentialised depiction of Orang Asli cultural heritage that does not conform to the dynamic cultural practices of the Orang Asli today. As native customary rights are established through maintaining a historical connection to the lands, this has even motivated a revival of land- and resource-based shamanistic practices among the Orang Asli (Subramanian and Edo 2016). In Sabah, PACOS Trust has been supporting Indigenous people in challenging the Sabah State Government and the Land Office, as well as private companies, for the illegal possession of their native customary lands and territories (Cooke 2013; Forest People Programme 2016). Despite some successes, Indigenous people still face an uphill battle in getting the Malaysian government to recognise their native rights, due to issues such as unfulfilled promises, inconsistent handling of compensation, and the hostility of the Malaysian Federal and State Governments towards court rulings (Aiken and Leigh 2011b; Cooke 2013).

In Peninsular Malaysia, the bigger issue impeding the Orang Asli from claiming their customary rights is the status of the Orang Asli as wards of the Malaysian state, a guardian-ward relationship that has its roots in the colonial construction of the Orang Asli as underdeveloped Malays and Malay subjects, and later enshrined in domestic laws, which empower the state to determine priorities for the Orang Asli and their welfare (Andaya 2008; Idrus 2010; Subramanian 2011). If it were to recognise Orang Asli customary rights according to UNDRIP standards, the Malaysian state would need to reduce its powers of 'wardship' over the Orang Asli and their lands, a position that is not tenable from the perspective of the Malaysian state, as it sees these controls as a means to align Orang Asli to national priorities and ensure that Orang Asli enjoy the benefits of national development (Subramanian 2011). This situation highlights the incompatibility of collective rights based on evoking Indigenous status with equal citizenship (Kuper 2003; Idrus 2010).

In Sabah, where native titles were already recognised under a system of native administration, which was established during the colonial period as part of indirect rule, Indigenous people articulated their claims to the ancestral lands and resources, by mobilising their 'place-based imaginaries' (Cooke 2013: 513), and emphasising their connections to the lands and their right to moral justice arising from their historical marginalisation. As such, they drew upon the historical conceptualisation of Indigeneity based on primordiality and autochthony, and self-idealisation as 'ecologically noble savages' as a tool for political activism. However, contrary to this, the

Indigenous people in Sabah are not anti-development, but rather, they perceive land as a productive asset and would like to be consulted on development plans for the native lands, which is evident in the dubious deals that Indigenous people have made with capitalist brokers for lands over which they eventually gained customary rights through the legal process (Cooke 2013). This resonates with what Li (2000) considers as a strategic articulation and positioning of Indigenous identity to negotiate resource politics, and the contradictory dualism between development and anti-development in Indigenous advocacy (Kirsch 2007; Clifford 2013; Kallen 2015).

Indigenous tourism and sustainable development in Malaysia

With the emergence of Indigenous consciousness in Malaysia in the 1980s, the concept of Indigeneity has taken on positive connotations, becoming 'a marker of global identity, associated with mainly positive ideas about cultural wisdom and integrity and with politically significant claims to self-determination' (Niezen 2003: 217). The dominant rhetoric concerning 'culture for development' and associated discourses on Indigenous museums as arenas for community involvement and Indigenous self-determination have also inspired a growing interest in developing Indigenous cultural tourism in Malaysia, as the Malaysian government and the Indigenous people themselves come to realise that cultural heritage can be valorised for identity building and economic generation. The cultural economy and the commodification of heritage seem to have offered Indigenous people in Malaysia a visibility and status that offers some leverage in respect of Indigenous advocacy and self-determination, albeit with ambiguous outcomes.

Since the 1980s, the Malaysian government has recognised the economic potential of cultural tourism. The first museum focusing on Indigenous cultural heritage was the National Orang Asli Museum, nested within the Orang Asli heartlands of Gombak in the state of Selangor. First established in 1987 at the official residence of the former Director-General of JHEOA, the Museum was rebuilt in the vicinity in 1995, at a cost of Malaysian Ringgit (RM) 3.3 million (£605,000), funded by the Malaysian government. It re-opened to the public on 2 March 2000 (Orang Asli Museum n.d.a). In 2011, the Museum again closed for major refurbishment and re-opened its doors in February 2013, featuring new displays and dioramas about the everyday lives of the major Orang Asli groups living in Peninsular Malaysia, and the role of JAKOA in uplifting their lives (Figure 2.1).

It was only from the 2000s that the Malaysian government started to take a greater interest in capitalising on its cultural heritage for tourism development. Under the Eighth Malaysia Plan – the national development plan for Malaysia from 2001 to 2005 – aspects of Malaysia's cultural heritage, encompassing its Indigenous cultural heritage, were identified as its core

Figure 2.1 The National Orang Asli Museum at Gombak in the state of Selangor in Peninsular Malaysia. Photograph: Author.

tourism products, with emphasis placed on engendering greater community involvement to maximise the benefits and minimise the adverse impacts of tourism (Eight Malaysia Plan 2000). Cultural tourism was also considered as a form of 'sustainable tourism development ... that w[ould] provide the necessary balance among economic, social, cultural and environmental needs in all tourism planning and implementation' (Eight Malaysia Plan 2000: 367).

The emerging interest in cultural tourism as a form of sustainable development chimes with the proliferation of Indigenous cultural villages or cultural theme-parks that draw upon the cultural heritage of local populations across Southeast Asia (Wood 1984; Adams 1997; Dellios 2002; Erb 2007; Cohen 2008, 2016; Hoffstaedter 2008). The growth of such heritage parks in Southeast Asia can be attributed to several causes. First, national governments have construed ethnic tourism as an instrument of nation-building, especially in countries with a multicultural heritage, both to showcase a national identity based on a rhetoric of 'unity in diversity' and to cultivate better understanding across different cultural groups (Adams 1997; Kreps 2003). Second, national governments and Indigenous people seek to take advantage of the economic and developmental opportunities offered by cultural tourism by displaying the material culture and heritage of Indigenous people (Kreps 2003; Erb 2007). Third, the expansion of capitalist forms of production and marketing encourages a form of tourism entrepreneurship based on the commodification and exoticisation of Indigenous cultural practices (Su and Teo 2009; Cohen 2016).

Stasch (2015) coined the label 'primitivist tourism' to describe a form of cultural tourism that draws upon the ideological construct of Indigenous people and ethnic minorities as 'primitive people' living in primordial societies. Primitivist tourism frames Indigenous subjects as authentic 'noble savages' living in harmony with nature in a state of primordial innocence (Conklin and Graham 1995; Ellingson 2001), for the consumption of tourists, often masking their historical and contemporary marginalisation by both celebrating and stigmatising their differences as a commodified and exoticised spectacle. The historical construction of Indigenous people as 'noble savages' is still actively drawn upon by tourism operators to promote Malaysia as an exotic cultural destination. An advertisement from an international travel agency portrays Sabah as a 'lush land of tribal warriors, mysterious headhunters and far-from-home war heroes [that] has intrigued adventurers, anthropologists, and explorers for centuries' (Intrepid Travel n.d.).

Indigenous museums, including Indigenous cultural villages, are an institutionalised form of primitivist tourism, promoting the commodification and exoticisation of Indigenous people and their cultural heritage for tourist consumption. They are staged arenas exhibiting a version of Indigenous cultural heritage, which not only conforms with tourists' imaginaries of the exotic, primitive people but also embodies the Indigenous people's self-imaginaries that they wish to meld with those of the tourists (Salazar and Graham 2015). A Malaysian tour operator, for example, promotes the Monsopiad Cultural Village as a 'headhunter's tour [in the] heartland of the Kadazan tribe set amidst serene hills, [offering an] up-close encounter with Monsopiad's "trophies" [at] Monsopiad's house in ... its well-preserved ancient dwelling' (Amazing Borneo Tours n.d.). This demonstrates how the historical construction of Indigenous people in Malaysia as 'primitive tribes' and 'noble savages' continues to shape modern tourism imaginaries about them (Salazar 2009, 2010; Bergmeister 2015).

As can be surmised from this historiographical account of Indigeneity in Malaysia, Indigenous people have been discursively constructed and reified as an inferior and underdeveloped race relative to Europeans and other racial groups in Malaysia through colonial ethnographic accounts and censuses. This has continued to be perpetuated in Indigenous policies and developmental politics from the colonial period to the present, although the Indigenous people in East and Peninsular Malaysia have been treated differently due to the perceived differences in their degrees of primitivism and relative autochthony. In the following four chapters, I explore how the colonial construction of Indigeneity is mobilised within four Indigenous cultural villages – sites of primitivist tourism – in Malaysia by different stakeholders to fulfil multiple interests and diverse agendas producing complex ramifications and uneven outcomes for the Indigenous people that complicate the positive rhetoric surrounding the 'culture for development' discourse.

Notes

1 Anthropologically, the term 'pygmies' has been used to describe an ethnic group with endemic short stature. Today, this term is generally regarded as derogatory.

2 The Department of Aborigines was renamed the Department of Orang Asli Affairs [Jabatan Hal Ehwal Orang Asli] (JHEOA) on 16 September 1963 at the formation of the Federation of Malaysia, and was later renamed the Department of Orang Asli Development [Jabatan Kemajuan Orang Asli] (JAKOA) in 2010.

3 Singapore was subsequently expelled from the Federation of Malaysia on 9 August 1965, two years after its formation.

4 In 1992, the native Penan people of Sarawak in East Malaysia staged a protest against the incessant clearance of tropical rainforests in Borneo, which was encroaching onto their native customary lands, territories, and resources at the Earth Summit in Rio de Janeiro, Brazil. Their plights attracted the interest of Indigenous rights activists, environmentalists, and celebrities from different parts of the world, who waged an international campaign on their behalf against the oppression of the Indigenous people and the global loss of biodiversity (Brosius 1997a, b, 2003). The pressures exerted by the international community on the illegal logging in Sarawak eventually led to the suspension of timber imports from Sarawak into the key markets such as the European Union and Australia.

3 Capacity-building as a modern civilising mission

Introduction[1]

The Mah Meri Cultural Village (Figure 3.1) presents a case study of the complex dynamics within a typical government-initiated community-based cultural project that is established to provide capacity-building for the local communities. I argue that community-based cultural projects can cultivate a culture of dependency between the brokers managing the projects and the intended beneficiaries of these projects, based on a form of 'patron-client' relationship that existed historically, leading to the marginalisation of the local communities in the hands of the brokers. What is promoted as a community-based capacity-building project for the Indigenous people today appears to resonate with the colonial civilising mission of the twentieth century, rooted in the historic 'patron-client' relationship that conceptualises Indigenous people as backward, undeveloped, and inferior relative to the white Europeans and other ethnic groups on the evolutionary hierarchy.

The workings of these cultural projects, as the case of the Mah Meri Cultural Village demonstrates, are further complicated by the lack of homogeneity and unity in the conceptualisation of 'community'. What is deemed as a collective community is made up of individuals with different agendas, allegiances, and interests to the projects, which may or may not align with one another. As such, these cultural projects become arenas where diverse interests and agendas are played out, giving rise to power politics and contestations over issues of identity and claims to representation. Within these cultural projects, Indigenous cultural heritage come to be mobilised by different stakeholders to fulfil diverse objectives in ways that may fulfil the needs or compromise the positions of the Indigenous people, depending on the politics of brokerage and representation.

The Mah Meri Cultural Village, which is established as part of the Malaysian government's national development plan to capitalise on its Indigenous cultural heritage for sustainable tourism development, is intended to serve as a model for Malaysia's wider adoption of UNESCO's 'culture for development' discourse. As a community-based museum development, the Mah Meri Cultural Village seeks to draw on cultural heritage as a

Figure 3.1 Compounds of the Mah Meri Cultural Village. The Mah Meri Cultural Village is sited on the ancestral lands of the Mah Meri people at Kampung Sungai Bumbun on Carey Island in Peninsular Malaysia. Photograph: Author.

resource for the socio-economic development and Indigenous empowerment of the Mah Meri people. It can be construed as an Indigenous museum that draws on Indigeneity and customs as 'a source of authority and power' (Stanley 2007: 16) to help the Mah Meri people cope with changes brought by the modern world. According to UNESCO's (2010b: ii) report *Community-Based Approach to Museum Development in Asia and the Pacific for Culture and Sustainable Development*, community-based museums enable 'members of such communities, often marginalised in previously dominant museum practice or in society as a whole, [to be] given greater opportunities to negotiate the representation of their memory or heritage in ways they deem appropriate in such institutions'.

The Mah Meri people, also known as *Besisi* by early researchers, are one of the Orang Asli groups under the category of Senoi that reside mainly in Selangor Mainland and Carey Island (Karim 1981). Although the Mah Meri people believe that they originally come from Indo-China, they are known to have occupied areas in the south of Selangor, mainly in Johore and Malacca, over the last two centuries (Karim 1981). The Mah Meri ancestors were mainly fishermen and mangrove hunter-gathers, but the Mah Meri people now undertake small-scale sedentary agriculture and waged labour for their livelihoods (Rahim 2007; Chan 2012). Of the 178,197 Orang Asli people surveyed by the Department of Orang Asli Development (JAKOA) in 2011, the Mah Meri people numbered 3,799, or about 2 per cent of the total Orang Asli population (Orang Asli Museum n.d.b.).

The Mah Meri Cultural Village was established in July 2011 on the ancestral lands of the Mah Meri people at Kampung Sungai Bumbun on Carey Island in the state of Selangor in Peninsular Malaysia. It has an on-site exhibition gallery narrating the history and cultural heritage of the Mah Meri people, a room for the display of priced Mah Meri woodcarvings, a community hall for cultural performances and ritual demonstrations, as well as life-size models of a wooden boat, a spiritual altar, and a spirit house used by the Mah Meri people on display within its garden compounds. The cultural village runs a full-day cultural tour for tourists at a charge of RM 85 (£16) per person. The day includes a guided tour of the exhibition gallery, detailed explanations of the Mah Meri rituals and craft demonstrations, as well as cultural performances, including a staged wedding ceremony performed by the local Mah Meri villagers.

Developed through a public-private partnership, the infrastructure of the Mah Meri Cultural Village was implemented with funding of RM 3 million (£566,000) from the Ministry of Tourism, Arts and Culture (MOTAC). It was built by the Corporation Asli Selangor Private Limited – a company linked to the government and run by Indigenous people from the state of Selangor – after which it was handed over to a government-endorsed ethnic Malay broker to manage its day-to-day operations. The Mah Meri Cultural Village is intended to serve the triple objectives of capitalising on the economic potential of cultural tourism, preserving the Mah Meri cultural heritage, and improving the livelihoods of the Mah Meri people by creating employment through tourism. According to then Minister, Datuk Seri Dr Ng Yen Yen, the Mah Meri Cultural Village is to be promoted as an artisan village to 'attract high-end tourists who are willing to fork out thousands of RM for the unique pieces' (*The Star Online*, 2 February 2012).

Contexts, personalities, and interests

While the Mah Meri Cultural Village was intended to benefit the collective Mah Meri community living on Carey Island, only two out of five main villages[2] – Kampung Sungai Bumbun and Kampung Rambai – are involved in its day-to-day operations. The inhabitants of a third village, Kampung Sungai Judah, shared information about their cultural heritage. According to a Village Headman, whose village was not involved with the Mah Meri Cultural Village:

> When the idea of a cultural village was first raised, all the *Tok Batins* (Village Headmen) of the Mah Meri villages on Pulau Carey were invited for a meeting. It was discussed that each village would take turns to perform at the cultural village. But later, when I found out that the management of the cultural village was an outsider, I did not want to be involved.

Similar to other community-based museums in the Asia-Pacific, which have been set up with various support mechanisms to help local communities with little expertise in museum management (UNESCO 2010b), it was intended at the conceptualisation of the project that the broker would train the local Mah Meri villagers during the first three years to prepare them to take over the management and operation of the cultural village and run it as a community-owned project.

Mired in a complex web of local politics, the initial contract held by the broker ended in 2014 but up until 2020, there is no handover plan in sight. No one seems to know the future plan for the Mah Meri Cultural Village. The villagers at Kampung Sungai Bumbun, where the cultural village is located and whose cultural heritage the site is based on, are dismayed with the situation. One member of the Committee of Village Development and Security, known colloquially as the JKKK (Jawatan Kuasa Kemajuan dan Keselamatan Kampung), lamented:

> We have plans to take over the management of the Mah Meri Cultural Village, but we have no government support and we are not ready due to the lack of training. He should give us training, but he only makes us low-pay workers. JAKOA can't take action, because the Mah Meri Cultural Village is under MOTAC, and the minister there likes him.

Meanwhile, the broker has alternative plans for the Mah Meri Cultural Village. Since late 2014, he has been making presentations to MOTAC about re-branding the cultural village as a discovery centre, as he feels that a revamp is due. He is confident of retaining the management of the cultural village, as he said to me:

> I have many years of experience running such cultural villages. I used to manage a similar cultural centre at Bukit Lagong in Perak that was bigger than the Mah Meri Cultural Village. The communities thought they could run the centre on their own. They took over and converted it into a training camp for youths, and it failed miserably. If they [the government authorities] wanted me to leave, they could come up with many reasons to make me leave, but they didn't.

He added that it would be a colossal task to decide who within the Mah Meri villagers would be a suitable party to take over the management of the cultural village, as there were different factions within the villages who could not get along with one another. He commented that the villagers did not know how to speak with the Minister or do administrative work, and hence they were lacking in the tacit skills essential to the effective management of the cultural village. He added that the cultural village was presented to him by the Malaysian government in place of a similar Indigenous cultural centre at an Orang Asli village in Bukit Lagong, also in the state of

Selangor, of which he was asked to give up the managership at the instigation of the local community.

The local realities about who within the Mah Meri community would take over the management of the cultural village, who would be given the opportunity to work at the cultural village, and whose version of Mah Meri cultural heritage ought to be represented in the cultural village point to the problems of conceptualising the Mah Meri people as a collective community with a common purpose and a clear position on the management of their cultural heritage. The notion of community has been criticised as too vague to be useful as an analytical framework (Bauman 1996; Dwyer 1999; Amit and Rapport 2002; Crooke 2008; Golding and Modest 2015). What is deemed of as the collective Mah Meri community is made up of different groups of social networks that cut across different situations, categories, and allegiances, each existing in its own right and operating in a distinctive manner (Amit and Rapport 2002). This complicates the working dynamics of the cultural village.

While the Mah Meri Cultural Village was established with the developmental needs of the Mah Meri people in mind, the cultural village has come under the management of the broker, who oversees the long-term strategy as well as the day-to-day operations of the site. As mentioned earlier, it was originally intended that the broker would train the local Mah Meri villagers to prepare them for taking over the management and operation of the cultural village, so that they could reap the benefits of cultural tourism. In particular, the broker was expected to transfer his previous experience and expertise of managing a similar Indigenous cultural centre at Bukit Lagong to the local villagers, inculcating in them the skills both to manage and operate the cultural village, as well as to translate and mediate between the tourism industry and the local village economy on their account. This transfer of knowledge and expertise has not occurred.

In classic brokerage terms, the broker at the Mah Meri Cultural Village is mediating and translating between the tourism industry and the local village economy to attract tourists to the cultural village, to meet the intended objectives of capitalising on the economic potential of cultural tourism, to promote the Mah Meri cultural heritage, and to improve the livelihoods of the local people by creating employment for them through tourism. However, the villagers from Kampung Sungai Bumbun, who are employed as performers at the cultural village, do not appear to enjoy such improvements, as they are mainly employed as low-skilled and cheap casual workers, given work only when their labour is required. In contrast, the broker appears to earn a decent income from the cultural village. A villager from Kampung Sungai Bumbun, who worked as a cultural performer at the cultural village, said of their dissatisfaction with their work conditions:

For every busload of tourists that we perform for, we are paid RM 40 (£7.55) if we make new costumes, or RM 35 (£6.60) if we use old costumes. This is decided based on the colours of the leaves used in the making of the costumes. Green colour: new costumes, and yellow colour: old costumes. However, if there are two busloads of visitors and we have to do two performances, we are only paid RM 5 (94p) more, but we feel we should be paid double because we do the performance twice.

The villagers are also frequently not paid on time:

For the recent Association of Southeast Asian Nations (ASEAN) Ministerial Meeting on 19 and 20 September 2014, we were promised RM 50 (£10) for the cultural performances, and RM 15 (£2.80) for each rehearsal we attended. In fact, he had a discussion with us and our *Tok Batin*, and we agreed on the payment, but until today, we have not received the payment.

Although perceived as generating additional income for the Mah Meri villagers, the Mah Meri Cultural Village has not significantly increased their income from the level of earnings prior to the establishment of the cultural village. It has merely changed the source of their income, as another villager working for the cultural village said:

Each month, we take home about RM 900 (£170) from the performances at the Mah Meri Cultural Village and doing some weaving on the side. Due to the sporadic nature of the performances, we cannot take up other more stable jobs, so there is an opportunity cost to us.

Meanwhile, the broker feels that the cultural village has played a significant role in elevating the standard of living of his workers through capacity-building, as he explained:

I am very strict with them to toughen them up to cope with the challenges of the real world out there. For example, I show them how to wash the plates properly. I tell them this is not clean and show them how they should wash the plates properly to conform to our standard of cleanliness. I also help them overcome their fears of finding out about new things. Many of them start off in the village without knowing what a toilet is, and the kids are very scared to ask. Later, they learn what toilets are and how to use them.

The broker adopts a paternalistic approach to his Mah Meri workers, conceptualising them as underdeveloped Malays and Malay subjects with limited capacities to cope with the challenges of the outside world, and therefore, in need of coaching to help them survive in modern Malaysia. This demonstrates how the colonial conceptualisation of the Orang Asli as inferior and underdeveloped, relative to Malay-Muslims, continues to influence how they are perceived and treated in contemporary Malaysia. What is couched as capacity-building at the Mah Meri Cultural Village appears to resonate with the colonial civilising mission of the twentieth century, rooted in the historical construction of the Orang Asli as primitive, backward, and uncivilised relative to the 'more civilised' ethnic Malays – an ethnic category to which the broker belongs – and therefore in need of help to achieve a higher rung on the evolutionary hierarchy.

Recognising that he has a role entrusted to him by MOTAC to improve the lives of the Mah Meri people through the Mah Meri Cultural Village project, the broker supports the needs of the local villagers where he can, especially where it can lead to mutually beneficial collaborations for him and the villagers. For example, he sponsored the funeral rites of a late Mah Meri elder from Kampung Sungai Bumbun in 2013, in exchange for documenting them so that they could become a display at the cultural village. He has also been soliciting donations for developing a library within the cultural village for the Mah Meri villagers, although the level of access that the local villagers will have to the library will be subject to his discretion.

Despite the broker's self-declared activist leanings, he has some reservations regarding other activist groups working with the Mah Meri villagers on Carey Island, preferring to avoid land-related conflicts, as he commented on the alleged encroachment of the Mah Meri native customary lands that took place in September 2014:

> There is an activist group provoking a conflict over land rights between a Mah Meri villager and some Indian developers. The police have been called in to intervene. While the land involved is part of the Mah Meri traditional lands, there has not been any document justifying ownership. If anything, it seems that the developers hold legal titles to the land. I am not interested in human rights or land rights struggles. My aim is to help promote and develop the cultures of the Mah Meri communities. You shouldn't get involved with the activists. If you work with me, you can't work with them, and if you work with them, you can't work with me. The people demanding compensation and land rights are lazy people. They need to work for their money. I will not get involved in the case, but if the man involved is jailed, I will be prepared to help him by supporting his family financially.

The broker's lack of interest in Indigenous activism, even as he advocates for the positive value of culture for development, contradicts the dominant rhetoric in the tourism literature on the positive impacts of Indigenous cultural tourism on Indigenous activism. Weaver (2010) argues that the exhibitionism and exploitation of Indigenous cultural heritage, while representing the nadir of Indigenous control, can foster strategies of resistance among Indigenous people, which later give rise to Indigenous empowerment. He proposes a six-stage Indigenous tourism model, purporting that, at the third stage, Indigenous people develop overt and covert strategies of adaptation and resistance to cope with the disruptive impacts of cultural commodification arising from Indigenous tourism. Eventually these morph into a form of quasi-empowerment at the sixth stage, during which Indigenous people actively assert their native rights to their ancestral lands and territories. This is supported by a shadow Indigenous tourism economy, in which developers are obliged to make concessions for Indigenous rights in other aspects of economic development, achieving a state of sustainable development (Weaver 2010).

While Weaver's (2010) six-stage Indigenous tourism model purports that Indigenous people develop overt and covert strategies of adaptation and resistance in the process of engaging in cultural tourism, which later give rise to a form of quasi-empowerment for the Indigenous people, the broker seems to consider Indigenous activism as a distraction to the promotion of culture for tourism and development. His lack of support for Indigenous activism is unsurprising, as strengthening the level of Indigenous consciousness and activism among the Mah Meri villagers may weaken his authority at the cultural village. The rhetoric of Indigenous empowerment may encourage the villagers to seek greater involvement and self-determination in the management and operation of the cultural village.

The prevailing structure of Mah Meri Cultural Village, which extends significant authority to the broker in the management of the cultural village, exacerbates the marginalisation of the local Mah Meri villagers. It serves to extend the prevailing paternalistic approach adopted by the Malaysian government towards the Orang Asli, rather than to improve their livelihoods and capacity for self-determination. This resonates with Ferguson's (1994) observation for the World Bank-sponsored Thaba-Tseka project in Lesotho that 'development' apparatus is established not to eliminate the poverty of marginalised people, but to deliberately reinforce and expand the exercise of bureaucratic state power. The Mah Meri Cultural Village thus serves to entrench a structural relationship that perpetuates a culture of dependency or a form of 'patron-client' relationship, based on a historical understanding of the Orang Asli as Malay subjects that existed even before colonial era. As a result, the Mah Meri Cultural Village has become a vehicle for perpetuating long-standing inequalities and facilitating the continued marginalisation of the Mah Meri villagers. The cultural village, therefore, complicates idealised notions about Indigenous museums and the positive role of culture, which are often uncritically reproduced in the museological literature and broader 'culture for development' discourse.

Transformation, representation, and interpretation of culture

At the Mah Meri Cultural Village, there has been a transformation of Indigenous cultural practices into commodified cultural heritage for the 'tourist gaze' (Urry 1990). The cultural village has become a staged arena, where

certain aspects of Mah Meri cultural heritage are constructed and represented for tourist consumption. This is negotiated by different stakeholders,
including the broker, the Mah Meri villagers, and tourists, to conform to
tourists' imaginaries about the Mah Meri people as exotic noble savages,
which are, in turn, shaped by historically inherited stereotypes about them
(Salazar and Graburn 2015). Here, I explore the complex dynamics surrounding the process of heritage-making at the Mah Meri Cultural Village
through examining the commodification of Mah Meri woodcarving and
the staging of a Mah Meri wedding ceremony, in order to understand the
politics of this instrumentalisation of heritage.

Contemporary Mah Meri woodcarving would seem to be a classic case of
commodified cultural heritage. The commercial folk-art carvings one can see
being made and sold at the Mah Meri Cultural Village (Figure 3.2), while
adapted from earlier woodcarving practices, emerged in the 1950s as a creative response to the forces of globalisation and modernisation. In common
with other Mah Meri cultural practices on display at the cultural village, I
argue that woodcarving too may be understood as a kind of 'staged' cultural
heritage, mediated through multiple channels, including the tourist art market (Steiner 1994; Scott 2017). While there was documentation of Mah Meri
wooden sculptures and masks in early ethnographic literature, which attests
to the practice of woodcarving dating back to the early twentieth century
(Skeat and Blagden 1906a, b; Karim 1981), these early wooden sculptures
and masks are markedly different in size, purpose, and material compared
with the commercial folk-art presented as Mah Meri woodcarving today.

Figure 3.2 A Mah Meri villager with the award-winning Chained Tiger Ancestor woodcarvings on sale at the Mah Meri Cultural Village. Photograph: Author.

The early wooden sculptures and masks are usually small in scale, made of lightweight but durable *tengkho* wood (*Alstonia* sp.), and are mainly used for ritual purposes. The *patong* (wooden sculptures), valorising images of their *Moyang* (ancestors), are produced for worship in their Mother Temples. The *topeng* (wooden masks), also valorising images of their ancestors, are used in their 'traditional' *Jo-oh* dance performances during festival celebrations such as *Hari Moyang* (Ancestor's Day). These wooden masks are believed to represent the spirits of the ancestors mentioned in customary Mah Meri songs (Karim 1981). They are usually painted and embellished with plaited *nipah* or bark cloth hair, as well as with eyebrows and moustaches made from goat hair (Rahim 2007).

According to one of my hosts, Diana Uju, the Mah Meri people carry out woodcarving as part of their ritual practices, with inspirations for designs drawn from their dreams, legends, and their everyday interactions with the forest and the sea. As she explained:

> Our ancestors redeem themselves for taking from the forests and the seas by doing woodcarving and praying. For example, fishermen will make woodcarvings for what they take from the sea. My father does not do woodcarving, but my grandfather does woodcarving. Two of my brothers learn woodcarving from my grandfather because they have passion and interest in woodcarving.

Since the late 1950s, the art of woodcarving has undergone significant transformation, from a community-based cultural practice to a commercial folk-art genre, largely through the intervention of a broker figure, the late Malaysian artist Hoessein Enas (1924–1995). Enas, who was the Assistant Protector of Aborigines in the Department of Aborigines in the 1950s, encouraged the Mah Meri people to carve large sculptures and masks for sale as a new source of income (Rahim 2007). As the lightweight *tengkho* wood had become very rare on the island, the Mah Meri carvers turned to using the heavier and more abundant *nyireh* (*Xylocarpus moluccensis*) wood for their carvings (Rahim 2007). The dark red hue of the *nyireh* wood produced a fine-grain and polished surface, which soon became a favourite among collectors in the art market, as they better conformed to the elements of Western aesthetics in art such as proportion, unity, and harmony, and hence, they were canonised and absorbed into the system of Western 'art-culture' (Clifford 1988; Steiner 1994; Forni 2017).

Enas later arranged for a few Mah Meri woodcarvings to be exhibited at the second exhibition organised by the Society of Malaysian Artists in Kuala Lumpur, which took place in 1959 (Shahrum 1971). This initial display of woodcarvings in 1959 aroused much interest in Mah Meri art. Twenty-six woodcarvings made by 12 carvers were later put on display at the Fifth Exhibition of the Exposition of Arts held at the British Council in Kuala Lumpur in August 1962, in association with the

Society of Malaysian Artists (Shahrum 1971). In the 1960s and 1970s, Enas, through the Department of Orang Asli Affairs (JHEOA), arranged for the Mah Meri carvers to display and market their works at exhibitions around Malaysia. The 'staging' of these Mah Meri woodcarvings at different important exhibitions in Malaysia significantly enhanced their visibility and hence generated awareness and interest in these new artistic forms, especially among art collectors and museums in Malaysia, including the National Museum of Malaysia and the University Asian Art Museum. The former acquired 16 examples of Mah Meri woodcarving in the 1960s: five were purchased at the aforementioned Fifth Exhibition of the Exposition of Arts; three were acquired during a visit to Kampung Sungai Bumbun by the staff of the National Museum of Malaysia in October 1964; seven were acquired at a subsequent visit to the village in February 1965, and one was received from JHEOA in March 1965 (Shahrum 1971). The acquisition of Mah Meri woodcarvings by the National Museum of Malaysia at that time not only legitimised the status of Mah Meri woodcarving as an 'authentic' art form representing the cultural and artistic heritage of the Mah Meri people as an Indigenous group but also communicated Mah Meri woodcarving as collectible art, which carried a tangible, long-term financial value for its owners.

The publication of ethnographer Ronald Werner's 484-page catalogue *Mah Meri of Malaysia Art and Culture* (1967), which documented a large collection of Mah Meri woodcarvings, the legends of the spiritual guardians portrayed on them, and the names of their carvers, contributed further to the discursive production and endorsement of Mah Meri woodcarving as an 'authentic' Indigenous art form. Specifically, the legends of their spiritual guardians portrayed on the woodcarvings emphasised their Indigenous origins as belonging to the Mah Meri people, an Indigenous group with their own belief system and cultural practices, as well as the mystical qualities associated with the Mah Meri Indigenous cosmologies. The catalogue served as a form of authentication and endorsement of this contemporary, folk-art genre. Coming from an 'expert', it thereby increased the demand for and hence enhanced the market value of Mah Meri woodcarving, especially in the museum sector and amongst the art collectors.

Since the 1960s, the cultural representation of Mah Meri woodcarving as an Indigenous cultural practice with mystical qualities has been discursively deployed in the promotion of it as a commercial folk-art genre around Malaysia and internationally. The acquisition of these Mah Meri woodcarvings by important museums and private art collectors in Malaysia, and, significantly, the publication of Werner's catalogue on Mah Meri woodcarvings in 1967 enhanced its authenticity and appeal, and Mah Meri woodcarving was absorbed into the tourist production system and recast as a commodity (Britton 1991).

Figure 3.3 The craft hut of a Mah Meri woodcarver Gali Adam by the main road leading through Kampung Sungai Bumbun on Carey Island. Photograph: Author.

By the 2000s, the popularity of Mah Meri woodcarvings led to the emergence of woodcarving as a lucrative occupation for many Mah Meri men in Sungai Kampung Bumbun. This was also in part due to the active promotion of Mah Meri woodcarving by the Malaysia Handicraft Development Corporation (MHDC), which implemented a series of initiatives that increased the visibility of Mah Meri woodcarvings locally and abroad, fuelling greater market interest and demand. To capitalise on the touristic demand for Mah Meri woodcarvings, MHDC provided funding for the establishment of craft huts for Mah Meri villagers engaging in woodcarving (Figure 3.3), with the intention of converting Kampung Sungai Bumbun into a tourist destination demonstrating Mah Meri woodcarvers at work, and for facilitating direct trade between the Mah Meri woodcarvers and prospective buyers. This can be interpreted as an effort to emphasise the authenticity of the woodcarvings, by allowing buyers to penetrate to the back regions of the marketplace (Steiner 1994).

Several Mah Meri woodcarvers have also been designated as *Adiguru Kraf* (Master Craftsman) by the MHDC, and regularly represent Malaysia in craft exhibitions overseas to exhibit their works. For example, they have represented Malaysia at the Shanghai Exposition 2010, and have exhibited their works at the UNESCO headquarters in Paris on several occasions with the Malaysian government's sponsorship. International bodies, such as UNESCO, also play a role in legitimatising this commercially responsive genre as authentic Mah Meri cultural heritage. Several pieces of Mah Meri woodcarving, including the *Moyang Harimau*

Berantai (Chained Tiger Ancestor), were awarded UNESCO's Seal of Excellence for Handicraft Products in 2012 (Jeyabalan and Hutagalung 2015), an award aimed at

> raising the international awareness of ASEAN handicraft ... [which] serve[s] as a quality control mechanism and marketing device for the promotion of hand-made traditional or innovative craft products from the region which conform to a rigorous standard of cultural, environmental and production excellence.
>
> (UNESCO-Bangkok n.d.)

On learning about UNESCO's Seal of Excellence for Handicraft Products scheme, the broker at Mah Meri Cultural Village encouraged several wood-carvers to apply for the accreditation with him as a joint applicant and offered to sponsor the registration fees amounting to around RM 1,000 (£190). Today, it is only possible to acquire Mah Meri woodcarvings with the UNESCO accreditation at the Mah Meri Cultural Village or through the broker's networks. From these sales the broker earns a significant commission, while the Mah Meri woodcarvers receive only around a quarter or a third of the market price. Although UNESCO's accreditation scheme has well-meaning intent – to give recognition to Indigenous crafts and their producers – the scheme does not prevent broker figures from benefitting more than the producers of these crafts, due to the cumbersome administrative and financial requirements of the application process, which makes it inaccessible to producers.

Although the designs of Mah Meri woodcarvings in the past were based on the woodcarvers' dreams and legends or their interactions with the natural environment, many Mah Meri woodcarvers today adapt their designs to fit market demand, producing more of the works desired by collectors. Ronald Werner's book (first published in 1967 and reprinted in 1997), which documents Mah Meri wooden sculptures and masks, was a regular feature in every woodcarver's craft hut in Kampung Sungai Bumbun that I visited. The woodcarvers use the book as a design catalogue in discussion with potential buyers. According to Diana Uju:

> In the past, the designs come from the mind. But now, it is impossible to come up with new designs, so we refer to the Ronald Werner book for inspirations. The book was first printed in 1960s but was reprinted in 1997 by the University of Malaya Press. But there are exceptions, like my brother, who still draws on his inspirations to find new designs.

Steiner (1994) argues that the concept of authenticity in non-Western art is a Western construction with economic and cultural motives. The commercial folk-art genre of Mah Meri woodcarving may also be understood as a product of economically driven 'strategic creativity' coupled with market awareness (cf. Forni 2017). Appadurai (1986) suggests that the value creation of tourist art or ethnic art lies in the status and identity of its producers. As Mary Katherine Scott (2017) has argued in relation to 'traditional-yet-contemporary' Maya tourist art, the value that the buyers attach to the Mah Meri woodcarvings does not lie in their material use, their imagery, or the technical mastery of the woodcarvers; rather, the carvings personify the Indigenous status of the woodcarvers themselves. For Mah Meri woodcarvings, it is the biographical narratives of their Indigenous makers and their Indigenous knowledge, especially the rituals surrounding the practice of woodcarving that feed into the consumers' desire for authenticity, that are crucial in constructing the commercial folk-art genre of Mah Meri art by elevating market demand and transactional values. These narratives are not only deliberately created in response to buyers' quests for authenticity but also actively embraced and reified by brokers and the Mah Meri woodcarvers themselves, both materially and discursively. Such historical entanglement of artisan production, authenticity, and Indigeneity is also observed in Africa and Latin America (Steiner 1994; Field 2009; Brulotte 2012).

A recent article in a Malaysian newspaper promoting the art of Mah Meri woodcarving painted a romanticised narrative of a woodcarver's personal journey into the profession. The author reified the commercial folk-art genre of Mah Meri woodcarving as an Indigenous knowledge, handed down from generation to generation and embodying mystical qualities that reflected Mah Meri Indigenous cosmologies:

When you come from a family of carvers, it seems that only special circumstances would justify hanging up your gloves. For Kemi anak Khamis' grandfather, it was when he became blind in both eyes. Such is the dedication to their craft among the Mah Meri folks who live on Pulau Carey in Selangor, where wood carving is seen as more than a mere trade or profession. To them, it is a vocation that has been passed down from their fathers and their fathers before them. Kemi himself has fond memories of his first contact with the spirit wood carvings that his community is so well-known for. 'I was around 12 years old when I started helping my father put the finishing touches to his masks, like sandpapering, which can take up to several days to complete,' he relates. The Mah Meri talk about their carvings with great pride. It is an especially exciting time now as there is growing interest in their works coming from far beyond this place they call home. For Kemi, who is now in his early 40s, it wasn't too long after his first brush with what would end up becoming a lifelong passion that he embarked on his first solo project. 'I carved a few masks which were quickly snapped up by tourists who really like my work. It was very encouraging,' he says, adding that he has never looked back since.

(Lin 2016)

The Indigenous rhetoric is also actively being mobilised to commodify tourist art as an Indigenous tradition handed down from the past. Appadurai (1986: 46–47) suggests that ethnic art or tourist art

> constitutes a special commodity traffic, in which the group identity of producers are tokens for the status politics of consumers, [in which] goods were reconceived as products, and the "gaze" (in Foucault's sense) of the consumer and the trader had given way to the "gaze" of the producer.

In particular, the cultural tropes of Indigeneity are actively drawn upon by different stakeholders for the formation of an eco-system for tourist art, embedding these works into the tourist production system as commodities by feeding into consumers' desires for authenticity (Britton 1991; Steiner 1994; Velthuis 2005; Thornton 2008).

The Mah Meri woodcarvers draw on their ritual practices to enhance the mystical qualities and hence authenticate their woodcarvings as an Indigenous practice to increase their transactional value. Here, they take on the role of internal brokers, mediating between the tourist art market and their local village economy. As Gali Adam explained:

> Before we cut down a tree, we must observe one taboo. First, we knock on the wood with a piece of iron. If it makes a sound like this, we are allowed to cut the tree. But if it's a noise like this, then we are forbidden to cut it. Because there is a spirit living in that tree. It's the spirit's home. We also have to perform a ritual before cutting a tree. We burn incense, pray for blessing from our ancestors, and ask for permission from the 'landlord'. By 'landlord', I mean the spirit entity on that land.
> *(The Star TV, 3 February 2016)*

The cultural tropes of Indigeneity are also actively drawn upon by museum institutions – which can also be conceptualised as broker institutions – to promote Mah Meri woodcarvings. A recent exhibition on Mah Meri woodcarvings, *Mah Meri Unmasked*, organised by the Centre for Creative Content and Digital Innovation (3CDI) at the University of Malaya and held at the University Asian Art Museum (from November to December 2013), discursively portrays Mah Meri woodcarving as an Indigenous art that has been practised by the Mah Meri people for generations. Specifically, the first gallery of the exhibition opened with a re-enactment of the *Hari Moyang* celebration, showcasing how the Mah Meri *topeng* were used in the *Hari Moyang* rituals, before tracing their production process from sourcing of the *nyireh* wood in the mangrove forests, to the carving of the Mah Meri masks and concluding with oral interviews with two Mah Meri carvers from Kampung Sungai Bumbun. The narrative of the video implied that the Mah Meri woodcarvings on display in the exhibition were the same as those used in the *Hari Moyang* rituals. This suggested that the contemporary folk-art genre of Mah Meri woodcarving had existed for a long time and had been used in *Hari Moyang* rituals for generations, thus drawing dubiously on Mah Meri ritual traditions to create a sense of authenticity for the Mah Meri woodcarvings in the Museum's collection. These exhibition narratives thus perpetuated the idea that commercial Mah Meri woodcarving had existed for a long time, which contributed to the material and discursive production of Mah Meri woodcarving as an 'Indigenous' art form.

As Thornton (2008, xiv) said about the production of artworks: 'great works do not just arise; they are made – not just by artists and their assistants but also by the dealers, curators, critics, and collectors who "support" the work'. Mah Meri woodcarvings are actively produced by the Mah Meri woodcarvers, as well as the Malaysian government, mass media, NGOs, museum curators, art dealers, and collectors, who play brokerage roles by communicating non-economic values, such as the status of the carvers, the identities of the collectors, the promotional roles of the art dealers and media, and the endorsement effect of museum curators, which all contribute to the value creation of commercial folk-art genre Mah Meri woodcarving as an Indigenous art (Appadurai 1986; Velthuis 2005). Through the staging process of heritage instrumentalisation, the art of Mah Meri woodcarving has been transformed from a community-based cultural practice to a commercial folk-art genre. This involves a dialogic process of heritage production and framing by multiple stakeholders, including the Mah Meri woodcarvers themselves, who are actively staging their identities to emphasise their Indigenous connection in their work to appeal to consumers' desire for authenticity (Scott 2017).

While the integration of the commercial folk-art genre of Mah Meri woodcarvings into the tourist production system has led to the revival or reinvention of the cultural practice, the community-based practice of woodcarving has been radically transformed through the processes of staging and cultural commodification (Greenwood 1989). Once sacred objects used for ritual and worship in their smaller forms, woodcarvings have taken on new personas as pieces of tourist art that serve no spiritual function. The wooden masks made from *nyireh* wood are now kept for display and collection purposes, as they are too heavy to be used in the *Jo-oh* dance performances or worship. Rather, these woodcarvings are reconnected with their spiritual aura through the invented cultural tropes and market narratives that bestow and reify these cultural practices with spiritual meanings in order to satisfy consumers' desire for authenticity (Forni 2017).

Today, the art of woodcarving has emerged as a form of heritage instrumentalisation exercised by the Mah Meri people, both as an important source of economic livelihood and as an avenue by which to maintain and reify their cultural differences in the face of cultural and social marginalisation in mainstream Malay-Muslim society and assert their marginalised identity locally and abroad, for example, through representing Malaysia at the Shanghai Exposition 2010 and the UNESCO Paris events. It has also acquired an 'emergent authenticity' (Cohen 1988) through the staging process, as it is internalised and embodied by the Mah Meri people as an emblem of their Indigenous identity and cultural practices. The commodification process contributes to a rediscovery and reconfiguration of Indigenous identities and cultural practices (Abram et al. 1997; Theodossopoulos 2015) and facilitates the reinvention of Mah Meri cultural products as tourist art (Glass 2006; Brulotte 2012). This demonstrates how Mah Meri woodcarving as a 'staged' performance takes on a subjective sense of authenticity depending on the prevailing circumstances: while they are historically inauthentic as an outcome of contemporary processes of modernisation, tourism, and Indigenous politics, these woodcarvings are at the same time deemed to be authentic by the Mah Meri woodcarvers themselves, who self-essentialise their cultural heritage to capitalise on the benefits of this commodification for personal interest. In an interview about Mah Meri woodcarving with a foreign media outlet, Mah Meri master woodcarver, Pion Bumbon said of the woodcarvings:

> These carvings help us live. If you don't want the wind to blow away your roof, you carve a tornado spirit, if you want safety when at sea, there is the anchor spirit.
>
> (Koswanage 2010)

Grunewald (2002) documents how the Indigenous Pataxo Indians of Brazil initially resurrected their craftworks and cultural practices to meet tourism demands, but later come to embrace them as authentic representations of their Indigenous cultural identity and heritage. Tourism also serves as a platform for the Indigenous Pataxo Indians to reassert their marginalised identity by reminding (predominantly white) tourists of the colonisation and exploitation suffered by the Indians at the hands of their ancestors (Grunewald 2002). In the case of the Mah Meri villagers, the cultural commodification of the contemporary folk-art genre of Mah Meri woodcarving offers the Mah Meri people a means of asserting their social and cultural identities in the face of marginalisation by maintaining difference (Gingging 2007; Fiskesjo 2015).

In this Similar to Canessa's (2012) observation in Latin America that tourism can lend legitimacy to Indigenous cultural practices, the commodification of Mah Meri woodcarving has lent political and economic legitimacy to their cultural heritage, thus pressuring the Malaysian government to make them seriously. The Mah Meri people of Kampung Sungai Bumbun have drawn upon their woodcarving practice to lobby against the encroachment on their native customary lands on Carey Island by palm oil plantations (Koswanage 2010). As one of my hosts Gali Adam told a reporter from Reuters about the restrictions placed on them by the palm oil plantation owners operating on Carey Island:

> Palm oil has given us development but it should not change our way of life. In the past, we would go in to the mangroves and make offerings to the spirits and get their permission to cut down just one tree. Now we have to get written permission from the estate manager before we can do anything.
>
> (Koswanage 2010)

Although Indigenous people seem to be represented and commodified as the exotic and primitive Other through tourism, they are also actively involved in the self-construction of their primitive personas and reputations to capitalise on tourism to promote their own objectives and agendas (Adams 1997; Schiller 2001; Bunten 2008). Here, the Mah Meri villagers skilfully drew on the discourse of loss and endangerment to their woodcarving heritage through a foreign media outlet to resist encroachment on their ancestral lands and territories and assert their Indigenous rights. Rather than rejecting their Indigenous personas, the Mah Meri people are actively involved in the discursive production of their Indigeneity to capitalise on its benefits and promote their own agendas. However, this reflects the 'intractable double binds' of Indigeneity (Clifford 2013), in which the Mah Meri people need to be positioned and perceived as Indigenous 'noble savages' to add authenticity and value to their woodcarvings.

Turning from the 'staging' of innovative and commercially responsive craft products as Indigenous cultural heritage to an example of performative 'intangible' cultural heritage, a three-day wedding ceremony is staged at the Mah Meri Cultural Village, compressed into a three-hour cultural performance for tourist consumption. The selection of rituals and the way the marriage ceremony is performed reflect the outcomes of the complex negotiations between different stakeholders to ultimately present a commodified wedding ceremony that conforms to tourists' desires and expectations about the Mah Meri people as the primitive Other. Drawing on a comparative study of a staged wedding ceremony at the Mah Meri Cultural Village performed in October 2014 and the wedding ceremony of one of my hosts, Diana Uju, conducted in November 2014, I consider the complex negotiations surrounding the commodification of the ceremony as it is performed at the Mah Meri Cultural Village.

The wedding ceremony is a major community affair among the Mah Meri people. Preparations for the three-day wedding ceremony can take months, involving the soliciting of funds for building a house extension and constructing a temporary wedding venue, as well as the making of customary bark cloth costumes for the couple and members of the community participating in the ceremony. Ahead of the wedding ceremony, the couple attends an engagement ritual, presided by the *Tok Batin* and the *adat* (customs) community[3], its purpose is to declare the status of the couple, and compensation will need to be paid by the party who has been married previously. The first day of the wedding ceremony involves an ostentatious display of wealth. The groom sends his gifts to the bride's home to express his appreciation to the bride's family for raising her to adulthood. On the following day, the couple participates in a series of rituals including teeth-filing, henna-staining of fingers, as well as a *bersanding* (bride display) ritual, during which the couple engages in of a cleansing ritual conducted by a ritual specialist while seated on a dais (Figure 3.4), so that the spirits can see and recognise the marital union.

The final day of the wedding ceremony begins with a symbolic martial arts competition, during which the groom's team must lose three consecutive rounds to the bride's team to symbolise the groom undertaking challenges to win over his bride. The groom will also have to identify the outstretched hands of his bride, who would be wound up in a tube cloth along with other women after circling seven times around the tube cloth. The ritual, known as *berarak* or bride parade, symbolises the groom searching for his bride and eventually finding her. This is followed by the *sambut menantu* (reception) ritual, in which the bride's mother will wash the feet of the groom, while the groom's mother will wash the feet of the bride, signifying acceptance of the groom and bride into each other's families. Two large urns of water were then poured onto a piece of

Figure 3.4 The Mah Meri wedding ceremony of Sharitaudin Bah Tuin and Diana Uju held at Kampung Sungai Bumbun on Pulau Carey in November 2014. The groom and bride are sitting on a dais after the *bersanding* ritual. Photograph: Colin Nicholas from COAC.

white fabric placed over the couple's heads, in what known as the bunga mandi (flower bath) ritual. A lunch reception for the guests marks the end of the wedding ceremony.

The wedding ceremony staged at the Mah Meri Cultural Village is an abridged version of the three-day wedding ceremony, with several rituals left out or shortened in the interests of time. While the Mah Meri villagers are agreeable to the staging of their wedding ceremony for the consumption of tourists, and participate in the staged performance as part of the wedding entourage, they do not play the roles of the bride and groom. They believe that this will compromise their own destinies, as they may be seen, in the eyes of the spirits, to not take marriage seriously. By holding back in this respect, they resist the commodification of their wedding ceremony in order to maintain the efficacy of their wedding rituals. Instead, tourist volunteers are selected to play the roles of the Mah Meri groom and bride, offering them an opportunity to be involved with the staged performance, and thus facilitating a sense of fun and fulfilment among tourists through personal experience. The staged wedding ceremony is carried out in the Mah Meri language by the Mah Meri performers and translated into English or Malay languages by the broker. This extends the 'performative authenticity' (Zhu 2012) of the staged wedding ceremony from the perspective of the tourists. However, this also renders the process susceptible to misrepresentation, as Mah Meri villagers have no control over what has been conveyed to the tourists.

The *sambut menantu* ritual has been omitted from the staged wedding ceremony but appropriated as a ritual to welcome the visitors to the Mah Meri Cultural Village. Tourists to the Mah Meri Cultural Village are welcomed with a feet-washing ritual. An intelligence test for the groom, involving a customary Mah Meri game of *jerat tupai* (squirrel game), is also included in the staged wedding ceremony, alongside the *merisik* (enquiry) ritual, during which the attributes of the groom and bride are declared. While the *merisik* ritual was probably useful for the arranged marriages of the past, it is no longer deemed necessary, as couples normally get to know each other before deciding to get married. Hence, the staged ceremony appears to have included rituals that have been practised in the past by the older generation of Mah Meri people but have now been excluded in contemporary marriages due to changes in dating and marriage norms. Furthermore, the sequence of *berarak* and *bersanding* rituals has been switched. The sequence adopted in the staged wedding ceremony appears to be a more logical process, as it is likely that one will first ascertain the bride through the *berarak* ritual, and later announce and declare the union through the *bersanding* ritual. This suggests that modifications may have been made to contemporary wedding rituals that do not conform to their ritualistic antecedents.

The staged ritual practices in the Mah Meri Cultural Village have also modified contemporary Mah Meri marriage practices. For the *berarak* ritual, the broker has created a wooden structure to hold up the tube cloth encircling the bride and other women participating in the ritual, instead of having the villagers hold it by hand. The wooden structure has been adopted by the Mah Meri villagers from Kampung Rambai in their wedding ceremony. This provides an example of how contemporary ritual practices of Mah Meri ceremonies evolve over time, incorporating innovations introduced through the touristic staging of culture. This attests to the multifaceted, dynamic, and ever-evolving manifestations of cultural representations that are socially and culturally constructed and negotiated by different stakeholders depending on context and interpretation (Harrison 2013).

Frictions, tensions, and issues

The popularity of Mah Meri cultural practices has rendered their cultural heritage susceptible to appropriation by other Orang Asli groups, who look to Mah Meri cultural heritage to revive their own. While the Mah Meri villagers are proud that they are well-regarded among the Orang Asli for their cultural heritage, they also recount with dismay how their cultural practices have been appropriated by other Orang Asli groups. As a Mah Meri villager of Kampung Sungai Bumbun recounts:

> The Temuan people, another Orang Asli group living in the hill region of Selangor, use coconut leaves for their weaving in the past, but now, they use *nipah* leaves, like us. It is unlikely that they adopt *nipah* leaves naturally, because the Temuan are mountain people and they use mountain leaves such as coconut leaves. Only the sea people like the Mah Meri and Orang Seletar use *nipah* leaves.

The Temuan people have also replicated the Mah Meri *mandi bunga* ritual practised during Mah Meri wedding ceremonies, although they conduct the ritual baths at wells, rather than on a dais like the Mah Meri people. The same villager also explained how the Mah Meri people's cultural practice of making bark cloth has been replicated by other Orang Asli groups in Malaysia:

> Among the Orang Asli groups in Malaysia, only the Mah Meri use bark cloth to make our costumes, as we are the only one with the knowledge to do so. The other Orang Asli groups did not use bark cloth. They use leaves to cover themselves. But some of the Orang Asli groups have started to use the bark cloth to make their costumes since the 1950s, copying the Mah Meri when our costumes become known to other Orang Asli groups through our cultural performances around Peninsular Malaysia.

As the instrumentalisation of Indigenous cultural heritage rests on the construction and reification of cultural differences, the appropriation of certain Mah Meri cultural practices by other Orang Asli groups compromises their use, in this respect, by the Mah Meri people. This complicates the Mah Meri people's mobilisation of their Indigenous cultural heritage for their own agendas vis-à-vis other Orang Asli groups, while strengthening the visibility of Orang Asli cultural heritage and identity more generally in Malaysia. The use of bark cloth costumes has, for example, come to be associated with a collective Orang Asli cultural identity and heritage.

Besides other Orang Asli groups, there are others, such as filmmakers, who misappropriate Mah Meri cultural practices for their own projects and personal gains. An example of this is the representation of Senoi dream practice in a film entitled *Mimpi Mah Meri* (Mah Meri Dream). The Mah Meri is a subgroup of the Senoi, and there has been considerable debate among anthropologists of the Indigenous lucid dreaming practice (aka 'Senoi Dream Theory'), by which people learn to exert control over their dreaming to reduce fear and derive pleasure (see Domhoff 2003; Benjamin 2014). The film, which won first prize at the 2013 Malaysian Student Film and Video Festival, was lambasted by the broker at Mah Meri Cultural Village, who commented on the film as we watched it on a laptop.

> This is a Temair traditional house, not a Mah Meri traditional house. Although the film refers to the Senoi Dream Theory, a belief system that the Mah Meri also subscribes to, the way the dream is presented is distasteful, especially with the ancestral figures staring at the Mah Meri girl in the film. In one scene, the Mah Meri villagers at Pulau Carey are featured in their temple ritual; then in another scene, there are a few girls dancing on the central stage as a reinterpretation of the temple ritual. This juxtaposition of the two scenes again refers to the gross misinterpretation of the Mah Meri culture. I have written to the producers to complain that they have presented the Mah Meri culture wrongly and in negative light, but I have yet to receive a response.

While the Mah Meri people have been successful in instrumentalising their Indigenous cultural heritage for asserting their cultural identity, this staging has made their cultural heritage increasingly visible, rendering it susceptible to misappropriation by other stakeholders, who also instrumentalise Mah Meri cultural heritage for their personal agendas. This has raised questions of infringement of intellectual property rights (see Geismar 2005, 2013). In the *Mimpi Mah Meri* film, some of these appropriations portray the Mah Meri people in a negative light by featuring them in skimpy clothes falsely represented as Mah Meri costumes and engaging in contemporary dance performances misleadingly represented as Mah Meri cultural dances. In this instance, the broker joins the Mah Meri villagers in condemning the misappropriation of their cultural heritage by filmmakers, as portraying Mah Meri cultural heritage in a positive light is important for the reputation of the Mah Meri Cultural Village.

At the Mah Meri Cultural Village, a major source of tension between the broker and the Mah Meri villagers lies in the representation of some aspects of Mah Meri cultural heritage. This has led to a level of 'heritage dissonance' (Tunbridge and Ashworth 1996), with the broker claiming his authority based on his 13 years of cultural interaction with the Mah Meri people, while the villagers claim their authority to represent their own cultural heritage according to their ancestry. In setting up the Mah Meri Cultural Village, the broker sought the permission from the *Tok Batin* and consulted with some Mah Meri villagers on the proposed location of the various facilities within the cultural village such as the placement of the spiritual altar and the spirit house. However, the final authority on the representation of Mah Meri cultural heritage in the cultural village lies with the broker. Much of the interpretation of Mah Meri cultural heritage presented at the Mah Meri Cultural Village is also derived from his own research using academic resources on Mah Meri cultural heritage, as well as his interactions with the Mah Meri people over the years.

There are, for example, tensions surrounding the interpretation of some Mah Meri cultural practices between the broker and the Mah Meri villagers of Kampung Sungai Bumbun. The Mah Meri villagers claim that the broker has misrepresented the divorce procedures of the Mah Meri people. According to a villager from Kampung Sungai Bumbun:

> He tells the tourists we wear a coconut around the neck and go to each house to declare that the marriage is now over. This is not true at all. According to our tradition, couples who wish to divorce should consult the *Tok Batin* and *adat* community to decide on the payment of the fine. We will meet in the community house to discuss. Who and how much to pay is based on the fault of the marriage. If the husband beats the wife, the husband will have to pay the fine. The *Tok Batin* decides on the payment after consulting with everyone.

According to the same villager, the broker has also misrepresented the customary Mah Meri game of *jerat tupai* as an intelligence test for the groom at the staged wedding ceremony:

> According to our tradition, we carry it when we go into the forest, and try to solve the puzzle to calm ourselves when we get lost in the forest. But he tells the tourists that this is used to test the intelligence level of the groom. These are games we play, but they are not part of our wedding rituals.

The broker has, however, included the game of *jerat tupai* as part of the staged wedding ceremony at the Mah Meri Cultural Village because he wanted to increase the number of rituals within the wedding ceremony from six to seven, an auspicious number based on Mah Meri cultural beliefs. As he explained to me at the end of my fieldwork, when I asked him if he knew about the Mah Meri villagers' view of his misinterpretation of the *jerat tupai* game:

> The groom circles around the curtain seven times for their *berarak* ritual. Their auspicious number is seven. But there are only six steps in the staged wedding ceremony. I need one more ritual to make up the seven steps, so I add in *jerat tupai* as the extra ritual.

Due to incidents such as these, the Mah Meri villagers feel that the broker has misrepresented their cultural heritage and they have not been given sufficient agency to represent their own heritage at the Mah Meri Cultural Village. Nevertheless, they are complicit in the misrepresentation of their cultural heritage through their continued participation in the staged performances, which perpetuate what they perceive as a misrepresentation of their cultural heritage, suggesting that the Mah Meri villagers have conformed to their expected roles in order to derive benefits from the cultural village (Doolittle 2004). Contrary to UNESCO's 'culture for development' rhetoric, the Mah Meri Cultural Village has not provided the Mah Meri people with greater opportunities to negotiate the representation of their shared memory or heritage but has created a structure that perpetuates their marginalisation in the hands of brokers who have the final authority on the representation of Mah Meri cultural heritage.

Despite the fact that the Mah Meri villagers have conveyed to the broker that some interpretations of the Mah Meri cultural heritage in the Mah Meri Cultural Village are not correct, he has presented these as authentic representations based on his observations. As he told me when we first met at the start of my fieldwork:

> The Mah Meri are shy and timid people. The Mah Meri people, like the other Orang Asli groups, have a deep mistrust for people. They develop the mask tradition, so that they can take on different personas. They also have two names, an ecological name and a given Malay name. They may disagree with you in their hearts, but they will say yes to you. They have this internal system, and they will not tell you everything about their cultural heritage. I have lived with the communities for many years, and I observe them and decipher their cultural heritage. And I found out that there is a reason for them to do things. The Mah Meri has this game called the *jerat tupai* that they play for fun. After interacting with them, I learn that this game can be categorised as an

IQ test for their in-law to-be since the game will reflect on the ability of their would-be son-in-law. Also for the divorce procedures, many people think that the Mah Meri cannot divorce. Actually they can. I observe that when they divorce, the husband wears a coconut around his neck, goes to each house, knocks on the door, and tells everyone in the house that he is divorcing.

The broker considers his interpretation of Mah Meri cultural heritage to be legitimated by the knowledge he has accumulated through his long-term interactions with the Mah Meri people, an accumulation of what Steinmetz (2008) calls 'ethnographic capital'.

Meanwhile, the broker also has reservations about the villagers from Kampung Sungai Bumbun, who have established what he regards as a competing craft centre located opposite to the Mah Meri Cultural Village:

> The craft centre opposite the Mah Meri Cultural Village, which the villagers set up on their own with JAKOA funding, poses competition to the Mah Meri Cultural Village. I mean, if the government is interested to set up another cultural village, they should choose another Orang Asli group elsewhere to work with, not crowd in Pulau Carey.

However, the Mah Meri villagers at Kampung Sungai Bumbun expressed surprise when asked if the craft centre was set up to challenge the Mah Meri Cultural Village, as a villager clarified:

> The craft centre was built in 2009/2010 by JAKOA, before the Mah Meri Cultural Village. In fact, we have been doing cultural performances for a long time, and our cultural group, *Tompoq Topoh*, has been coordinating the dances for quite some time. The craft centre was not affected by the Mah Meri Cultural Village, as business was brisk anyway prior to the establishment of the Mah Meri Cultural Village.

Due to the underlying tensions between the broker and the villagers of Kampung Sungai Bumbun, tourists to the Mah Meri Cultural Village are driven to the craft centre at another Mah Meri village, Kampung Rambai (Figure 3.5), located ten minutes away by car, for craft demonstrations. Notwithstanding, a road sign leading to the Mah Meri Cultural Village refers to both the Mah Meri Cultural Village and the craft centre in Kampung Sungai Bumbun as a single destination, suggesting these two venues were probably intended to be developed in tandem. This highlights how the original intent of the Mah Meri Cultural Village, as a vehicle to promote the socio-economic development of the Mah Meri people, has been compromised due to tensions between the broker and the Mah Meri villagers.

Figure 3.5 The Mah Meri craft centre at Kampung Rambai built by JAKOA and visited by tourists of the Mah Meri Cultural Village. Photograph: Author.

Despite their dissatisfaction with the broker, the villagers of Kampung Sungai Bumbun continue to work at the cultural village, albeit with less motivation and a lacklustre attitude, as they see value in generating awareness about their cultural heritage and asserting their Indigenous cultural identity through the Mah Meri Cultural Village. According to one villager, who served as a liaison with the broker for the cultural performances at the Mah Meri Cultural Village:

> We still support Mah Meri Cultural Village because it is located in our village, and it is representing our cultural heritage. We have no other income. It is not from the willingness of our hearts, but we still do it.

The Mah Meri villagers have, however, developed several coping strategies or what Scott (1985) considers as 'weapons of the weak', highlighting that they are not passive agents to the unequal relationship, but are negotiating their marginalised positions with creativity and agency. When asked if there was any difference between them performing at the *Hari Moyang* festival – the villagers' own ritual ceremony – and at the Mah Meri Cultural Village, another villager replied:

> The feeling is not the same. At *Hari Moyang*, there are lots of food and blessings from the ancestors, so we perform with more energy. But at the Mah Meri Cultural Village, we are less motivated, so the music is less spirited and slow.

The villagers' lacklustre attitude towards working for the cultural village was also keenly felt by the broker, who complained that the villagers were very unreliable in the provision of their services. He once said to me:

> I hope you will maintain some distance from the communities. Once they get too close to you, it may affect their work. There was once an occasion when the communities did not turn up for work in order to celebrate the visit of a foreign researcher whom they knew. This cost a lot of problems for me, because I had already taken bookings for cultural performances on that day and I had to refund all the visitors because the communities didn't show up to perform.

Besides trivialising their work commitments at the Mah Meri Cultural Village, the villagers also developed other coping strategies to deal with their dissatisfaction towards the broker. One strategy was to laugh off the misinterpretation of their cultural heritage, as another villager employed at the cultural village said:

> Sometimes we feel angry. Sometimes we feel funny. Like when he tells the tourists how we grind our teeth as part of our marriage rituals to look like Dracula, the tourists ask us why we are laughing. We just smile. We dare not explain to them why we are laughing. And the tourists believe what he said. We already told him this is not the way, but he just does it his way.

Another strategy was to accept that the broker's misrepresentation of their cultural heritage was something beyond their control and to recognise that the tourists would be rational enough to judge for themselves. According to the same villager:

> We are a bit confused because the Mah Meri Cultural Village does not follow Mah Meri customs. Actually, he can tell the tourists the truth, but he doesn't want to. He knows the truth. It doesn't matter to us if he doesn't tell the truth. But we prefer him to tell the truth because it is a centre that shares our heritage with tourists. It will affect people's perception of Mah Meri if the truth is not told. But it also depends on the tourists what to believe in the Mah Meri Cultural Village. If the tourists are interested, they can ask the villagers.

Although this involved the commodification of their cultural heritage for tourist consumption, the villagers did not perceive authenticity of the cultural performances to be problematic for their cultural beliefs, as they had rationalised the re-enactment of their performances within their belief systems. As another villager said:

Moyang (Ancestors) understand that we need to make money. A local tourist guide who visited the Mah Meri Cultural Village once told me: we need to create something to find food and income. It is fine to make fake wedding, but at *Hari Moyang*, you must perform at least three songs for the *Moyang* if you can't perform seven songs for them. So the cultural performances at the Mah Meri Cultural Village do not affect our beliefs. But for us, we cannot participate in the fake marriages as grooms and brides ourselves, as this will affect us in the future.

Similar to what Doolittle (2004) had observed at rural development projects in Sabah, the Mah Meri villagers self-consciously conformed to their expected roles in order to receive the benefits from the Mah Meri Cultural Village, however meagre these were, albeit with some resistance and negotiation.

These dynamics underpinned another moment of friction that was played out during the *Hari Moyang* celebration at Kampung Sungai Bumbun in March 2015, to which I was invited to attend by my host families (Figure 3.6). What was originally intended to be a village celebration attended only by a handful of visitors invited to the event by the villagers ended up being mobbed by tourists. Without informing the villagers, the broker brought three busloads of almost 100 visitors to attend the village celebration, positioning it as an appreciation event for tourists who had made donations to the Mah Meri Cultural Village for the development of a village library. Based on village practices, the tourists were expected to make monetary or food contributions to the celebration, which would be

Figure 3.6 The Mah Meri annual *Hari Moyang* celebrations at Kampung Sungai Bumbun in March 2015. Photograph: Author.

communally consumed after the rituals. However, as the broker had told the tourists that it was an appreciation event organised by the grateful villagers for their donations to the Mah Meri Cultural Village, they came empty-handed but nevertheless joined the communal feast, leaving many villagers hungry. The broker appeared to have given tourists the impression that their monetary contribution to the Mah Meri Cultural Village would go to the Mah Meri villagers at Kampung Sungai Bumbun, but this was not the case. These donations formed part of the finances of the Mah Meri Cultural Village managed by the broker, and there was no plan to transfer any contribution to the villagers.

The episode drew much anger and concern from the Mah Meri villagers at Kampung Sungai Bumbun, as they were worried that their ancestors might be offended, which would adversely affect their destinies in the forthcoming year. Several villagers expressed their displeasure:

> The tourists need to respect us. This morning, there was a lack of respect from the tourists who visited us at *Hari Moyang*. But they are from different backgrounds, different cultures, so we cannot blame them. But the people who bring them here should brief them so that they respect our culture. This is a once-in-a-year celebration, and we are a superstitious people. Tourists say wrong things at sacred places. We do not want bad things to happen to our village because of these tourists.

> I don't care how much the tourists donate to the Mah Meri Cultural Village. They cannot come here and make it their own event. This is our event, and they should respect us. This is a very horrible thing. We don't want any bad thing to happen to our village because of these disrespectful tourists. Because we are Orang Asli, we are superstitious, and we believe in these things very much.

The concerns of the Mah Meri villagers reveal that even though they are complicit in the commodification of their Indigenous cultural heritage at the Mah Meri Cultural Village, which is the source of their economic livelihoods, they still believe in the ritual efficacy of their cultural practices and remain deeply rooted in their Indigenous beliefs. The annual *Hari Moyang* celebrations are occasions where the Mah Meri villagers exercise an active resistance to the commodification of their Indigenous cultural heritage. Yet, at the *Hari Moyang*, the villagers continue to face pressures to open up their 'back stage', as these village celebrations are actively portrayed and marketed by brokers as occasions where the 'authentic' rituals are performed vis-à-vis the commodified rituals on show at the Mah Meri Cultural Village.

These were not the only challenges that the Mah Meri villagers at Carey Island face in safeguarding their cultural identities and livelihoods. On my first visit to Carey Island, I spent a night with a handful of guests at the Amverton Cove Golf Course and Island Resort, a luxurious 50-room resort, which is also the only available accommodation on the island. Its existence on the island is a little incongruous, as there is only one tourist attraction in the vicinity: the Mah Meri Cultural Village. Carey Island consists of a large palm oil plantation owned by a Malaysian conglomerate, Sime Darby Corporation, and a small handful of Mah Meri villages, nestled within the large plantation and its processing plants. On crossing the bridge to the mainland Malay Peninsula, the town of Banting is a large industrial estate with several residential settlements. I was later told by the resort staff, none of whom came from the nearby Mah Meri villages, that its guests are mainly well-heeled Malaysian businessmen and politicians who usually visit the resort at weekends to play golf.

It was only later after I met with my host families at Kampung Sungai Bumbun, and negotiated a long-term stay with them, that I found out about the disdain and dismay held by the Mah Meri villagers for the luxurious accommodation in which I had stayed. The Amverton Cove Golf Course and Island Resort was built by an ethnic Malaysian Indian businessman on the ancestral lands of the Mah Meri people in 2011, despite much resistance from the Mah Meri villagers of Kampung Sungai Bumbun. The villagers were unsuccessful in resisting the development, which not only encroached on their native customary lands and waters but also affected their ritual practices by blocking off their access to the mangrove swamps that were an integral part of their ritual practices. As a villager told me:

> The Amverton Cove Golf and Island Resort has affected our rituals. As part of our rituals, we are supposed to cross a bridge over the river to get to the mangrove swamps. But the access is now blocked due to the Amverton development, and we are not able to get across to the other side of the river. The people from Amverton even said we have stolen from their coconut trees although these coconut trees are planted by our ancestors, as the development is on our traditional lands.

They were also unsuccessful in seeking compensation from the developer, although the development had led to the pollution of the area and the dwindling of resources such as *nipah* leaves used for weaving and *nyireh* wood used in woodcarving. This severely affected their livelihoods. As another villager said:

> Our Orang Asli lands are getting smaller and smaller. Access to the mangrove swamps has been cut off by development, and the fisheries levels have dropped due to pollution. The clearing of forest land in Pulau Carey has led to the loss of our traditional rivers, as well as the *nipah* leaves used for our weaving. *Nyireh* wood is also becoming difficult to find, and the low quality of wood is affecting the quality of our woodcarvings. The better wood is hardy, more polished and will sell

better. In the past, we could see fireflies every night, but now, there is no more firefly because there is too much light and development.

She underscored the long-term impacts of such encroachment:

In the past, when the storms came, we could see the fishes and the sea creatures in the swamps because the waters were so clear. But now, the waters are so polluted that we can no longer see the fishes in the waters. Even the Mah Meri children don't know about our traditional animals and sea creatures now. The dwindling resources have also affected our incomes, as we can no longer catch enough seafood to eat or collect enough plant resources to sell to make a proper living.

The Mah Meri villagers are susceptible to such land encroachment because they do not have secure titles to their native customary lands and territories, as these have not been gazetted by the Malaysian government as Orang Asli Reserve Land. According to another villager:

The lands that our kampung sits on are still questionable in terms of ownership. My grandparents have applied to JAKOA to gazette the lands for their ownership since the 1970s, but the application has not been processed. Today, we have no idea whether the land falls within Sime Darby ownership or state ownership, as the authorities have not been able to provide the details.

Even though the Mah Meri villagers of Kampung Sungai Bumbun received the gazette of the lands on which their village sits in April 2015, this was a small area relative to their native territories, much of which had been encroached by the state or had been sold by the state to commercial entities such as Sime Darby Corporation and the Amverton Cove Golf Course and Island Resort.

The plight of the Mah Meri villagers caught the attention of Colin Nicholas of the Center for Orang Asli Concerns (COAC), Malaysia's most influential Orang Asli NGO, who produced a documentary film entitled *The River Must Flow* in 2011 on the encroachment of Amverton Cove Golf Course and Island Resort. In the film, the circumstances of the encroachment were narrated through interviews with the Mah Meri villagers, who described how they had come to learn about the development plan on their ancestral lands and rivers after speaking to the ethnic Indian workers who were clearing the land for development. The workers told them about the impending golf course development and the large bungalows to be constructed on the cleared land.

The documentary focused on the loss of the villagers' customary river, the River Bumbun, from which the village had derived its name, which had been blocked up by the developers. As the villagers lamented:

The water is not flowing in, our boats cannot move as well. What can we do when the river is blocked? This is the river. It is blocked. The area was blocked by YS Company. Until recent years, the golf company came in to start an agricultural project. I am not sure about that. Now this area is closed. What's left are just the remnants of the Bumbun River. The river used to be the main pathway of the river. This is a historical place, because this is where the village got its name from. I understand that the area will be a golf course and bungalows over there. That's what I've been told by the company's workers. They said, 'Uncle, this is where bungalows will be built.' (Any officer from the authorities came to inform you?) 'None. None at all.' We got all the information from the workers. They told us that they will build bungalows here. This is where it is. If this area disappears, our generations, traditions and customs will be gone too. And also, the culture of the people from Bumbun River.

(COAC 2011)

The Mah Meri villagers drew on the discourse of loss and endangerment, alluding to the depletion of the river, to resist the encroachment of their ancestral lands and territories. They instrumentalised their cultural heritage in relation to River Bumbun, through the mediation and facilitation of Colin Nicholas, to give persuasive force to their resistance to the encroachment of their native customary lands and territories.

The documentary provided oral evidence for the breach of the Free, Prior and Informed Consent (FPIC) principle which was enshrined in the UNDRIP Convention, as the Mah Meri villagers were neither informed nor consulted on the development. Importantly, the villagers themselves drew upon an essentialised conceptualisation of Indigeneity, performing their Indigenous cultural heritage on film to advance their Indigenous rights to the lands and territories. By alluding to the loss of their historic River Bumbun, the Mah Meri villagers articulated their Indigenous position, based on the polythetic definition widely recognised in international discourses premised on four criteria of Indigeneity – first-come, non-dominance, cultural difference, and self-ascription (Saugestad 2001: 43) – even though the concept was really 'an ideological and social construct recognised by those who claim the status, by anthropologists who support their cause and no doubt by the educated public at large' (Barnard 2006: 7).

Colin Nicholas can be constituted as a broker who mediates and translates the local Indigenous politics of Malaysia into the global Indigenous rhetoric well-understood within the activist circles of the broader transnational Indigenous rights movement. He recalls how he came to be acquainted with the Orang Asli and decided to fight for their causes.

I was a scout and I was writing a manual about jungle-trekking, so my weak point was surviving in the forest, jungle survival skills. So when I chose the Orang Asli for my master's research, I wanted to learn from them how to trap animals and identify food and all those stuff. Not for anything else, and I was working for the bank and I was on scholarship from the bank. So I told them 'Yes, I will go and study how the markets can penetrate the Orang Asli.' But obviously, I wanted to study the Orang Asli, and they surprisingly agreed. So that's how I got involved with the Orang Asli. But as anyone who has worked with any community, once you stay with them and get to know them, the issues come up and you have a choice either to communicate them or continue to do what the bank wants you to do. So, it is a choice to do what you are doing.

By recording the marginalisation of their Indigenous rights in a digital format, which was posted to YouTube, Colin Nicholas enabled the Mah Meri villagers at Kampung Sungai Bumbun to reach out to an international audience through the mass media. Under his strategic curation of the documentary narrative, the Mah Meri villagers drew upon environmental politics concerning the ecological destruction of their ancestral lands for their Indigenous rights advocacy, alluding to the convergence of Indigenous and environmental discourses in what Conklin and Graham (1995: 697) call the 'global ecological imaginary'. There is a strategic alliance between Indigenous activists and environmental activists, where Indigenous people are cooperating with the transcultural, transnational imagined community of Western environmentalists Indigenous rights advocacy, while environmentalists draw upon Indigeneity to legitimise their environmental advocacy, reflecting the entanglement between Indigenous activism and environmental politics (Dove 2006; Ghosh 2006; Kirsch 2007; Zips and Zips-Mairitsch 2007; Athayde 2014).

Faced with increased encroachment of Indigenous lands and territories by national governments and private developers, the environment has emerged as a focal point for the enactment and perpetuation of political, economic, and social inequalities. Indigenous people, in turn, resist and negotiate these inequalities by positioning themselves or are positioned by others as 'natural conservationists', in order to legitimise their claims to their ancestral lands and territories (Conklin and Graham 1995; Brosius 1999; Nadasdy 2005). The mobilisation of Indigeneity to resist dam construction, deforestation, and other ecological violations on ancestral lands rests upon the strategic articulations of Indigenous people as 'ecologically noble savages' (Redford 1990). This is a concept grounded in the idealised European vision of the inhabitants of the non-Western world, 'who use environmental resources in ways that are non-destructive, sustainable and mindful of the effects on future generations' (Conklin and Graham 1995: 697). The documentary thus drew upon the image of the Mah Meri villagers as 'ecologically noble savages' (Redford 1990) to assert their Indigenous rights to their native customary lands, territories, and resources at

Kampung Sungai Bumbun (Conklin and Graham 1995; Hames 2007). This was also a role that the Mah Meri villagers themselves were eager to forge in order to promote their own agenda of asserting their Indigenous rights to the encroached lands and territories.

In contrast with the ongoing friction between the Mah Meri villagers at Kampung Sungai Bumbun and the broker at the Mah Meri Cultural Village, Indigenous activists such as Colin Nicholas have played a more positive brokerage role in instrumentalising Indigenous cultural heritage to serve the altruistic needs of the Mah Meri people, drawing upon the strategic essentialism of Indigeneity and Indigenous cultural heritage to advance their self-determination and advocacy. Motivated by their personal sense of social justice to draw on cultural heritage to champion for the empowerment of the Indigenous people, Indigenous activists such as Nicholas mediate and translate between the vernacular world of the Orang Asli and transnational Indigenous activism circles. They play a positive brokerage role in fostering a more equal partnership, leading to the self-determination and empowerment of Indigenous people and fulfilling the ethos lauded in the 'culture for development' discourse.

Despite the intervention of COAC through Colin Nicholas, the Mah Meri villagers' resistance towards the encroachment on their lands remained weak due to the different allegiances of the villagers with regard to JAKOA. This calls attention to the problems of conceptualising the Mah Meri villagers as a collective community with a common allegiance and agenda. Most of the Mah Meri villagers chose to cooperate with JAKOA as a way of negotiating their marginalised status covertly, rather than to resist their marginalised status overtly. As Diana Uju, who is the secretary to the local JKKK, explained:

> Since the setup of JKKK, we feel that our needs are better communicated to JAKOA. JKKK is a citizen consultancy committee and serves as an intermediary middleman between the Mah Meri communities of Kampung Sungai Bumbun and JAKOA. JKKK provides feedback on the needs of the communities in terms of facilities, welfare, etc. The JKKK President and Secretary have a monthly allowance from JAKOA, whereas for the other members, the allowance is given according to the attendance at the meetings.

With the financial support of JAKOA, some Mah Meri villagers have also received educational grants to pursue higher education in Malaysian universities and training institutes, while others have received new JAKOA-built cement houses with electricity and piped water in place of their wooden houses which lack such amenities.

While JAKOA has offered some financial support for the Mah Meri villagers, it appears to be helpless in addressing any perceived injustice towards the Orang Asli regarding land matters. On 16 September 2014, a

Mah Meri villager, Roslan, was detained overnight by the Malaysian police following an altercation with several ethnic Indian workers (COAC 2014b). The workers were clearing a cemetery belonging to Roslan's family in order to build an Indian shrine at the site. According to a villager in Kampung Sungai Bumbun, who knew about the case:

> For the recent land encroachment, it was the ethnic Indian workers who attacked Roslan with their spears and wooden planks first, then Roslan retaliated by using blowpipes to attack the Indian workers, but it was Roslan who got arrested by the police. Despite that Roslan's mother-in-law was buried on the land, the Indian workers continued to dig on the land although Roslan told them to stop. JAKOA's response? JAKOA only asked the affected villager to apply for the grant 'Dasar Pemilikan Tanah' (Land Ownership Policy).

While the Village Headman and the villagers knew about the encroachment issue, they were noncommittal in their responses to help Roslan and did not stand alongside him in resisting the land encroachment. There were even rumours that the Village Headman had given his approval for the Indian workers to encroach on the lands. As the same villager lamented:

> We are not as united as the Mah Meri communities in Kampung Sungai Kurau and Kampung Kepau Laut. Many villagers in Kampung Sungai Bumbun did not want to get involved with the case.

The reluctance of some Mah Meri villagers in Sungai Kampung Bumbun to be involved in resisting land encroachment is understandable, considering that some of them are recipients of the government's financial support through JAKOA, and will not want to be antagonistic towards their sponsors. However, their lack of unity has considerably weakened the collective assertion of their native customary rights over their ancestral lands and territories.

Conclusion

The Mah Meri Cultural Village, which was established to promote the developmental needs of the Indigenous Mah Meri people through cultural tourism, has come to be managed by a broker figure, who appears to benefit economically from the site more than the people who 'own' the cultural heritage that the cultural village represents. However, the prevailing structure of the cultural village, which extends significant authority to the broker in the management of such initiatives, seems to perpetuate a patron-client relationship between the Indigenous Mah Meri villagers and the broker, based on historical inequalities between the Orang Asli and Malays, and contributes to the continued marginalisation of Orang Asli in mainstream Malay-Muslim society.

In this case study, I have drawn attention to the structural 'patron-client' relationship between such broker figures and Indigenous people in cultural villages or community-based cultural projects in general. These hierarchies perpetuate long-standing inequalities and complicate the dominant rhetoric on the positive impacts of such projects. What is promoted as community-based capacity-building for the Indigenous people at the Mah Meri Cultural Village appears to resonate with the colonial civilising mission of the twentieth century, rooted in the historic 'patron-client' relationship that conceptualises Indigenous people as backward, uncivilised, and inferior, relative to other non-Indigenous groups, and therefore, in need of external assistance to achieve a higher rung on the evolutionary hierarchy. Due to the politics of brokerage and representation, I argue that such community-based cultural projects cultivate a culture of dependency between the brokers managing the projects, and the intended beneficiaries of these projects, which exacerbate the marginalisation of the Indigenous people, rather than contribute to their capacity-building and sustainable development. This complicates the positive rhetoric about the roles of Indigenous museums and 'culture for development' discourse widely promoted in the museological and academic literature. Crucially, it brings to question the effectiveness of decentralising developmental aid provision through brokers, a popular approach to aid deliverance in the current neoliberalist age.

The case study of the Mah Meri Cultural Village makes a significant contribution to Indigenous museology, especially in the Southeast Asian context, by demonstrating how Indigenous museums are sites of negotiation and contestation, where struggles over identity, representation, self-determination, and resource access are played out, producing complex ramifications for the Indigenous people and their cultural heritage. Although the Mah Meri Cultural Village draws upon the historical construction of Indigenous people as exotic noble savages, the villagers are not passive about their commodification and exoticisation through tourism, but are actively involved in the self-essentialisation of their primitive personas to capitalise on the benefits of this commodification for their own ends, either by becoming willing accomplices to the broker or by acting as brokers themselves in the commodification of their cultural heritage, or in the promotion of their woodcarving, for example, as an Indigenous craft handed down for generations. They are also actively contesting and negotiating their marginal positions in the cultural village covertly and overtly by adopting various strategies of resistance, while collaborating with the broker when it was in their interests to do so. Their position, however, is much constrained by the fragmentary nature of the Mah Meri community, as different villagers have their own interests and allegiances.

In contrast with the broker at the Mah Meri Cultural Village, Indigenous activists such as Colin Nicholas seem to play a more positive brokerage role in instrumentalising Indigenous cultural heritage to altruistically serve the needs of Indigenous people. They draw upon the strategic essentialism of Indigeneity and its connection with environmental politics to advance Indigenous self-determination and advocacy. These activists mediate between the local politics and the broader transnational Indigenous rights movement, enabling Indigenous people to reach out to an international audience in order to champion Indigenous empowerment and social justice. However, the lack of unity amongst the Mah Meri community compromises the collective assertion of their native customary rights over their lands, territories, and resources, which points to the complexities of conceptualising Indigenous people as a unified whole with similar interests and agendas. By critically examining the diverse roles different brokers play in the mediation and translation of cultural heritage, the case study of the Mah Meri Cultural Village expands on the literature on brokerage in museum and heritage studies.

Notes

1 Some materials used in this chapter have been published in Cai (2017).
2 There are currently five main Mah Meri villages on Pulau Carey, namely Kampung Sungai Bumbun, Kampung Sungai Judah, Kampung Sungai Kurau, Kampung Kepau Laut, and Kampung Sungai Rambai (Rahim 2007). Some of the villages are comprised of smaller riverine hamlets, for example, Kampung Sungai Bumbun is made up of three riverine hamlets, namely Kampung Sungai Bumbun, Kampung Sungai Mata, and Kampung Sungai Salang (Rahim 2007).
3 Each Mari Meri village will appoint an *adat* community, a group of community representatives that assists the *Tok Batin* in upholding their customs and traditions. The *adat* community decides on and carries out the rites and rituals for the community, including the *Hari Moyang*, marriage, funeral, and other rituals in the village.

4   Indigeneity as an intractable double-bind

Introduction[1]

The Orang Seletar Cultural Centre (Figure 4.1) is a case study of a cultural project which has been mobilised for Indigenous activism and self-determination to resist a threat to their livelihoods and an encroachment to their native customary lands and waters. While the Orang Seletar villagers have full ownership and management rights of the cultural centre, the project did not emerge organically from within the villagers themselves but was the vision and initiative of an external broker. The villagers also rely on another external broker – the owner of an eco-tourism business – to bring tourists to the cultural centre and realise the benefits of this cultural project. By highlighting the prominent roles brokers play in the mediation of these so-called community-based cultural projects, I demonstrate how cultural projects, including those owned and managed by the local communities

Figure 4.1 The Orang Seletar Cultural Centre is sited within Kampung Sungai Temon in the state of Johor in Peninsular Malaysia. Photograph: Author.

themselves, can still cultivate a culture of dependency between the external brokers and the intended beneficiaries.

There is also a paternalism in evidence at these community-based Indigenous cultural projects, in that they capitalise on the exoticisation of the Indigenous people as the 'primitive Other' to draw in tourists by conforming to their imaginaries about the exotic noble savages. While these cultural projects such as the Orang Seletar Cultural Centre offer an opportunity for the Indigenous people to complicate this historical conceptualisation and to mobilise their essentialised portrayal as Indigenous people for staking native claims to their ancestral lands, territories, and resources, this nevertheless reproduces and reinforces their colonial construction as an inferior race relative to the white Europeans. As such, this strategic essentialisation of 'Indigeneity' can serve as a 'double-bind' (Kallen 2015) for the Indigenous people.

The Orang Seletar are an Indigenous group who are known to have occupied the lands and waters around Singapore Island and the Johore Strait since the nineteenth century.[2] Skeat and Blagden (1906a: 88), citing an account from Thomson published in 1847, noted that 'they numbered in all 200 people, or 40 boats, and were subject to a *Batin* or petty chief, under the sovereignty of the Sultan of Johor', and that they had taken their name from the Seletar River, a mangrove creek on Singapore Island. By 1971, there were three settlements of Orang Seletar – two settlements in Johor and one settlement in Singapore – numbering around 300 people in total (Carey 1976). In 1986, due to the development of the Seletar area by the Singapore government, the Orang Seletar people in Singapore resettled in Johor Bahru at the invitation of the Sultan of Johor, with whom the Orang Seletar people had a long-standing patron-client relationship (Ali 2002).

Based on Department of Orang Asli Development (JAKOA) 2011 survey of the Indigenous population in Peninsular Malaysia, there are about 1,620 people who identify themselves as Orang Seletar people, constituting less than 1 per cent of the Orang Asli population (Orang Asli Museum n.d.b). Classified by JAKOA under the subgroup of proto-Malays (Carey 1976), they are mainly scattered across nine Orang Seletar villages,[3] located along the southern coast of Johor, of which seven are located within the Iskandar Development Region (IDR) (COAC 2014). Of these, only two villages, namely Kampung Bakar Batu and Kampung Simpang Arang, have been partially gazetted as Aboriginal Reserves under the Aboriginal Peoples Act 1954 (Act 134) (COAC 2014). The other villages do not have secure land titles and are, at best, 'tenant-at-will', which means that their continued occupation of the lands is dependent on the will of the state and they can be evicted if the state needs the lands for development (Nicholas 2000).

The Orang Seletar Cultural Centre which presents the cultural heritage of the Orang Seletar people, is situated within the Indigenous village of Kampung Sungai Temon in the state of Johor in Peninsular Malaysia. Established in 2011, the site is an independent cultural centre, wholly owned by the Orang Seletar community in the village. The centre features a collection of photographs from British photographer, naturalist, ethnologist, documentary filmmaker, and medical doctor, Dr Ivan Polunin, who lived in Singapore and Malaysia from the 1950s until his death in 2010. It also presents maps and photographs depicting aspects of the cultural heritage of the Orang Seletar people and marine wildlife found in the area, and replicas of hunting tools and customary boats used in their daily lives.

Featured in the Centre's exhibits are displays concerning contemporary issues faced by the Orang Seletar villagers in Kampung Sungai Temon. These include news reports of community involvement in the establishment of the cultural centre and their ongoing lawsuit against the private landowners, property developers, and state agencies involved in a waterfront development at Danga Bay that has encroached on their ancestral lands and waters. In addition, the Centre has a wooden stage for cultural performances, which take place mainly on Saturday nights, to complement the museum exhibits. Both the Centre and the village as a whole are under threat of eviction, as the villagers do not possess legal land titles to the village. According to the Village Headman of Kampung Sungai Temon, Salim bin Palon, the Orang Seletar Cultural Centre has a number of objectives, including ensuring that 'the traditional Orang Seletar culture is preserved', that 'the younger generation do not forget their roots', showing that the Orang Seletar 'have stayed in this area for many generations', and that 'development should not come at [their] expense or encroach on this land' (Yap 2011 n.p.).

The Orang Seletar Cultural Centre was established by the now-deceased Choo Chee Kuang, a Malaysian Chinese marine biologist and environmental activist associated with the Malaysian Society of Marine Science (MSMS). While conducting research on seahorses in the Johore Strait, Choo encountered the Orang Seletar people. Saddened by their plight, he gathered together a group of 10 friends, with the aim of establishing the needs of the Orang Seletar people, and later lobbied an international non-governmental organisation (NGO), the Global Environment Facility (GEF), for one-off funding of RM 60,000 (£11,300) to establish the 2,500 square foot Orang Seletar Cultural Centre (Yap 2011). In an interview with a Malaysian radio station in August 2011, Choo spoke about his objectives for setting up the Centre with the villagers:

> We mainly conduct work on the community capacity-building for the Orang Seletar people. So, we help them to preserve their culture and create some subsistence income through tourism activities. This is because the Seletar people are affected by development projects that destroy their source of livelihoods, mainly the mangroves that are scattered along the southern corner of the Johore Strait.
>
> (*The Business Station*, 24 August 2011)

The establishment of the Orang Seletar Cultural Centre resonates with UNESCO's 'culture for development' discourse, which posits that Indigenous culture can contribute to the socio-economic development of Indigenous people through sustainable tourism. In the face of urbanisation and pollution, which threaten the Orang Seletar people's customary livelihood as fishermen, the Orang Seletar Cultural Centre is intended to serve as an alternative means of income for the villagers so that they can reduce their dependency on the sea.

Choo said that his encounters with the Orang Seletar people and his desire to raise awareness of their existence as a distinct ethnic category motivated him to set up the Orang Seletar Cultural Centre with his friends and the Orang Seletar villagers:

> I was doing research to gather information about the Orang Seletar, and I got to know them. I went through their villages, scattered around nine locations in Southern Johore, and I interacted with them. I really feel for them, when I understand their plights and hardships. There is something urgent that you must help them. And since they are the least known Orang Asli group in Malaysia, there is very little documentation about the Orang Seletar tribes. So, people are hardly aware of their existence.
>
> (*The Business Station*, 24 August 2011)

Sympathetic to the plight of the Orang Seletar people and determined to alleviate their hardships, Choo played a positive brokerage role by lobbying for funds from GEF to set up the Orang Seletar Cultural Centre. Choo was mediating and translating between the development aid sector and the Orang Seletar village economy, strategically aligning the villagers' needs with the funding priorities of GEF to secure a budget for building the Centre. In the early days of its establishment, the Orang Seletar Cultural Centre was managed by Choo in consultation with the Orang Seletar villagers. Since Choo's premature death in 2013, the Centre has been fully managed by the Village Headman's second son, Jefree bin Salim, who is tasked with overseeing the management and operation of the Centre on behalf of the villagers.

Contexts, personalities, and interests

Once hailed by *Time Magazine* as 'one of the most ambitious development projects in the world', Iskandar Malaysia is a US$28 billion (£23 billion) project to transform Johor Bahru, located at the southern tip of Peninsular Malaysia, into an integrated waterfront development comprising port, commercial, residential, industrial, and tourism facilities (Chowdhury 2012). Established in 2006 as one of three regional corridors in Peninsular Malaysia conceived under the Economic Transformation Programme, the

IDR aims to become 'a strong and sustainable metropolis of international standing by the year of 2025' (Iskandar Malaysia 2016).

Since 2010, the Danga Bay area and its surroundings, where some of the Orang Seletar villages are located, have gradually been sold to private developers for massive reclamation and the development of high-rise waterfront properties as part of the IDR vision. The IDR development has damaged or destroyed much of the natural environment in the Danga Bay area, severely threatening the Orang Seletar people's subsistence as fishermen and their conventional way of life. Eddy bin Salim, the Village Headman's eldest son, spoke about their hardships:

> Since the development of Danga Bay in 2010, the fishery catch has been severely affected. The farming of green mussels is also severely affected. Twelve years ago, we can get 30 to 40 kilograms of green mussels every six months due to the rich nutrients in the waters of Johore Strait. Now, in one year, we get perhaps one to three kilograms of green mussels, certainly less than five kilograms.

As fish stocks have dwindled due to pollution and the destruction of their natural habitats, the Orang Seletar Cultural Centre has become the basis for the development of eco-tourism as an alternative means of livelihood for the Orang Seletar villagers. Since 2014, the villagers of Kampung Sungai Temon have been running eco-tourism tours around their village in partnership with a Malaysian eco-tourism enterprise known as Nature Classroom. These tours are aimed at increasing awareness of the villagers' cultural heritage and natural environment. The eco-tourism tours enable the Orang Seletar villagers to draw on their cultural heritage and tacit knowledge of the seas and lands.

Nature Classroom was founded by a Penang-based Malaysian Chinese environmental educator, Wong Yun Yun. The eco-tourism enterprise runs nature tours around Malaysia, focusing mainly on Penang, aimed at inculcating greater awareness and appreciation of Malaysia's rich biodiversity. As a broker, Wong mediates and translates between the nature tourism sector and the Orang Seletar village economy to bring tourism benefits to the Orang Seletar villagers of Kampung Sungai Temon and herself. Wong works with the Orang Seletar villagers through Jefree, who also oversees the operation of the Orang Seletar Cultural Centre, to coordinate with the Orang Seletar villagers for these eco-tourism tours around Kampung Sungai Temon. In this respect, we can see how Jefree serves as an internal broker for the Orang Seletar villagers of Kampung Sungai Temon, liaising with external brokers such as Wong, and coordinating internally with the other villagers in Kampung Sungai Temon for the eco-tourism tours around their village.

Wong hopes to increase public awareness of the Orang Seletar villagers and promote multicultural tolerance and diversity through these eco-tourism tours, and to confront preconceived notions that non-Indigenous Malaysians often have of Indigenous people. As Wong has said:

> I would like to facilitate better understanding of the Orang Seletar people, and to get people engaged with the natural environment, especially the lush mangrove habitats. Many people in Malaysia still don't know about the Orang Asli. They think that the Orang Asli live in the forests in very backward and primitive conditions. I want to bring people to interact with the Orang Seletar to let them know that they are just like one of us.

A full-day eco-tourism tour with Nature Classroom, consisting of a maximum of 30 participants and costing about RM 75 (£15) per person, typically begins with a morning briefing on the history and lifestyle of the Orang Seletar people through a tour of the Orang Seletar Cultural Centre, followed by a walk around the village to view their houses. Throughout this tour, the Orang Seletar villagers' 'past' is staged in the cultural centre, while their 'present' is staged around the village for the participants' consumption. The tour, thus, offers both an essentialised and a dynamic view of their culture, linking present practices with their cultural heritage. This is then followed by the assignment of an Orang Seletar child to the participants, who they have been asked to sponsor. The child accompanies the visitors on a boat trip around the mangrove swamps of the Johore Strait, guided by the villagers of Kampung Sungai Temon. During the boat trip, participants are introduced to the fauna and wildlife in the area (Figure 4.2). They are also asked to collect natural materials that they will be using for a craft session later. After a meal prepared by the villagers of what is described as 'home-cooked Orang Seletar food', comprising rice with three dishes of chicken rendang, curried mussels, and curried papaya, the participants adjourn to the cultural centre for a craft-making session, before the evening conclusion of a gift presentation session and the sharing of thoughts among the participants with the villagers.

At an eco-tourism tour with Nature Classroom in which I took part, the participants, mainly Malaysian Chinese living in Johor Bahru, said that they enjoyed the tour, and the experience changed their views of the Orang Seletar people:

> The Orang Seletar children are so brave. The Orang Seletar girl [that accompanied us] is only five years old, yet she jumps into the mangrove swamps to chop down the leaves for our crafts with a cleaver without fear. I think they can take care of themselves at such a young age, because they are exposed to these dangerous tasks. Comparatively, my children are so protected.

> I am very envious of their childhoods of being close to nature, so carefree. In Malaysia today, it is hard to find this kind of lifestyle.

> I am quite surprised that the *Tok Batin* lives in a big bungalow that looks spacious and luxurious, and possibly bigger than my house.

Figure 4.2 Visitors on a boat trip to see the mangrove swamps at Johore Strait, guided by the Orang Seletar villagers from Kampung Sungai Temon. Photograph: Author.

While such eco-tourism tours are perceived as a form of sustainable tourism that can lead to the socio-economic development of local communities, there is nevertheless a paternalism in evidence that capitalises on the exoticisation of the Orang Seletar people as the 'primitive Other'. The opportunity to dispel notions of the Orang Seletar villagers as exotic noble savages is, however, emphasised by Wong as a key objective of the tour, highlighting how tourists' imaginaries of the Orang Seletar people are actively mobilised, but also complicated by these tours. In this sense, the historical conception of the Orang Seletar as a backward, uncivilised, and underdeveloped people is employed as a 'hook' for attracting tourists to these eco-tourism tours, with the objective to challenge this very historical conception of the Orang Seletar people through presenting tourists with both their 'past' cultural heritage on display in the Orang Seletar Cultural Centre and their 'present' cultural practices through the tour of the village. This has, to a certain extent, been achieved, not least with a tour participant expressing surprise at the Village Headman's spacious bungalow house, which probably contrasts with their preconceptions of the Orang Seletar as being poor, backward, and underdeveloped, which demonstrates how colonial and post-colonial representations of Indigenous people as the primitive Other continue to influence contemporary imaginings in present-day Malaysia.

Drawing from MacCannell's (1973) use of dramaturgical analysis, the 'front stage' manifested in the 'essentialised past' on display at the Orang Seletar Cultural Centre and the 'back stage' manifested in the 'dynamic present' of the vernacular lives of the Orang Seletar villagers are staged for the participants' consumption, mobilising and yet complicating tourists' imaginaries of the Orang Seletar people as a backward, underdeveloped, and uncivilised ethnic group relative to Europeans and non-Indigenous Malaysians. The Orang Seletar villagers of Kampung Sungai Temon are willing to open up their 'back stage' for tourist consumption as a means of negotiating their constructed imaginaries as the primitive Other.

Although the eco-tourism tours at Kampung Sungai Temon are generally popular, Wong does not organise them regularly as it is inconvenient for her to do so, since she is based in another Malaysian state. Wong has a cordial working relationship with Jefree, although she has commented that it has taken her a while to build trust to be able to work with him to bring participants to Kampung Sungai Temon. At present, although she tries to organise these tours at least once every two months, the potential of these eco-tourism tours serving as an alternative source of livelihood for the Orang Seletar villagers at Kampung Sungai Temon is limited due to their infrequency. As Jefree still works predominantly as a fisherman, he does not promote the eco-tourism tours pro-actively since they only constitute his subsidiary source of income. Despite this well-meaning relationship, Wong nevertheless fosters a sense of paternalism and perpetuates a culture of dependency among the Orang Seletar villagers.

Transformation, representation, and interpretation of culture

Like many Southwest Pacific museums that featured in Stanley's (2007) edited book, the Orang Seletar Cultural Centre was initiated by an external broker, Choo, who sought funding from GEF to pay the Orang Seletar villagers for its construction. It was not a project that emerged organically from within the Orang Seletar villagers. Nonetheless, the cultural centre made a useful contribution to villagers by offering them alternative livelihoods in cultural tourism and eco-tourism in the face of rapid urbanisation and pollution brought about by the IDR development. The Centre also served as an arena for asserting their Indigenous identity and native customary rights in their class action lawsuit against the IDR development in the Danga Bay area, notably when the judge was brought on a tour to the Centre to learn about their cultural heritage and their historical connections to the lands and territories from which they are under threat of eviction.

During my fieldwork in Kampung Sungai Temon, I became acquainted with Ah Chek, an ethnic Chinese Malaysian who has run a provision shop in the village for almost 20 years. Ah Chek offered a contrasting perspective on the Orang Seletar Cultural Centre, which cast doubt on the idealised view of the external sponsorship of community-run cultural institutions as a tool for development. In his opinion, the Orang Seletar Cultural Centre was merely an economic opportunity for the Orang Seletar people. As he explained:

When Choo was setting up the cultural centre, he also sought my views. I felt that the effort put in by the Orang Seletar villagers did not justify the funding given to the project. Did you know that wages were paid to the Orang Seletar villagers to gather the materials and set up the cultural centre? The villagers did not set up the cultural centre for free, but they were later given the cultural centre for free. It was such a good deal for the villagers, but they did not value it by keeping it in a tip-top condition. Instead, they allow it to languish. Given the lack of care of the villagers over the cultural centre, I did not think it was a worthwhile effort.

In Ah Chek's view, community-based cultural projects such as the Orang Seletar Cultural Centre served merely as mechanisms to offer aid to the beneficiary communities in ways that might not fulfil their genuine needs. Ah Chek also cast doubt on the authenticity of the heritage represented by the cultural centre:

> The cultural centre was not authentic, as this was based on research and not their everyday lived experiences. 10 to 20 years ago, the Orang Seletar villagers would hang out and dance every evening – those were the authentic Orang Seletar dances. To understand their lives in the past, you should consult the oldest Orang Seletar women, who are still alive in Kampung Bakar Batu. The cultural dances performed at Kampung Sungai Temon are not authentic; they were recently invented.

As Ah Chek rightly highlighted, the Orang Seletar cultural dances currently performed by the villagers of Kampung Sungai Temon are created by an Orang Seletar man who act as a songwriter-cum-dance choreographer for the villagers (Figure 4.3). These cultural performances speak of the current experiences of Orang Seletar people in twenty-first-century Malaysia, and of a sense of community spirit and resilience to cope with the raft of changes they have experienced through the years. There is, for example, a performance about their plight as a community faced with dwindling resources due to rapid urbanisation and land reclamation on their ancestral lands. There is another piece of performance that speaks of the carefree lifestyle they once had, based around the sea, interacting with sea creatures, which were and are still so central to their lives. Intricately connected to their contemporary vernacular lifestyles, these staged performances are actively embraced as a part of the Orang Seletar villagers' evolving cultural heritage and communicate their resistance to the broader marginalisation they face within the contemporary politics of Danga Bay. Thus, they also serve as a vehicle for Indigenous empowerment.

Musical instruments and dance movements are also frequently revised by the songwriter and dance choreographer. Although the Orang Seletar cultural performances are contemporary creations, this has not stopped

Figure 4.3 The Orang Seletar villagers at Kampung Sungai Temon performing a dance on stage beside the Orang Seletar Cultural Centre. Photograph: Colin Nicholas from COAC.

them from winning first prize in the national dance competition at the Orang Asli Entrepreneur Carnival 2014, suggesting that these are generally accepted as an authentic expression of Orang Seletar culture by JAKOA, which is the organiser of the carnival. This is an example of how contemporary cultural practices can acquire 'emergent authenticity' (Cohen 1988) and alludes to the dynamism of Indigenous cultural practice in the everyday lives of the Orang Seletar people. This contrasts with the essentialised notions of Orang Seletar cultural heritage as portrayed in the displays of material culture at the cultural centre.

The Orang Seletar Cultural Centre seems to resemble an Indigenous museum, as it fulfils many characteristics highlighted by Stanley (2007) in his seminal book on Indigenous museums in Southwest Pacific. It is small in scale and has known 'publics' who are the Orang Seletar villagers at Kampung Sungai Temon. It also focuses on the use of the collection to transmit cultural heritage rather than the safeguarding of its objects from wear and tear to ensure their posterity. This is evident from the absence of any form of climatic control in the Centre, where damaged objects are replaced rather than professionally conserved. The Orang Seletar Cultural Centre also discusses the contemporary issues faced by the Orang Seletar villagers in its exhibits, by presenting news reports of the community coming together to build the Centre, and their ongoing court case against the state agencies, private landowners, and property developers involved in the waterfront development at Danga Bay that has encroached on their native customary lands and waters.

When I last visited Kampung Sungai Temon in February 2018, the Orang Seletar Cultural Centre was in a dilapidated condition. Its lights were no longer working, and the wooden hut looked neglected. The future of the Centre is in limbo pending the outcome of their appeal against the court's judgement for their resettlement in another part of Malaysia in return for a monetary compensation. Kreps (2007) suggests that the larger concern over Indigenous museums is whether they have contributed to sustaining the Indigenous people's cultural lives and their socio-economic developments. In this sense, the Orang Seletar Cultural Centre has made a useful contribution to the political, economic, cultural, and social lives of the Orang Seletar villagers by offering them an alternative livelihood in heritage tourism and serving as an avenue for asserting their native customary rights.

Frictions, tensions, and issues

In 2012, the villagers of Kampung Sungai Temon chanced upon the desecration of their ancestors' graves due to the clearing of lands for IDR's development, and learned that the land on which their village sits had been sold to private developers without their knowledge (COAC 2014). This chance discovery triggered a class action lawsuit proposed by Eddy bin Salim, Salim bin Palon, and Mat bin Inder on behalf of themselves and another 185 Orang Seletar villagers from Kampung Sungai Temon and Kampung Bakar Batu in December 2012, which sought to stop Iskandar Development Region Agency's (IDRA) development on their native customary lands and waters (COAC 2014).

Although the possession of registered land titles defines the right to remain 'in-place' at the Danga Bay area, by no means is this the only grounds on which contestation over land occurs. As Cresswell (1996) demonstrates, being 'in-place' or 'out-of-place' entails not only legal but also moral and aesthetic judgements about who belongs and does not belong to place. The legal considerations, with regard to the threatened displacement of Orang Seletar villagers in the Danga Bay area, are also bound up with the broader political and cultural contexts. The moral code defines who has a right to be 'in-place' and carries 'expectations about behaviour in place [which] are important components in the construction, maintenance, and evolution of ideological values' (Cresswell 1996: 4).

Since the launch of the class action lawsuit, the private landowners and property developers who seek to redevelop the Danga Bay area have sought to settle the matter by offering different plans for the resettlement of the Orang Seletar villagers in the hope that the case can be resolved out of court. Different members of the Village Headman's family, who hosted my stay at Kampung Sungai Temon, discussed this emotive topic with me at length on several occasions, and each time they spoke with fury and anxiety. They told me in exasperation:

Why can't we be allowed to stay where we are? The private developers can spend some money to beautify our village, if they think we are incompatible with their developments. They can make us a tourist village as part of their developments, where tourists can come here to have dinner, and do an eco-tourism tour.

The Orang Seletar villagers are under threat of eviction from the Danga Bay area because of their status as underdeveloped, backward, and uncivilised Indigenous people. Their spatial manifestation in the rural and dilapidated environment of Kampung Sungai Temon and Kampung Bakar Batu (Figure 4.4) is perceived by the state authorities to be incompatible with the IDR's vision of modernity and urbanity. The presence of the Orang Seletar villagers in the Danga Bay area is deemed a form of transgression, ideologically inappropriate, and aesthetically 'out-of-place' with the grand vision of IDR. Hence, they have to be evicted to conform with the appropriate moral order and aesthetic judgement associated with the IDR.

The incompatibility of the Orang Seletar villagers within the moral and aesthetic landscape of IDR underpins the wider discrimination towards the Orang Asli within the social and political realms of Malaysia. This remains deeply entrenched in the contemporary attitudes of the political Malay elites towards the Orang Asli in Malaysia, who are often critical of their resistance to the government's developmental efforts. Jamilah Ariffin (2014: 227), the wife of the former Chief Minister of Johor, writes condescendingly of the Orang Seletar's 'inhibiting attitudes and mindsets' in a book documenting her research on the Orang Seletar people in Johor, particularly their reluctance to undertake waged work as factory workers or labourers.

Figure 4.4 The wooden houses of the Orang Seletar villagers at Kampung Sungai Temon at Danga Bay in Peninsular Malaysia. Photograph: Author.

An analysis and verification of these accounts has led me to conclude that, among the factors inhibiting the Orang Seletar's progress is the presence of some form of attitudinal 'mental block'. To begin with, there appears to be an innate sensitivity against being 'corrected' by 'outsiders', coupled with a tribal sense of unity in the face of such criticism – even to their own detriment. As one respondent notes, 'The young people are very sensitive. If they are reprimanded by their bosses, they will walk away at once and not even return for the money.' There have been accounts by employers in nearby towns on how groups of Orang Seletar employees can just quit en bloc and walk away when one of their number is admonished. This perhaps is their demonstration of tribal unity. In addition, their cultural inertia to become factory workers or labourers ('Coolie') can, perhaps, be explained by the apparent 'shame' of being employees of outsiders or someone not of the *Kon Seletar*[4].

Rather than acknowledging the underpinning political and social structures that account for Orang Seletar people's marginalisation in modernising Malaysia, Ariffin (2014) draws upon their culture to explain their economic marginalisation, or in her words, their 'cultural inertia' towards waged work. Ariffin (2014) attributes the marginalisation of the Orang Seletar to a supposed 'anti-development' sensibility inherent in their culture, even though the Orang Seletar villagers have clearly expressed a desire for development through initiatives such as developing their seafood supplies and restaurant businesses as a means of supporting their livelihoods.

Ariffin (2014: 232) also criticises the Indigenous activists for their biased stances towards the Malaysian government, alluding to the instrumental value of Indigeneity that has been drawn upon by Indigenous scholars and activists to further their agendas:

> These sentiments of the young respondents resonate with the prejudiced notions held by a few NGO groups and some academic writers from outside the Seletar community (as revealed through the judgemental slant in their writings). They remain unconvinced of the sincerity of the State Government of 1995–2013 and the then Chief Minister in uplifting the living standards of the Orang Seletar. They continue to harp on the usual complaints, namely the lack of attention for those 'forgotten sea gypsies' and the encumbrance of the 'red-tape' in the bureaucracy. However, they do not attempt to contribute constructive suggestions on how to remedy the situation.

Ariffin's (2014) accusations towards these NGOs and academics are largely unjustified, as several scholar-activists for the Orang Asli have repeatedly lobbied for their political representation and self-determination in managing their customary territories and their lives by demonstrating how the

Orang Asli's marginalisation is underpinned by the political and social structures of contemporary Malaysia (Dentan et al. 1997; Nicholas 2000; Nicholas et al. 2010; Aiken and Leigh 2011a, b; Subramaniam 2011, 2014; Nordin and Witbrodt 2012). Resonating with Ferguson's (1994) observation in Lesotho, Ariffin's stance, reflecting those of the political elites in Malaysia, shows how developmental projects, such as the IDR, serve to expand the bureaucratic powers of the Malaysian state and sidestep Indigenous resistance on the politics of land and resources as obstacles to development.

In December 2014, amidst the ongoing court proceedings, the private landowners and private developers offered two options to the Orang Seletar villagers living in Kampung Sungai Temon: first, each family would be offered monetary compensation to purchase an alternative property of their own; second, the whole village could move to a new site as a community. The villagers discussed the options available to them, and communally decided that as a minority group, they would need to live together if they were to continue living as an identifiable Indigenous group with distinct cultural practices and heritage. Hence, they indicated their preference for the second option. Wong (of the Nature Classroom enterprise) underscores the need to keep the Orang Seletar villagers together as a community.

> Keeping the communities together and preserving their traditional ways of life are crucial to safeguarding their cultural heritage and identity. Because they are a minority, they are at a greater risk of losing their cultural heritage and assimilating into the majority cultures. However, if they choose to urbanise, and adopt an urbanite lifestyle, such as become a taxi driver or work in factories, they are at risk of losing their cultural heritage, since these elements are no longer relevant to their current lives. Unlike the majority cultures such as the Chinese or Malays, even when some of the communities don't practise their cultural heritage, there is bound to be others that will practise them. But for the Orang Seletar, because their population bases are very small, if they no longer practise their cultural heritage, they are at risk of losing their cultural heritage completely. Hence, for a marginalised or fringe culture like the Orang Seletar, it is all the more important for them to stay together, and to retain their natural environment so that their cultural heritage continues to remain dominant and relevant to their lives.

My host family explained that they had been brought to view six possible sites for resettlement. Although they were promised large, beautiful houses at these alternative sites, they did not agree to the resettlement since these sites were not only located inland but also nested within Malay-Muslim villages which were incongruent with their customary livelihoods as fishermen and where as non-Muslims they would nevertheless have to abstain from eating pork and adapt to other food practices. A coastal site near

Puteri Harbour, also in Johor Bahru, was eventually offered, which they found acceptable for resettlement. The villagers collectively decided that although they would need to erect their own houses on the site, they felt that they could continue with their customary livelihoods as fishermen and keep running their seafood restaurant businesses. This resettlement site was, however, rejected by the state authorities for political reasons that were not clearly articulated. Meanwhile, my host family was adamant in their resistance to the powers of the political elite. As the Village Headman's wife said:

> Everything is not decided yet. If the compensation is good, we will move; if the compensation is not satisfactory, we will not move. The lawyers will help us negotiate the deal.

The plight of the Orang Seletar villagers and their customary land claims were, however, completely white-washed by the private developers of Danga Bay, as my visit to one sales gallery in Singapore revealed. One prominent development at the Danga Bay area is the Country Garden Danga Bay development, a 57-acre mixed-use integrated waterfront development comprising residential, commercial, and leisure components, situated along the Johore Strait, six kilometres from Singapore via the Johor–Singapore Causeway (Country Garden n.d.). Launched for sale in August 2013 by a Chinese developer who bought the land from the Johor State Government in 2012, the luxurious development also boasts a private beach of fine white sand imported from Sabah and ample mooring areas for private yachts. Its sales gallery in the central district of Singapore is impressive, complete with mock-ups of the furnished apartments, along with a series of incentives to entice foreign buyers. As one of the earliest developments in the Danga Bay area, the complex is exempted from a ruling that mandates a minimum price of RM 1 million (£189,000) for foreign ownership.[5]

As the salesperson tried to impress upon me the desirability of the new development by listing the major investors in the Danga Bay area, including many prominent Singaporean and Chinese developers, I casually brought up the Orang Seletar land claims and asked how these might affect me should I purchase an apartment. The salesperson confidently reassured me:

> There is nothing about the Orang Asli land claims in the Danga Bay area. Even if the lands were indeed part of the Orang Asli customary lands, the state, which would hold the strongest power, would have the final say. Anyway, the developers bought the lands from the Johor State Government and had clear titles to the lands. In any case, it would not affect the development of the Country Garden Danga Bay.

Such is the sad reality of the Orang Seletar villagers and their customary land claims in Malaysia. The Orang Seletar villagers at Kampung Sungai Temon and Kampung Bakar Batu are facing the threat of eviction from their native customary lands in Danga Bay, not only because they do not hold the registered land titles but also because their physical existence is deemed 'out-of-place' with the modern vision of the IDR under the capitalist neo-liberalisation of Malaysia. Their marginalisation is largely dismissed by Malaysian political elites and capitalists who attribute their economic and social marginalisation to their anti-development 'cultural inertia', rather than the wider political and social contexts in Malaysia that have led to their current plight. This again highlights the entrenched perception of the Orang Asli as inferior and backward people, which continues to have implications in their current treatment in contemporary Malaysia.

This instance of Orang Seletar villagers turning to the courts to assert their Indigenous rights should not be seen in isolation, but instead as part of a broader international set of developments that have become increasingly prominent since the late 1990s. As part of the transnational Indigenous movement, ideas and practices with regard to human rights, produced at United Nations conferences, in courtrooms, or elsewhere, have circulated globally through policy statements, legal precedents, and the work of activists and other brokers (Merry 2006). There is also a growing awareness that landmark rulings in cases such as Delgamuukw in British Columbia,[6] the Mago and Wik Peoples in Queensland,[7] the Miriuwung and Gajerrong in Western Australia,[8] and the Amodu Tijani in southern Nigeria[9] can be used to strengthen the claims of Indigenous people in other places, including Malaysia (Bunnell and Nah 2004).

These global connections with the transnational Indigenous movement enable a sense of collective experiences to be forged with Indigenous minorities elsewhere. As Yogeswaran Subramaniam, one of the plaintiffs' lawyers, explained:

> The Orang Asli have realised that they are part of the global Indigenous rights movement. In Sabah and Sarawak, Indigenous groups are more advanced in their activism, with a lot of them participating in conferences, workshops, and dialogues with international Indigenous people where they are made aware of developments on Indigenous rights. The Orang Asli have since joined the fray which I feel has prompted the increase in complaints and legal action. If you don't know your rights, it would be unsurprising if you were to assume that you have little or no rights.

The increased awareness by Indigenous people of their rights, coupled with the exhaustion of other avenues such as dialogue and negotiation to make their concerns heard, and the successes of the Indigenous people in seeking compensation for infringement of their native rights through legal jurisprudence elsewhere have encouraged many groups of Indigenous people in Malaysia to turn to the courts to address alleged breaches of their land and resource rights (Nicholas 2000; Idrus 2010; Aiken and Leigh 2011a).

Two landmark cases – the Adong Kuwau case in 1996 (Adong bin Kuwau & Ors v Kerajaan Negeri Johor & Anor, 1997) and the Sagong Tasi case in 2002 (Sagong bin Tasi & Ors v Kerajaan Negeri Selangor, 2002) – were crucial in establishing the legal precedence for Indigenous claims in Malaysia. The Adong Kuwau case of 1996 (Adong bin Kuwau & Ors v Kerajaan Negeri Johor & Anor, 1997), in which the Indigenous Jakun people of Johor won their case against the Johor State Government, which had prevented them from foraging on their ancestral lands that had been set aside as a reservoir to supply water to Singapore, was significant in demonstrating that native title could be accommodated within Malaysian law (Aiken and Leigh 2011a). More specifically, the Adong Kuwau case affirmed that Indigenous people in Malaysia hold native title, which

> is the right of the native to continue to live on their land as their forefathers had done", a right "acquired in law" and not based on any document or title ... [and] that "future generations of the aboriginal people would be entitled to this right of their forefathers.
>
> (Nah 2008: 228)

For the Jakun people, the case resulted in significantly higher compensation than what was otherwise offered by the Malaysian government for the loss of their fruit trees, crops, and homes. The compensation proposed by the court for the loss of their ancestral lands and territories included consideration of the deprivation 'of heritage land, of freedom of inhabitation or movement, of produce of the forest, of future living for the plaintiffs and their immediate families, and of future living for their living descendants' (Nah 2008: 228).

The Sagong Tasi case of 2002 (Sagong bin Tasi & Ors v Kerajaan Negeri Selangor, 2002), in which the displaced Temuans of Selangor received compensation for their ancestral lands acquired by the state for constructing a highway leading to Kuala Lumpur International Airport, was significant in demonstrating that the state recognised the proprietary rights of Indigenous people to their native customary lands even though these lands had not been gazetted (Bunnell and Nah 2004; Nah 2008; Idrus 2010; Aiken and Leigh 2011a). The judgement also reaffirmed that Indigenous people could acquire

> rights over the said lands by land use and occupation through customs, original possession and usufructuary derived from their forefathers and still continuing up to the present time ... [by showing] that they speak an aboriginal language, follow an aboriginal way of life as well as aboriginal customs and beliefs.
>
> (Bunnell and Nah 2004: 2459)

In the Sagong Tasi case, the Temuan plaintiffs presented evidence of their *Lembaga Adat* (Tribal Council) that they claimed had existed for generations up to the present day, and their *Adat Tanah* (Customary Lands) by marking their landmarks, such as ancestors' graves and geographical features, onto existing survey maps using Global Positioning System (GPS) equipment. This enabled them to challenge the defendants' argument that they no longer practised their culture (Bunnell and Nah 2004). Importantly, the Sagong Tasi case identified how land rights for Indigenous people could be acquired by providing evidence of their continued practice of Indigenous cultural heritage, which indicated a connection to the lands and territories. The use of the term 'aborigines' in the court ruling, to refer to the Orang Asli, highlights how nineteenth-century conceptualisations of Indigenous people as primordial and autochthonic continue to influence contemporary conceptualisations of Indigenous people in Malaysia.

Litigation for the Orang Seletar class action lawsuit commenced on 23 February 2014, and formally ended on 29 March 2016, with the submission of court documents due on 27 July 2016. During the trial proceedings, the Orang Seletar had been successful in securing several court injunctions to halt all work on the sites until the case was settled (COAC 2016). During my fieldwork in Peninsular Malaysia from September 2014 to March 2015, I attended six full days of court proceedings as an observer at the Johor Bahru High Court on 14 and 15 October 2014, 11 November 2014, 8 December 2014, 5 February 2015, and 29 March 2015. The court proceedings for the Orang Seletar class action lawsuit can be conceptualised as encounters of friction and disjuncture (Tsing 2005), embedded in networks of unequal power relations. A large entourage of well-heeled lawyers representing 13 rich private landowners, property developers, and state agencies were teamed against the Orang Seletar villagers, represented by a group of pro-bono lawyers from the Malaysian Bar Council.[10] At these sessions, witnesses representing the Orang Seletar villagers, as well as the private landowners, property developers, and state agencies, took turns on the stand to be cross-examined by lawyers from both the plaintiffs' and the defendants' sides.

The court proceedings served as an arena for the complex interplays of power relations between the different stakeholders, who wrestled over the control of the lands on which the villages of Kampung Sungai Temon and Kampung Bakar Batu sit. The Orang Seletar villagers claimed rights to remain on the lands based on their native customary rights, while the private landowners, property developers, and state agencies claimed rights to own and develop the lands based on their legal titles. Lawyers and witnesses on either side strategically mobilised state apparatuses such as institutional practices, constitutions, and regulations, as well as representations of Indigeneity and Indigenous cultural heritage to stake their claims to these lands, territories, and resources.

In these high-stake power exchanges between the Orang Seletar plaintiffs and the defendants of private landowners, property developers, and state agencies, the pro-bono lawyers from the Malaysian Bar Council and the Orang Asli activist, Colin Nicholas, played important brokerage roles, which facilitated the translation and mediation of Orang Seletar villagers' simple oral accounts of their customs and traditions into the complex legal terminologies used in the court proceedings. The brokerage roles of the lawyers and activists involved a strategic selection and interpretation of a body of oral accounts and literature that related to the Orang Seletar villagers' historical connections to their ancestral lands and waters.

In the court sessions that I attended, during which the defendants presented their case, there was an architect representing the Johor State Land Office, who was highly confident and eloquent and framed her statements carefully so that she did not commit herself more than she needed to. There was another representative from the District Land Office who was less eloquent. She said she knew about the presence of Indigenous people in the Danga Bay area but did not know that they belonged to the Orang Seletar group. There was also a representative from the IDRA, the agency tasked with drawing up the development master-plan and coordinating its implementation for the IDR, who clarified that while there was a committee set up within IDRA to look into the socio-economic aspects of the IDR development, it had a limited role as the IDRA was not mandated under its constitution to consider issues of economic and social 'uplifting'. The testimony nonetheless led to the discontinuation of the Orang Seletar villagers' claim against the IDRA, as it was realised that the organisation was merely a planning agency appointed to develop the lands and did not have any ownership or fiduciary duty over the management of the land.

The longest cross-examination of government officials was reserved for the JAKOA representative in a session that took place on 8 December 2014. Jumaat Misman, an ethnic Malay officer, wrote a report on Orang Seletar cultural heritage during his tenure at JAKOA. He was the defendants' expert witness on the Orang Seletar people's history and cultural practices. Pitted against Colin Nicholas, who served as the plaintiffs' pro-bono expert witness on the historical contexts of the Orang Seletar villagers' claims, Jumaat Misman's credibility was put to test by the cross-examination of lawyers on both sides, who each wanted their respective expert witnesses to be regarded as the more credible. One of the plaintiffs' pro-bono lawyers, Yogeswaran Subramaniam, admitted after the trial that they had experienced a dilemma over whether they should attempt to discredit Jumaat Misman, as his report established that the Orang Seletar people have a long connection to the Danga Bay area and included historical information about the settlement of the Orang Seletar on lands, which would be advantageous to their claim that the Orang Seletar people have native claims to their ancestral lands and waters.

Colin Nicholas was earlier cross-examined at a session on 7 February 2014, based on his 28-page expert report, which detailed a comprehensive collection of historical information on the Orang Seletar people and Malaysian government policies on the Orang Asli, derived from books, dissertations, and journals dating back to the nineteenth century (Nicholas 2014). While I was not present at the cross-examination, as the earlier court sessions took place before the commencement of my fieldwork, I had the opportunity to review the judgement which was made available on 7 July 2017. The judgement contained the respective arguments and defences from both the plaintiffs and defendants. The defendants' lawyers had attempted to discredit Colin Nicholas by highlighting his role as an advocate and lobbyist for the recognition of native customary rights among the Orang Asli, especially his belief that the Orang Asli have been systematically discriminated against by the Malaysian government and its pro-Malay-Muslim policies (Johor Bahru High Court 2017). The plaintiffs' lawyers refuted the charges, citing that Colin Nicholas is an acknowledged expert on Orang Asli matters, with his testimonies previously accepted by Malaysian courts and that being an activist does not render his evidence unreliable (Johor Bahru High Court 2017).

Notwithstanding the probative value of Jumaat Misman's evidence to the Seletar claim, there were parts of the cross-examination where the Orang Seletar observers in the audience could be seen shaking their heads in disapproval, for example when Jumaat Misman claimed that the Orang Seletar were different from the Orang Laut,[11] and were considered proto-Malays under JAKOA's classification of Orang Asli. These Orang Seletar observers appeared to disagree with the answers of Jumaat Misman on their cultural practices, which gave weight to their overt scepticism regarding Jumaat Misman's credibility as an expert witness. The dissonance between Jumaat Misman and the Orang Seletar villagers highlights how cultural heritage is shaped by power relations and is embroiled in questions of ownership and representation, including who has the right to represent it, and for whom it is represented. The court proceedings took a surprising turn at the last session on 29 March 2015, when the judge requested a private mediation between the Orang Seletar plaintiffs and the defendants. The private mediation, led by their respective lawyers, failed to agree on an amicable solution. The parties involved then unanimously agreed that the legal proceedings should take their natural course and that the judge should make a ruling on the claims of both sides.

As part of the court proceedings, the judge was taken on a tour of the Orang Seletar Cultural Centre situated within Kampung Sungai Temon, and other sites of customary significance in the vicinity (Figure 4.5). With its representations of an essentialised Orang Seletar identity associated with customary territory, the centre thus became a resource that was instrumentalised in the court case. By articulating their historical connections to the lands, made visible through the narratives and material cultural heritage displayed in the centre, as well as geographical landmarks such as ancestors' graves and culturally significant geographical features connected to Indigenous cosmologies, the Orang Seletar villagers and their lawyers were able to support their claims to customary rights through 'place-based

Figure 4.5 The judge and lawyers on a visit to the Orang Seletar Cultural Centre situated within Kampung Sungai Temon and other sites of customary significance in the vicinity. Photograph: Colin Nicholas from COAC.

imaginaries' (Cooke 2013), which were 'realised historically *in* and *through* place' (Bunnell and Nah 2004: 2459, original emphasis).

By alluding to Indigeneity as grounded in an idea of temporal and spatial presence 'from time immemorial', the Malaysian law has embraced an antiquated anthropological notion of Indigeneity based on primordiality and autochthony. This is evident not only through using terms like 'aborigines' in the court rulings, which imply that Indigenous people exist 'from time immemorial', but also through the emphasis placed on material cultural heritage and culturally significant geographical landmarks as evidence of Orang Seletar Indigenous identity and historical connections to the lands and territories. Since 'juridical systems of power *produce* the subjects they subsequently come to represent' (Butler 1990: 2 quoted in Birrell 2009: 222, original emphasis), a legal legitimacy is thus extended to this essentialised notion of Indigeneity premised on the production of cultural difference, thus rendering these differences as facts, rather than acknowledging their fluid and dynamic subjectivities (Barnard 2006; Birrell 2009). Despite its epistemological and ontological incongruity, the recognition of native titles and proprietary rights in and to native lands within the Malaysian law offers a channel for Indigenous people to redress their historical marginalisation and dispossession by instrumentalising an essentialised notion of their Indigenous culture to assert their native claims to ancestral lands and territories. Nevertheless, this still places the Indigenous people in a subaltern position, due to what Povinelli (2011) considers as 'governance of the prior', as Indigenous people will be subjected to the contrasting governing logic of the prevailing Malaysian judiciary system that is premised on non-Indigenous ontologies.

The hearings at the Johor Bahru High Court were always attended by a large contingent of Orang Seletar villagers, who showed up at the court wearing their 'native' headdresses woven from *nipah* leaves, representing their collective cultural identity and their assertion of native customary rights (Figure 4.6). Echoing the antiquated anthropological notion of Indigeneity as expressed in the law, Orang Seletar villagers displayed these headdresses as part of a staged performance of their cultural identities, instrumentalising and mobilising a notion of Indigeneity as a fixed anthropological notion to lend weight to their advocacy (Conklin 1997).

In connecting Indigenous activism with environmental advocacy, Indigenous people draw heavily upon their bodily politics through theatre, spectacle, and ceremonial acts that idealise their Indigenous ontologies of land as spiritual and embodying webs of interdependent relationships, as well as emphasising their Indigenous identities and sovereignty (Conklin 1997; Graham and Penny 2014; Diagle 2016). They put on elaborate costumes and ritual performances at protests and other sites of resistance to evoke and mobilise the Western ideological imagination that casts them as 'ecologically noble savages' (Redford 1990), who use environmental resources in a respectful and sustainable manner in contrast with the wanton exploitation of natural resources by capitalist interests.

As a form of spectacle, the headdresses not only function as an expression of Indigenous pride and political assertiveness but also serve as a visual

Figure 4.6 The Orang Seletar plaintiffs at the Johor Bahru High Court speaking with their lawyer, Yogeswaran Subramaniam. They were wearing leaf-woven headdresses, representing their collective cultural identity in their assertion of native customary rights. Photograph: Colin Nicholas from COAC.

symbol evoking the Western ideological imagination of exoticism and primitivism. They celebrate Orang Seletar culture and society as antithetical to the 'Western', bureaucratic, capitalist model of civilisation and modernity represented by the entourage of defendants (Conklin and Graham 1995; Conklin 1997). However, such essentialisation and self-essentialisation of the Orang Seletar people as 'ecologically noble savages' (Redford 1990), although involving an inversion of the historically pervasive idea of native populations as 'primitive', nevertheless reproduce and reinforce the colonial construction of Indigenous people as an inferior race relative to white Europeans.

While such performances of Indigeneity speak to the notion of 'survivance' (Vizenor 1999), Indigenous people often need to be exoticised as primitive and underdeveloped to advance their advocacy, a concept that Bateson (1956, quoted in Kallen 2015) considers as a 'double-bind', which can misrepresent their priorities and compromise Indigenous self-determination and agency (Conklin and Graham 1995; Kirsch 2007; Stoler 2016). This conundrum faced by Indigenous people is aptly conveyed by Conklin (1997: 713) in her discussion of the challenges faced by the Amazonian Indians in mobilising their Indigenous personas for activism:

> Amazonian Indians are represented as guardians of the forest, natural conservationists whose cultural traditions and spiritual values predispose them to live in harmony with the earth. A kind of essentialised image is created suggesting that primitive people are homogenous entities fixed in time. To be sure some native leaders welcomed this image and helped promote it both because of the struggles they are facing dealing with appropriation of their lands and from an appreciation that conservationists could aid them in their struggles. However, this image is false, maintained through symbolic activities of a few native representatives, and puts the interests of native peoples at odds with their national governments especially as it relates to their sensitivities of outside intervention.

Such performances of Indigeneity may also foreclose opportunities for intercultural interaction and creative innovation and leave little room for connecting their pasts with their presents, thus placing the 'authentic' Orang Seletar people outside of global trends of contemporary cultural changes and technological innovations (Conklin 1997; Mandelman 2014).

Like Indigenous movements in other parts of the world, the Orang Seletar villagers have instrumentalised an ambiguous conception of Indigeneity to assert their claims for native customary rights that are grounded in the historical marginalisation and dispossession they have been facing in modernising Malaysia. As explained by Yogeswaran Subramaniam:

> There is their dignity, which has been taken away through historical injustices and dispossession. I feel that this is the main driving force in

this case. The Orang Seletar feel that they have been treated in a most undignified way; they feel that they've been dispossessed from their lands, they feel that their culture has been trampled upon by other people. But if you look at their perspectives in terms of pragmatism and moving forward, they are pragmatic too.

Although drawing on an essentialised notion of Indigeneity to advance native customary rights through the legal process can offer Indigenous people opportunities to redress their historical marginalisation, this can carry some risks. Not only will this consume an immense amount of time and resources, a lost case may set a precedent that could jeopardise future class actions, both in Malaysia and elsewhere. As Yogeswaran Subramaniam highlighted:

> Losing the Orang Seletar case will have implications for the broader Indigenous rights movement in Malaysia, but it depends upon the way in which the case is lost, if it is lost. For example, if we lose due to the fact of lack of evidence, it is not so bad. But if the court goes on to rule that there is no such thing as 'customary land rights' for the Orang Asli and unravels Sagong Tasi and other similar precedents we are drawing on, that will be a blow to the Indigenous movement, not only here but potentially in other places. This precedent may be used in other jurisdictions to knock out Indigenous claims.

While the Orang Seletar villagers have drawn upon their local place histories for the assertion of native customary rights, they also simultaneously draw directly and indirectly upon international legal standards and landmark domestic and international cases on native customary rights. In turn, the outcome of their own case will itself have both local and international ramifications. For example, while the Sagong Tasi case cited successful precedents of Indigenous rights claims from Canada, Australia, and Nigeria to advance its argument, the case was, in turn, cited by the Supreme Court of Belize for the Indigenous rights claims made by the Maya villagers of Conejo and Santa Cruz, as a precedent to reaffirm the state's role in exercising fiduciary duties towards the Indigenous people under their charge (Anaya 2008). Through these translations of local histories into complex legal terminologies used in the court proceedings and the transfer of policy guidance and legal judgements across international boundaries by lawyers, activists, and other brokers, Indigenous cultural heritage, grounded in local place histories – in this case, those from the Danga Bay area – come to be mobilised as a form of 'counter-globalisation' against the hegemonic forces of economic neo-liberalisation. At the same time, Indigenous activism in Malaysia strengthens and is being strengthened by globalising transnational, Indigenous movements, through the transferability of policy documents and legal judgements across national boundaries and through the work of activists and other brokers as part of these transnational Indigenous networks.

In contrast to the broker at the Mah Meri Cultural Village discussed in the previous chapter, it may be argued that the pro-bono lawyers from the Malaysian Bar Council and the Orang Asli activist Colin Nicholas played positive brokerage roles. They mediated and translated between the Orang Seletar vernacular world and the transnational legal and Indigenous activism circles, to help the Orang Seletar villagers at Kampung Sungai Temon and Kampung Bakar Batu assert their native rights to their ancestral lands and territories. Through the many brokerage roles Colin Nicholas has taken on for the Orang Asli in Malaysia over the last two decades, he has also become a symbol of Orang Asli activism in his own right (Hinderaker 2002), for which he attracted fierce criticism from his opponents in this court case. Brokers are often caught in an uncomfortable position (Szasz 1994). Indeed, for Colin Nicholas, while he was successful in establishing the trust of the Orang Seletar villagers through his Indigenous advocacy work, his credibility as an expert witness on Orang Seletar matters came under attack from the defendants' lawyers precisely because of his advocacy and lobbyist stance.

Colin Nicholas has played a crucial brokerage role for the Orang Asli since the 1980s, first through the Peninsular Malaysia Orang Asli Association (POASM), during which time he lobbied alongside Anthony William-Hunt for the Orang Asli to champion for their Indigenous rights (1987), and later through the establishment in 1989 of the Center for Orang Asli Concerns (COAC) to organise the Orang Asli in bringing forth their concerns and campaign for their Indigenous rights. Since then, COAC through Colin Nicholas has taken on a research and advocacy role, serving as a support group for the Orang Asli, providing research and documentation on Orang Asli issues and heritage, as well as capacity-building and training for the Orang Asli to empower them to advocate for their own rights. As an anthropologist by training, Colin Nicholas has also served as an expert witness on Orang Asli history and heritage in court cases concerning Indigenous rights, as well as a mediator and translator between the Orang Asli in Malaysia and the transnational legal and Indigenous activism circles.

While Indigenous activists such as Colin Nicholas and Yogeswaran Subramaniam are playing a brokerage role, their role operates at a different scale and in a different form from those brokers at the cultural villages in a number of ways. First, their brokerage spans across networks of different scales, as they mediate between global Indigenous activism circles and the local vernacular worlds of Indigenous people in Malaysia. They embrace an international outlook that is evidently absent from the brokerage observed at the Indigenous cultural villages. The friendships between Colin Nicholas and other Indigenous activists such as Anne Lasimbang of PACOS Trust (see Chapter 5) seem to function as conduits for the transfer and exchange of ideas and know-how on brokering Indigenous advocacy, as well as providing a platform for collaboration on Indigenous activism in

Malaysia. Second, unlike the broker at the Mah Meri Cultural Village who manipulates and controls the workings of the cultural village, and subordinate the interests of Indigenous people, brokers such as Colin Nicholas and Yogeswaran Subramaniam give the power back to Indigenous people to determine their own agendas and interests. Rather than playing politics to achieve their own goals, which marginalise the needs of Indigenous people, brokers like Colin Nicholas exert their influence by shaping the agendas of Indigenous people through persuasion and forging collaborations that empower them. Third, their brokerage seems to rest on maintaining cordial and supportive relationships with Indigenous people. There is a sense of trust that these brokers will stand alongside Indigenous people in their resistance against the establishment.

Nonetheless, similar to the brokers at the Indigenous cultural villages, the brokers from these Indigenous NGOs also draw benefits from their brokerage. They derive a sense of personal satisfaction and affirmation from their brokerage, as well as earn the trust and respect of the Indigenous people. This translates into a positive professional reputation, what Steinmetz (2008) considers a form of 'ethnographic capital' that can enhance the power and influence of their brokerage. Indigenous cultural heritage, in this sense, has been instrumentalised to serve the economic, political, and social agendas of these activists in ways that empower Indigenous people to pursue the objectives they determine for themselves, in line with the positive and transformative role of culture promoted in the 'culture for development' discourse.

After almost two years of deliberation, the judgement was eventually issued on 28 February 2017. Applying the principles of the Commonwealth courts and two decades of domestic common law jurisprudence from the Malaysian courts, the judge for the case ruled that the Orang Seletar villagers of Kampung Sungai Temon and Kampung Bakar Batu have native rights not only to their ancestral lands but also to their customary waterways (IPHRD Network 2017). The judge also ruled that the Federal Government of Malaysia, Johor State Government, Land Office, and JAKOA have a fiduciary duty to protect the welfare and land rights of the Orang Seletar villagers, which they have failed to uphold (IPHRD Network 2017). These state agencies were ordered to pay compensation to the Orang Seletar villagers for the loss of their ancestral lands based on market values (Tan 2017). The Orang Seletar villagers have since appealed against the ruling and are still awaiting for the outcome, as they would prefer to have their ancestral lands returned to them rather than be compensated for their loss. This demonstrates how the Malaysian state has drawn upon legal jurisprudence to alienate the Orang Seletar people from their native customary lands and territories, albeit with monetary compensation, and attests to how such legal jurisprudence in the neoliberal realm can serve to expand the bureaucratic powers of the Malaysian state and sidestep Indigenous resistance.

Conclusion

Established with the objective to offer an alternative means of livelihood for the Orang Seletar villagers of Kampung Sungai Temon to reduce their dependency on the sea in the face of urbanisation and pollution, the Orang Seletar Cultural Centre is an exemplar of a community-based cultural project that endorses the 'culture for development' discourse widely promoted by UNESCO. Although the Orang Seletar villagers own and manage the cultural centre, it is a project set up by an external broker, Choo, rather than one that emerges organically from within the local community. The cultural centre also relies on the brokerage of another external broker, Wong, to bring visitors on organised visits to the cultural centre as part of the eco-tourism tours of Kampung Sungai Temon. In this case study, I would like to draw attention to the culture of dependency between the Orang Seletar villagers and the external brokers, as the villagers largely rely on these external brokers to realise the physical development of the cultural centre and the benefits the centre is purported to bring.

There is a paternalism in evidence at such Indigenous cultural villages like the Orang Seletar Cultural Centre that capitalises on the historical imagination of the Indigenous people as exotic noble savages to attract tourists in order to realise its benefits to the local communities. However, this exoticisation of the Indigenous Orang Seletar people is challenged through the tours, when Kampung Sungai Temon was transformed into a cultural village for tourist consumption, with the Orang Seletar Cultural Centre offering an essentialised representation of Orang Seletar cultural heritage, while the rest of the village represented the vernacular experiences of the Orang Seletar villagers in modern-day Malaysia. This mobilises, but also complicates, tourists' imaginaries of the Orang Seletar people. The Orang Seletar villagers capitalise on the strategic essentialisation of their Indigenous identity through the cultural centre, to assert their native rights to their ancestral lands and territories in the Danga Bay area. During the court proceedings launched to stop IDRA's development encroaching on their ancestral lands and waters, the judge was brought to the Centre to learn about Orang Seletar cultural heritage and understand the historical connections of Orang Seletar people with their ancestral lands and territories through 'place-based imaginaries' (Cooke 2013).

The essentialisation and self-essentialisation of the Indigenous people as 'ecologically noble savage', nevertheless, still construct and reinforce the historical imagination of the Indigenous people as the 'primitive Other'. By examining how Indigeneity and Indigenous cultural heritage are staged, mediated, and brokered at the Orang Seletar Cultural Centre to serve different agendas and objectives, this chapter makes an important contribution to Indigenous museology by critiquing the positive discourses on Indigenous museums and other community-based museum developments. Specifically, it demonstrates that Indigenous museums which are purported to promote the 'culture for development' discourse often lead to the marginalisation of the Indigenous communities due to the politics of brokerage and representation that cultivate and perpetuate a culture of dependency between the brokers and their intended beneficiaries.

Notes

1 Some materials used in this chapter have been published in Cai (2017).
2 The Orang Seletar people are also considered part of the Orang Laut, which literally means 'sea people' in Malay language. Orang Laut is a term used to denote the different groups of seafaring communities living around the waters of present-day Peninsular Malaysia, Singapore, and the Riau Islands.
3 The nine Orang Seletar villages are Kampung Simpang Arang, Kampung Sungai Temon, Kampung Bakar Batu, Kampung Teluk Jawa, Kampung Pasir Putih, Kampung Kuala Masai, Kampung Teluk Kabong, Kampung Sungai Tiram, and Kampung Sungai Papan.
4 *Kon* Seletar is an emic identification of the Orang Seletar people.
5 In most Malaysian states, foreigners are not allowed to own properties valued at less than RM 1 million (Bhatt 2018).
6 The Delgamuukw v British Columbia case of 1997 in Canada clarified how Aboriginal title could be claimed and how oral testimonies should be treated as evidence of historical occupation in such land claims.
7 The Wik Peoples v The State of Queensland case of 1996 in Australia clarified the co-existence of statutory pastoral leases and native title rights depending on the terms and conditions of the pastoral leases, but the rights of pastoral leases would prevail if there was a conflict with the native title rights.
8 The Western Australia v Ward (Miriuwung-Gajerrong) case of 2002 in Australia clarified on the nature and content of native titles, particularly what constituted or did not constitute native titles.
9 The Amodu Tijani v The Secretary, Southern Nigeria case of 1921 in Nigeria ruled that the cessation of its capital Lagos did not affect private claims to native land rights.
10 The number of defendants was reduced from 13 to 11 as the plaintiffs withdrew their claims from the local authority of Johor Bahru Tengah before the commencement of the trial, and from IDRA amid the trial after it was established that IDRA did not have any ownership or fiduciary duty over the management of the land (Johor Bahru High Court 2017).
11 Academic scholarship on Orang Laut, generally considers the Orang Seletar to be one of its subgroups.

5 Appropriation, reinvention, and contestation of Indigenous heritage

Introduction[1]

The Monsopiad Cultural Village (Figure 5.1) provides an example of a community-based cultural project that complicates the idealisation of Indigenous communities as unified and homogeneous wholes who have a clear direction on the management of their cultural heritage, and that Indigenous insiders will naturally act in the interests of one another against non-Indigenous outsiders. Here, the Indigenous elites who own the land and the collections on which the Monsopiad Cultural Village is based choose to rely on brokers for its management, and in so doing endorse a management structure that marginalises the Indigenous workers. By demonstrating how the categories of 'insiders' and 'outsiders' within these community-based cultural projects are fluid and open to negotiation, I argue that such projects entrench a culture of dependency that leads to the marginalisation of some members of the Indigenous community in the hands of others. As in the case of the Monsopiad Cultural Village, these community-based cultural projects become arenas where different agendas and contesting claims to heritage are played out, which may fulfil or compromise the position of the local communities whose cultural heritage is represented, complicating the 'culture for development' discourse widely promoted in the field of international development.

Indigenous cultural heritage come to be appropriated, reinvented, and mobilised by different stakeholders to fulfil different political, economic, social, and cultural agendas, such as capitalising on cultural tourism, asserting Indigenous identity, and staking claims to native customary lands, territories, and resources, as well as resisting their marginalisation in the dominant Malay-Muslim society of Malaysia. This mobilisation of Indigenous cultural heritage can lead to cultural renaissance and the strengthening of Indigenous self-worth, on the one hand, or a loss of cultural belief and ritual efficiency, on the other hand, as cultural practices become decontextualised and alienated from their original settings. By examining the complex politics and power plays in the negotiation and contestation of Indigenous cultural heritage, I seek to situate critical museology and heritage studies within the Indigenous discourse.

Figure 5.1 Entrance to the Monsopiad Cultural Village. The Monsopiad Cultural
Village is sited in Kampung Kuai-Kadazon in the District of Penampang
in the eastern Malaysian state of Sabah. Photograph: Author.

In Sabah, there are about 1.96 million people who identify as Indigenous
based on the 2010 census. They make up 61.2 per cent of the local population (Leonie et al. 2015) and can be broken down into 39 ethnic groups,
speaking over 50 languages and 80 dialects. The Dusunic, Murutic, and
Patanic groups form the majority (Leonie et al. 2015). The Kadazan are a
subgroup of the Dusunic people and are the largest Indigenous subgroup in
Sabah. Most of them reside in the District of Penampang on the west coast
of Sabah. Under the influence of foreign missionaries who came to Sabah
from the 1880s onwards, and the adoption of Islam as Malaysia's state religion since Independence, the majority of Kadazan people have converted
from animistic religions to Christianity or Islam.

The Monsopiad Cultural Village was established on 1 May 1996 in
Kampung Kuai-Kadazon in the District of Penampang in the eastern
Malaysian state of Sabah. The oldest cultural village in Sabah, it presents
the cultural heritage of the Kadazan people, focusing on the history of
Monsopiad, a Kadazan warrior who lived in the area some 300 years ago.
At the Monsopiad Cultural Village, a collection of 42 human skulls believed to have been captured by Monsopiad is actively marketed to tourists
as a major highlight, capitalising on the exoticisation of the Indigenous
Kadazan people for cultural tourists. The skull collection is now in the
custodianship of Gundohing Wildy Dousia Moujing, the seventh direct
descendent of Monsopiad, who is also the current Village Headman of
Kampung Kuai-Kadazon. He inherited the skulls in April 2016 after the
death of his father, the late Gundohing Augustine Dousia Moujing, the
sixth direct descendent of Monsopiad.

The Monsopiad Cultural Village also has life-size reconstructions of a granary, known as the *Tangkob*, and a Kadazan longhouse, a community hall for cultural performances, as well as an in-house café and a small souvenir shop. It displays the material culture of the Kadazan people, including equipment for the making of their 'traditional' alcoholic beverages, hunting equipment such as blowpipes and traps, as well as musical instruments such as gong ensembles. The Monsopiad Cultural Village offers a cultural package at a charge of RM 55 (£10) per person, and includes a tour of the cultural village, explanations of the cultural heritage, including the history of the *Gintutun Do Mohoing* menhir and the Kadazan headhunting practice and demonstrations of crafts, as well as cultural performances staged by a group of Indigenous young adults employed to work at the cultural village, some of whom come from the nearby Kadazan villages.

The Monsopiad Cultural Village was founded by a British entrepreneur who ran a diving resort in Sabah and his Kadazan wife, who is the cousin of Wildy Moujing, the custodian of the skulls. In the 1990s, inspired by the frequent visits made by tourists to see the ritual house and its collection of human skulls, the British man lobbied his wife's uncle, Dousia Moujing, to place the surrounding lands, the ritual house, and its collection of human skulls on lease to him for the establishment of the Monsopiad Cultural Village as a tourism attraction. As Wildy Moujing recalled:

Before Monsopiad Cultural Village existed, a representative from one tourist agency came and saw me, they wanted to bring the tourists to this house, so they asked me: 'How much are you going to charge?' I didn't know what to say, because this was my first experience. Then they brought the tourists here in a bus, and there were 42 tourists on the bus. They paid RM1 (19p) per person. That was in the 1990s, in the beginning. That's why they got the idea to set up the cultural village.

The direct descendants of Monsopiad, including Dousia Moujing, agreed to the proposal, as they perceived the partnership as a mutually beneficial collaboration that would capitalise on the British entrepreneur's experience and expertise of establishing and running a dive resort in Sabah. They envisaged that the establishment of the Monsopiad Cultural Village would bring development to Kampung Kuai-Kadazon in line with UNESCO's 'culture for development' discourse, create interest and awareness for the village's cultural heritage relating to Monsopiad, as well as provide them with a steady source of rental incomes through the lease of the lands and artefacts for the cultural village. Although established with an underlying profit-making mission, the Monsopiad Cultural Village lists as its aims to study, document, revive, and keep alive the culture and traditions of the Kadazan people.

Contexts, personalities, and interests

In the early years of its establishment, the Monsopiad Cultural Village facilitated the development of Kampung Kuai-Kadazon, as the Sabah State Government invested resources to build a link road from the village to the main town and provide other amenities such as telephone, water, and electricity lines to the villagers to support the new tourist attraction. As Wildy Moujing said:

> I know that once the Monsopiad Cultural Village is set up, the village will become very valuable. If you say your land is over here, it is very expensive. Because of Monsopiad Cultural Village, the lands here become prime land. We have telephone lines, electricity lines, streetlights, because of Monsopiad Cultural Village. You know why we have these? When the Minister of Tourism came to visit us here, we asked him to provide these amenities.

The British founder and his Kadazan wife can be conceptualised as brokers for the Monsopiad Cultural Village, mediating and translating between the tourism industry and the Kadazan village economy to set up the cultural village as a tourist attraction. Both have complex allegiances with the Indigenous communities of the Monsopiad Cultural Village. They are simultaneously perceived as 'insiders' on the account of the wife's familial relations with the direct descendants of Monsopiad, and as 'outsiders' due to the British founder's foreign nationality and ethnicity. Their daughter is also conceptualised as a broker with mixed 'insider' and 'outsider' allegiance on account of her mixed British-Kadazan ancestry and her marriage to a local Kadazan man.

After its establishment in 1996, the Monsopiad Cultural Village was mainly managed by the Kadazan wife, whom I understand to have led an extravagant lifestyle from the earnings of the cultural village when it was doing well through the 1990s and early 2000s. However, since the failure of the British founder's diving resort business and the onset of a chronic illness about a decade ago, business at the Monsopiad Cultural Village seems to have deteriorated, both due to its poor financial management and increased competition from new Indigenous cultural villages in Sabah. In the last three years, the cultural village has come to be managed by the couple's only daughter, who holds management rights. The Monsopiad Cultural Village continues to lease the lands and collections from the direct descendants of Monsopiad (Wildy Moujing), paying a monthly rent of RM 1,000 (£190) for two adjoining plots of land and a further RM 500 (£95) for use of the ritual house and its collection of human skulls. Leases for the land, ritual house, and its artefacts are due to expire in 2021, after which a new contract will have to be negotiated in order for business to continue.

At the time of my fieldwork in 2015, the Monsopiad Cultural Village was mired in a complex web of tensions and local politics, and was operating at a loss with significant outstanding debts. The operational model of the cultural village appeared to be unsustainable. It had relatively high overhead costs in terms of the rental arrears for the lands and artefacts, and a staff of around 14 people, mainly low-skilled Indigenous young adults from the nearby Kadazan villages, who were each paid between RM 600 (£113) and RM 800 (£150) per month and lived on-site in staff dormitories. As the cultural village only had in the region of 10–20 visitors per day, admission revenue was incommensurate with the high overheads. As a result, the Monsopiad Cultural Village had accrued rental and staff salary arrears, the latter resulting in high staff turnover and low morale. The employees were consequently not fully committed to their work at the Monsopiad Cultural Village and had to take on other jobs to supplement their meagre incomes. As the employees were frequently absent, the level of service as well as the quality of cultural performances and guided tours at the Monsopiad Cultural Village were severely affected, and travel agents would not recommend that visitors include the site in their itineraries. This only exacerbated the already poor attendance and low admission revenue. Infrastructure within the cultural village was also in a dilapidated condition and had not been maintained for some time. While the staff employed at the Monsopiad Cultural Village had not been paid, the founders appeared to lead comfortable lives.

The start of my fieldwork in April 2015 coincided with the appointment of a new General Manager to oversee the long-term strategic management and day-to-day operation of the cultural village. The British founder, who had been ill, asked the new General Manager, a long-time family friend, to help with the ailing business before his return to England for medical care. The General Manager, a French woman married to a local Kadazan man, had over 20 years of experience managing hotels and tourist attractions in the hospitality industry in Sabah and elsewhere. It was intended that the General Manager would activate her extensive network of contacts to bring more visitors to the Monsopiad Cultural Village and would draw upon her extensive experience and management skills to improve the administration of the site and enhance its offering to visitors.

Although the General Manager was employed to rectify the situation, she was not given the full authority to manage the Monsopiad Cultural Village's finances. While she had successfully secured several rather lucrative contracts for the staff to perform their cultural dances at external venues, she could not pay off the outstanding debts with the revenue earned. Her appointment was met with significant resistance from local Kadazan workers, who perceived her as an 'outsider' and frequently undermined her authority by not obeying her directives to carry out maintenance work. They were, however, more amenable to the founders' daughter, despite not receiving their monthly salaries, as they recognised that she held the overall decision-making power. The founders' daughter, as an 'insider', seemed to wield significant power and control the Monsopiad Cultural Village, which entrenched a structural relationship that marginalised the Indigenous staff working under the French General Manager, who had 'outsider' status as a non-Indigenous foreigner. Facing immense difficulty in her brokerage role between the founders' daughter and the staff of the cultural village, the French General Manager eventually left the cultural village at the end of my fieldwork period in June 2015, without receiving payment for her services.

While the owners of the lands and artefacts were owed rent, they chose not to exercise the right to repossess the Monsopiad Cultural Village after three months of non-payment but continued to pressurise the management of the Monsopiad Cultural Village. As Wildy Moujing put it:

> I'm not happy with the situation. I think the money spent is very poor. Then they're not going to make Monsopiad Cultural Village lucrative, like what other cultural villages do. If they do that, I will be very happy. Once their lease lapses, I think we're going to take back [the lands and artefacts]. The lease arrangement is something like, if they're not going to pay rental for three months, then we can enter the premises, and take over. This is inside the agreement. But we're relatives, we're cousins. So, if they don't pay us for three months, we will just keep quiet. For relatives, money don't count (laughs).

The Monsopiad Cultural Village was not always in such a dire situation. It had previously demonstrated immense potential as a lucrative business. As Wildy Moujing recalled:

> Last time, before the Monsopiad Cultural Village was set up, tourists used to come here to see the skulls. At that time, they pay only RM 1 (19p) per person, and we can even collect up to RM 5,000 (£943) per month. Then we wonder, if they charge RM 5 (94p) per person, how much more will that be?

As recently as late 2014, the founders of the Monsopiad Cultural Village managed to interest a local, non-Indigenous investor to take over and re-furbish the site as a means of managing its outstanding debts. However, the endeavour was sabotaged by the owners of the lands and artefacts, who requested a significant increase in their rental incomes, making the invest-ment unprofitable to the investor who eventually pulled out. The owners of the lands and artefacts wanted a greater share of the income that was projected to grow after the redevelopment of the Monsopiad Cultural Vil-lage. A staff member who was working at the site when the discussions with the potential investor were underway dismissed the viewpoint of the owners, citing the cultural values Kadazan people attach to lands used for cemeteries:

You know what? Monsopiad Cultural Village is built on an ancient graveyard. This is an inauspicious site, and they would need to conduct many rituals to cleanse the lands, which will be very expensive. Nobody, except foreigners, will pay a high rent for this kind of land. This is a worthless piece of land.

While the owners of the lands and artefacts see the founders of the Monsopiad Cultural Village as 'insiders' due to their familial relations, the local Indigenous people working for the Monsopiad Cultural Village tend to see the founders and investors of the cultural village as 'outsiders', who are not familiar with the cultural beliefs of the Indigenous people in Sabah. This alludes to the multiple allegiances, agendas, and beliefs among the different stakeholders of the Monsopiad Cultural Village, which complicate the working dynamics of the cultural village. This also shows that the categories of 'insiders' and 'outsiders' are fluid and open to negotiation, challenging the assumption that people with Indigenous ancestry are naturally insiders, who will act in the interests of their fellow Indigenous people.

In late 2015, the management rights of the Monsopiad Cultural Village were sold to two young, entrepreneurial local women of Kadazan heritage, who took over the management and operations of the site, and who continue to lease the lands, the ritual house, and its artefacts from the direct descendants of Monsopiad. At my last visit to the Monsopiad Cultural Village in August 2016, it seemed to have undergone a minor revamp, as several of the structures in the Monsopiad Cultural Village had been repaired and repainted. The site also appeared to be quite vibrant with a full strength of staff in attendance, attending to a constant stream of visitors.

The existing structure of the Monsopiad Cultural Village, which extends significant authority to the founders and their daughter, who hold management rights, serves to entrench a structural relationship that marginalises the Indigenous workers at the Monsopiad Cultural Village, rather than being an instrument for their Indigenous self-determination and empowerment. This structural relationship appears to be endorsed by the direct descendants of Monsopiad who own the lands and artefacts on which the cultural village is built and based around, as they choose not to interfere with the management and operation of the site, even though they have the power to repossess the lands and artefacts if they so wish (and thus changing the structural relationship). Rather, these Indigenous elites choose to rely on the founders to manage and operate the Monsopiad Cultural Village, cultivating a culture of dependency on the brokers, as they seek to capitalise on the site for their personal gain. This is evident from how they have sought to renegotiate the terms of the lease to derive more rental income from the proposed redevelopment. That some Indigenous people, particularly the founders of the Monsopiad Cultural Village and the direct descendants of Monsopiad, may not always act in the interest of other Indigenous people, especially those working at the Monsopiad Cultural

Village, complicates the typical representation of Indigenous communities in museological literature, which tends to idealise these communities and regard them as homogeneous and unified wholes.

Transformation, representation, and interpretation of culture

The 42 human skulls on display at the Monsopiad Cultural Village (Figure 5.2) are said to have been captured by Monsopiad in his headhunting raids and handed down to his descendants for generations. According to various oral and written sources, Monsopiad was a courageous Kadazan warrior who defended his village against roaming bandits who frequently robbed the villagers of their rice and farm animals (Phelan 1997; Majikol and Majikol 2000; Phelan 2001). His bravery attracted the jealousy of other warriors, such as Gantang from Kampung Minintod and Manggung of Kampung Nosoob, who tried to kill him. Monsopiad eventually died as a result of an injury to his right hand sustained during a fight and was buried on a small hill overlooking Kampung Kurai and Kampung Kuai-Kadazon, commemorated with a menhir[2] that still exists today.

For decades, the subject of headhunting in Borneo has intrigued many Western travellers and ethnographers, who have sought to explain the cultural practice and its associated cultural taboos (Furness 1902; Evans 1922; Krohn 1927; Rutter 1929; Wyn 1974; Hoskins 1996; Phelan 2001; Gingging 2007; Metcalf 2010). The cultural practice of headhunting was largely discontinued in the nineteenth century, as it was discouraged by the British

Figure 5.2 Forty-two human skulls at the Monsopiad Cultural Village. They are installed at the ceiling of the ritual house and are the main attraction of the Monsopiad Cultural Village. Photograph: Author.

North Borneo Company, which conceived of the practice as backward, barbaric, and uncivilised when it took over the administration of Sabah in 1881. However, the human skulls have emerged as an important marker of cultural difference in the last three decades, and they are increasingly mobilised by Indigenous people in Sabah, both to assert their marginalised identity and to reap the benefits of 'primitivist tourism' (Stasch 2015).

Rutter (1929: 182) has attempted to provide a context for this cultural practice in North Borneo by describing its emic motivations:

> Headhunting was never practised on so large a scale in North Borneo as it was among the Sarawak tribes, simply because the pagan communities were smaller; but its objects were similar, and it was held to confer benefits both on the individual taker of the head and on the community to which the taker belonged.
>
> The taking of his first head denoted a youth's entry into manhood. It proved him to be a tried warrior and he was then entitled to receive his first tattoo marks. The possession of a head also entitled him to win the favour of the young woman of his fancy and to press a suit which would have been less successful had he been unable to show any such material proof of his prowess. But this was not all. The souls of those whose heads have been taken were believed to follow their victors to the spirit world; and naturally the greater number of heads a man obtained the greater respect was he likely to win from his fellows both in this life and the next. That was undoubtedly the idea which underlay the custom of obtaining the head of an enemy, or of sacrificing a slave, on the death of a chief.
>
> In addition to the advantage accruing to the individual from the possession of a head, there were also definite advantages accruing to the community. In times of sickness or famine, a head feast[3] was considered necessary to avert the threatening disaster, and the association between headhunting and a fruitful harvest was close, and probably intimately connected with the primordial ideal of human sacrifice being necessary to placate the spirits of the crops.

Historically, the Kadazan people believed that the human skulls were their spiritual guardians, who would protect their families and properties from harm, ward off sickness, and ensure success in their various pursuits. They believed that the capture of a human skull signified the transfer of spiritual power from the victim's village to that of the new owner. The spirits of the skulls not only comprised the spirit of the deceased but also part of the spirits from the village from where the victim had come, with the strength of the spirits increasing proportionately with the social status of the victim (Phelan 2001). The ownership of more human skulls thus not only signified greater spiritual strength, and hence more protection for the owners, but also indicated the higher social status of their owners. To maintain their spiritual powers, the human skulls needed to be appeased every 40 years with a *Magang* ceremony: an elaborate ceremony comprising several days and nights of chanting, feasting, dancing, and sacrifices of different animals, conducted by a group of Kadazan ritual specialists known as *bobohizans*.

The human skulls captured by Monsopiad were moved from their temporary location in the family's granary and installed in the current building during a seven-day *Magang* ceremony conducted between 4 and 10 May 1974. The building was erected to replace an old family house on the same site (Phelan 2001). Brother Peter Phelan, an Irish Catholic pastor who migrated to Sabah in 1963 to teach at the La Salle schools in Kota Kinabalu, and later wrote several books on the Indigenous cultures of Sabah, documented the *Magang* ceremony held in 1974. When an earlier house was demolished in the 1960s, the skulls were temporarily moved to the family's granary in a ceremony that lasted for a night (Phelan 2001). Although the new family house was completed in 1969, the skulls were only moved into the house in 1974, as time and resources were needed to prepare and raise funds for the *Magang* ceremony, which was attended by around 500 relatives and friends. The ceremony was conducted by a group of nine *bobohizans*, led by a chief *bobohizan* – Bianti Gindal – known as the *bohungkitas*. Biandi Gindal was also the mother of the then caretaker of the human skulls, Dousia Moujing, and the grandmother of the current caretaker, Wildy Moujing. Dressed in their ritual regalia of long black dresses with brass and silver ornaments, over the seven days of the ceremony the *bobohizans* chanted long *rinait* chants, rang *sindavang* cymbals, performed the customary *sumazau* dance, made animal sacrifices, and went into trances when the spirits of the skulls took possession of their bodies (Phelan 2001). The highlight of the ceremony was on the second day, when the human skulls were physically transferred from the granary to the family house in an elaborate ritual supported by gong music, chanting, and dancing (Phelan 2001). Two cannons were fired near the house towards the end of the ceremony, marking the significance of the occasion (Phelan 2001). The ceremony was also supported by families and friends, who prepared the ritual paraphernalia and cooked the food, including the animals sacrificed for the ritual, for the ceremony participants.

Wildy Moujing spoke fondly of the 1974 *Magang* ceremony:

> In 1974, that is the *Magang*. Do you know why I remembered that one? Because I got engaged in May 1974. I still remember, my grandmother was the *bohungkitas*, and they slaughtered one buffalo and seven pigs for the feast. And this is held once every 40 years. You know why? Because this is a very big ceremony.

Wildy Moujing also explained that when the Monsopiad Cultural Village was established in 1996, the founders of the cultural village built another house on an adjoining plot of land for his father and mother, Mr and Mrs Dousia Moujing. They then converted the family house to a ritual house, which was branded as the 'House of Skulls' and presented as a major attraction of the Monsopiad Cultural Village. After the Monsopiad Cultural Village was set up, the family conducted a *Momohizan* ceremony lasting three days and two nights in January 1997. Taking place at the ritual house, the ceremony appeased the human skulls and strengthened the working relationship between the spirits and the people. During the *Momohizan* ceremony, a team of four *bobohizans* paid homage to the spirits of the ritual house, the human skulls, and the *nibong* plant, a sacred plant in the ritual house, with feasting, dancing, and sacrifices of animals. The spirits also participated in the proceedings by possessing the *bobohizans* who entered trances. Due to the expensive and laborious process of organising rituals and the challenges of finding ritual specialists to perform them, the family intended that this would be the last ritual ceremony for the spirits. Hence, during the ceremony, the *bobohizans* informed the spirits that there would be no further appeasement ritual and they were to look after themselves in the future. The spirits were also told that they would be free to attend weddings and other celebrations to amuse themselves but that they should not disturb people.

These ritual ceremonies for appeasing the human skulls are spiritually significant to the direct descendants of Monsopiad, who believe that the skulls may seek revenge if they are not properly managed. Indigenous people in Sabah still believe in the cultural taboos associated with these skulls, even though they may have converted to other world religions. Since the 1970s, due to the conversion of many Indigenous people from their animist religions to Islam or Christianity, neither of which condone the ownership and valorisation of human skulls, families with inheritances of human skulls have sought to dispose of them either by burying them or donating them to museums. In such cases, a ritual ceremony is performed by the *bobohizans*, so as not to offend the spirits of the human skulls. They believe that human skulls that are disposed of unceremoniously will seek revenge by bringing bad luck to the descendants of their owners, contributing to the downfall of their families. One account I collected tells of how the descendants of a Kadazan warrior, who dumped the family's inherited human skulls into a river, without conducting any ritual ceremony, had all either killed themselves or died suddenly in accidents, or had experienced mental health crises.

As Kreps (2014) has shown in the case of Thai monastery museums, where ritual prohibitions against the removal of an object or image serve as a form of safeguarding, certain cultural taboos can sometimes help to safeguard Indigenous cultural heritage in Malaysia. The belief in the efficacy of these cultural taboos and ritual prohibitions, especially the consequences for breaking them, establishes limits on and serves as a self-imposed deterrence against the instrumentalisation of certain forms of Indigenous cultural heritage. The cultural taboos surrounding the treatment of human skulls in Sabah ensure that they are disposed of in a manner that is culturally acceptable to the Indigenous people who own them.

Wildy Moujing continues to believe in their spiritual powers, although he has converted to Christianity. He spoke of a personal encounter with the skulls when he was young:

> During my school days, I liked to play football. I asked my grandmother Bianti jokingly, saying: 'Grandma, ask our ancestors or the skulls to follow me'. We won the game in Penampang. You know, the football game, all our opponents dropped down and collapsed when the game started. We didn't know why, but we won the game. The opponents said something was following us, and they thought we were very good players. I went home and my grandmother asked me: 'You're not rejoicing?' And I told her: 'Because we didn't play, as they fell down before the game.' My grandmother said: 'You didn't know, before the game, you asked me to ask the skulls to follow you, so I had been chanting for one night.' After the incident, I stopped asking the skulls to help me. I'm quite afraid, as I'm a religious man, and this is a conflict of faith.

Although he no longer seeks the intercession of the spirits of the human skulls, he believes that they still occasionally communicate with him through dreams:

> I occasionally have dreams. Something like a group of people come to the village to find us. They're going to kill us. We're scared. We're sleeping, then I suddenly wake up. The last time, because I put some holy water around the house, our neighbour next door dreamt of a big fire around this house. According to his dream, there were a lot of people in this house. Maybe our skulls are still here, the unseen spirits.

The incorporation of the human skulls as an attraction at the Monsopiad Cultural Village, and the performance of the *Momohizan* ceremony to appease the skulls and inform them that there will no longer be any appeasement ritual for them, is conceived by the direct descendants of Monsopiad as a spiritual settlement. According to Dousia Moujing, who agreed to the establishment of the Monsopiad Cultural Village in the 1990s:

> I told them [my children] *jangan kacau* (don't disturb them). They cannot surrender them to the museum, church or even bury them when I am gone. What they can do if they are sick of seeing the skulls or feel it in conflict with their new beliefs is to build a separate house and hang them there. After all, the skulls have accepted getting used to the rituals not being held regularly. So the question of feeding them does not arise. It is important to keep passing them down to future generations.

The moment anyone in my family tree in future surrenders them, our honour and that of Monsopiad will be no more.

(Sarda 1994 quoted in Phelan 2001: 55)

To the late Dousia Moujing, the establishment of the Monsopiad Cultural Village serves as a means of preserving family pride and legacy. He considers the incorporation of the human skulls in the cultural village as a better spiritual settlement than other available options, such as donating them to museums or churches, or burying them, as they remain within the ownership of the family. To him, the commodification process serves as a means of safeguarding his family's legacy and cultural heritage for future generations. Tourism is perceived here as an avenue for sustaining Monsopiad's legacy and the Kadazan headhunting heritage, which may otherwise disappear with the onslaught of modernisation (Cohen 1988).

Gingging (2007) argues in her study of the Monsopiad Cultural Village that the Kadazan people are actively embracing this essentialised self-portrayal and are willing to be exoticised for the assertion of their Indigenous identity. Drawing from Fiskesjo's (2015) study of the Wa people in China, which demonstrates how they draw on their headhunting tradition to express their martial prowess and superiority over the ethnic Han Chinese, I suggest that these human skulls similarly symbolise the same qualities of the Kadazan people in comparison with the dominant Malay-Muslims, while serving as a source of family pride for the Moujing family. Rather than rejecting the headhunting heritage as a symbol of their backwardness and barbarism, the direct descendants of Monsopiad have appropriated and reconfigured their headhunting heritage to maintain their distinct cultural identity as a way of asserting their Indigenous identity and resistance against assimilation into the dominant Malay-Muslim society. This strategic essentialism nonetheless constitutes a form of 'double-bind' (Kallen 2015), in which the Kadazan people need to be exoticised as undeveloped, uncivilised, and barbaric in order to assert their cultural identity and Indigenous rights.

This exoticised image of Kadazan headhunting heritage at the Monsopiad Cultural Village is sought after by tourists in search of an 'authentic' experience. The Monsopiad Cultural Village thus functions as an institutionalised form of 'primitivist tourism' (Stasch 2015), which draws upon the ideological construct of Indigenous people as 'primitive people' for tourist consumption. It is a staged arena exhibiting a version of Indigenous cultural heritage, which not only conforms to tourists' imaginaries of the exotic, primitive Indigenous people of Borneo but also embodies the Indigenous people's self-essentialisation, which they seek to meld into the tourists' imaginaries (Salazar and Graburn 2015). This is evident from the promotional materials of a Malaysian tour operator that advertises the Monsopiad Cultural Village as a 'head-hunter's tour [in the] heartland of the Kadazan tribe set amidst serene hills, [offering an] up-close encounter with Monsopiad's 'trophies' [at] Monsopiad's house in … its well-preserved ancient dwelling' (Amazing Borneo Tours n.d.).

While, by virtue of their display at the Monsopiad Cultural Village, the human skulls are now open to the 'tourist gaze' (Urry 1990), the direct descendants of Monsopiad request that respect is shown to the skulls. On entry to the 'House of Skulls', tourists are required to take off their shoes and politely ask for permission to enter the ritual house as a mark of their humbleness and respect. As Wildy Moujing advised:

> Before entering the ritual house, just greet the skulls: 'How are you? Good morning, good afternoon, good evening, or something.' Don't say anything that is offensive. You must not be rude, and respect everything. Go with the respect intention, and you must not have any intention for disrespect.

The performance of such rites of respect not only conforms to cultural expectations but also increases the perceived authenticity of the encounter from the tourists' perspective. This can be construed as a form of 'customised authenticity', which is mutually constructed between the hosts and guests in a tourism setting (Wang 2007). It can also be conceived as an instance in which Indigenous people resist the commodification and exoticisation of their cultural heritage by stipulating the practice of certain ritual observances.

Although there was an agreement with the spirits that there would not be any appeasement ritual for them from 1997 onwards, the direct descendants of Monsopiad agreed to a suggestion from Rita Lasimbang, the founder of the Kadazandusun Language Foundation (KLF), to host a one-day *Magavau* ceremony that was conducted in the ritual house in 2000. The Magavau ceremony is a rice-honouring ritual conducted in the rice fields by *bobohizans* to welcome the rice spirit, *Bambaazon*, and bring the strayed spirits of the rice home during the harvest season. The *Magavau* ceremony is part of the more comprehensive *Monogit* ceremony for the appeasement of the rice spirits, to secure their protection over the rice-growing process to ensure a good harvest. The family agreed to host the *Magavau* ceremony at the ritual house under the persuasion of Rita Lasimbang, who received a grant from the Toyota Foundation of Japan to document the language of the *bobohizans* from the District of Penampang from 2000 to 2003 and was willing to fund the ceremony in full.

Rita Lasimbang is a firm advocate and lobbyist for the preservation of Indigenous cultural heritage and especially Indigenous languages in Sabah. Previously a curator at the Sabah Museum, she established KLF as a non-profit organisation in 1995 with the 'objectives of preserving, developing, and promoting the Kadazandusun language as well as other Indigenous languages of Sabah' (Lasimbang 2004b: 10). KLF collaborates with Indigenous people in Sabah to undertake cultural and language documentation and to conduct training for local people on preserving the practice of their cultural heritage and the use of their Indigenous languages. In particular, KLF has played an instrumental role in the reintroduction of the Kadazan language in the curriculum of selected schools, which had been removed from the school curriculum in the late 1960s.

In recent years, Rita Lasimbang has played an important brokerage role in mobilising resources for the documentation of Indigenous rituals in Sabah. In particular, she has been successful in mediating and translating between the global developmental aid sector and the Indigenous activist sector in Sabah to seek foreign sponsorship for the documentation of Indigenous cultural practices in Sabah. She has also been successful in mobilising ritual specialists, village elders, and other stakeholders to conduct these cultural practices so that she can document them. The *Magavau* ceremony, conducted at the ritual house of the Monsopiad Cultural Village in 2000, was largely the result of her brokerage. Rita Lasimbang also documented a *Monogit* ceremony that was conducted in 2007 at the house of *bobohizan* Ina Gusiti in Kampung Sugud, funded by a grant from the American Embassy in Malaysia.

According to Rita Lasimbang, the *bobohizans* and Dousia Moujing (the caretaker of the human skulls at the time) were initially reluctant to carry out the ritual ceremony as it would renege on their oath to the spirits, who would be invited to 'attend'. However, they relented after she persuaded them that it was a worthwhile project to document the waning Kadazan ritual practices and they learned that she was the granddaughter of a late *bohungkitas*. Although KLF had originally intended to document the *Monogit* ceremony, a more comprehensive rice-honouring ritual, it was downsized to a *Magavau* ceremony due to the death of a senior *bobohizan* during the preparatory period, during which animals, such as buffalo, were reared to be sacrificed during the ceremony. The KLF team documented about 14 uninterrupted hours of chants and songs through photography and audio-recordings, during which two *bobohizans* and a group of 12 Kadazan elders performed a series of rituals that consisted of the *Magaagandai* ritual for winnowing the rice grains, the *Mangambai* ritual for tossing the rice grains into the air, and the *Mogkodim* ritual for summoning the *Bambaazon* (KLF 2005).

Until the 1970s, most of the Indigenous people in Sabah were rice-cultivators (Blood 1990). They followed a ritual complex structured around the cultivation of rice, with different stages of the growing process celebrated with its own ritual practices, all entangled within an Indigenous cosmology of spirits, ancestors, and non-human entities.[4] There was a close relationship between their social organisation and ritual practices in their everyday lives. It was not until the 1970s, when widespread rural to urban migration in Sabah led to the demise of rice cultivation in rural villages, that the intricate connection between ritual practice and rice cultivation began to be severed.

Today, rice is no longer grown on a significant scale in Sabah but is, instead, imported from neighbouring Thailand and Vietnam. As a result, many ritual practices associated with rice cultivation are no longer performed as part of the everyday lives of the Indigenous people in Sabah. This is exacerbated by the death of *bobohizans* due to old age and the conversion of Indigenous people to other religions such as Christianity and Islam, both of which discourage animist ritual practices. I had the opportunity to interview one of the three remaining senior *bobohizans* in Sabah, Ina Gusiti, via a member of my host family, Winnie Jimis, who served as an interpreter for the interview, which was conducted in the Kadazan language. Ina Gusiti spoke about the demise of Kadazan ritual practices and of the difficulties she has faced in passing on the craft.

> I'm very sad but I cannot do anything because we don't have any *bohungkitas* to continue the teaching and study. At the same time, most of the communities are turning to Christianity, some to Islam, some to other religions. And I personally cannot pass down the traditional knowledge because I've forgotten a lot of things. Even though I can remember some, I've forgotten others, so even if I pass down to another person, it's not correct because when people go for *Modsuut*,[5] and the *rinait* chants are not proper, then it's not good for that person.

Ina Gusiti also alluded to the simplification of the Kadazan rituals over the years, including how the *Magavau* ceremony has been relegated to a form of cultural performance:

> The rituals today are very simplified, because if you really follow the real rituals, then nobody can do that. So we have to make it very simplified, like the *Magavau* ceremony. It's not actually a real *Magavau* but it's just to show the culture. And since nobody can do the real rituals, I'm just happy that the *Magavau* is still practised, even if it's just a show for its symbolism. It's better than nothing.

The *Magavau* ceremony conducted at the Monsopiad Cultural Village can be conceived as a staged performance, where a version of the *Magavau* ceremony has been performed by ritual specialists to facilitate KLF's documentation of the ritual. It thus involves the displacement of the *Magavau* ceremony from the rice fields where it is normally held during the harvest season, to fit with the new conditions of time and space at the Monsopiad Cultural Village. In this *Magavau* ceremony, the 'back stage' becomes the 'front stage', in MacCannell's (1973) terms, as vernacular cultural practices are put 'on stage' for documentation purposes. Nevertheless, as a staged performance, the *Magavau* ceremony performed at the Monsopiad Cultural Village is mediated and negotiated by different stakeholders, including brokers such as Rita Lasimbang, *bobohizans*, village elders, and other stakeholders, to conform with their respective imaginaries about what constitutes an 'authentic' *Magavau* ceremony.

Since KLF's documentation of the *Magavau* ceremony in 2000 and the *Monogit* ceremony in 2007, Rita Lasimbang has published two short articles on the sequences of both ceremonies in the KLF's annual magazine. During my interview with her, although I was able to view a compilation of the photographs taken of the *Magavau* ceremony at the Monsopiad Cultural Village, which was presented as a report to the Toyota Foundation of Japan, my request for a duplicate copy of the report was rejected, and I was also not allowed to take photographs of it. The primary documentation of these ritual ceremonies remains in KLF's possession and can only be accessed with the permission of Rita Lasimbang. As I understand, the primary documentation has not been shared with other cultural bodies in Sabah that have a remit to safeguard Sabah's Indigenous cultures such as the Sabah Museum and the Kadazandusun Cultural Association (KDCA). During my interview with Rita Lasimbang, she spoke of KLF's plans to publish a book on Kadazan rituals, which would include the documentation of the aforementioned two ceremonies, and that she was looking for someone to transcribe and translate the *rinait* chants recited at both ceremonies from the old Kadazan language into modern Kadazan and English.

In the last decade, the *Magavau* ceremony has enjoyed a revival in Sabah as it is transformed from a ritual ceremony performed to serve the spirits in everyday life to a form of cultural performance that is symbolically staged for family celebrations as well as state carnivals organised by the Sabah State Government in major urban areas. The *Magavau* ritual, which celebrates a successful harvest, has become a symbol of Kadazan identity and values and is a major highlight of the month-long *Pesta Kaamatan* or Harvest Festival, celebrated around Sabah every year in May and June. Judeth John Baptist, the Senior Assistant Curator from the Sabah Museum, who explained to me the sequence of the *Magavau* performance during the opening of the *Pesta Kaamatan* held at the KDCA premises in 2015, said that the staged *Magavau* performance (Figure 5.3) typically features a group of Kadazan performers dressed in the customary costume of long black gown, melodically singing the relevant *rinait* chants. The performers first sing the chants while sitting in a circle formation, before standing up and marching in a single file formation, with each performer putting his or her hands on the shoulders of the performer in front of them, thus forming an unbroken line. The man at the head of the line wields a Kadazan sword, representing the Kadazan warrior. Together, the performance symbolises the action of threading through the rice fields in a single file to welcome the *Bambaazon* and to summon the spirits of stray rice grains. The performance concludes with the Kadazan *sumazau* dance, symbolising merry-making and celebration on successfully bringing the *Bambaazon* and other stray rice grains home.

Figure 5.3 The *Magavau* ceremony staged at the *Pesta Kaamatan* celebration at the Kadazandusun Cultural Association premises in 2015. Photograph: Author.

In the last five years, there has also been a revival of *Magavau* ceremony in the private spheres of urban Sabah, as families stage the ceremony at their celebrations for good luck and blessings. It appears that the staging of the *Magavau* ceremony in the public domain has come to be embraced by local Kadazan people in the private domain as a symbol of self-representation and cultural identity. It has, thus, acquired an 'emergent authenticity' (Cohen 1988). The *Magavau* ceremony was staged at two family *Kaamatan* celebrations at which I was in attendance. At these staged performances, a full-day *Magavau* ceremony performed by a group of *bobohizans* in the rice fields at the end of the harvest season was transformed into a 20-minute segment performed on stage by a group comprising both *bobohizans* and non-*bobohizans* who had learned the *Magavau* sequence and chants. Most of the ritual paraphernalia typically used in the *Magavau* ritual, such as winnowing trays, grass mats, pickled fish, banana flowers, rice wine, rice grains, and coconut leaves, amongst others (Sabah Museum 2001), are excluded from the staged version. While the *bobohizans* are expected to give out a war cry or *pangkis* on recovering any stray rice grains when in the rice fields, this has been excised from the staged version, which instead morphs into the elegant Kadazan *sumazau* dance that is not part of the *Magavau* ritual as practised in the fields.

In staging the *Magavau* ceremony, elements of the *Magavau* cultural practices have been remade, reorganised, and invented as they are transformed into the staged performance, mediated by the different stakeholders to conform with their expectations of what is deemed as representative of the *Magavau* ceremony. The Kadazan performers that I spoke to assured me of the integrity of the staged *Magavau* ceremony, as they have observed certain taboos when learning the *Magavau* chants. As one female performer said:

> Although we do not understand the meanings of the chants as they are in old Kadazan language, we take the learning process seriously to show appreciation for our ancestors and to preserve our culture. There are some taboos and superstitions about learning the *Magavau* ritual which we need to observe. For example, we cannot fool around when learning the chants, as the spirit of the rice will do something to us, or our family will have a bad year. We still observe these superstitions even though we have converted to Christianity, as Christianity teaches us to respect other cultures.

While the staged *Magavau* ceremony is culturally significant to the Kadazan people, there is no cultural prohibition on the number of times it can be staged on any one occasion. At one family *Kaamatan* celebration, the host asked for a second performance of the *Magavau* ceremony at the end of the celebration, albeit using a toy sword as the original Kadazan sword had been returned to the owner, so that I could document the performance.

In the last few years, the *Magavau* ceremony has also been transformed into a symbol of Sabah's cultural identity. At the Sabah Fest 2014 cultural festival, the *Magavau* ceremony was incorporated into a musical entitled 'Aki Nabalu',[6] curated by the Sabah State Museum and produced by the Sabah Tourism Board, which highlighted the ritual practices of seven different groups of Indigenous people in the region. A cultural group comprising *bobohizans* and non-*bobohizans* from the District of Penampang was invited to Sabah's largest cultural complex at the National Department for Culture and Arts [Jabatan Kebudayaan dan Kesenian Negara] (JKKN) to stage the *Magavau* ceremony as part of the 'Aki Nabalu' musical. This staged performance included a segment during which a group of performers, clothed in Kadazan dress, re-enacted the different stages of harvesting rice with rice stalks, winnowing trays, and woven basket props, which served as a prelude to the *Magavau* ritual by the same group of *bobohizans* and non-*bobohizans* who performed at the *Pesta Kaamatan* 2015. On this occasion, the *Magavau* ritual was further shortened to a five-minute segment, featuring the group marching in a single file formation, forming an unbroken line with a man leading the march while carrying a sword.

The 'Aki Nabalu' musical enables the ritual practices of Sabah to be made relevant to contemporary times, decontextualised from the original ritualistic meanings and symbolism. Detached from the village setting, the placement of the musical in an urban setting reflects the urbanisation of cultural heritage, through which rituals are re-interpreted to fit the economic development trajectory. Such a performance also helps to place Indigenous cultures in Sabah on a global stage and can be perceived as a vehicle for the political assertion of Indigenous identities, as well as an effort to capitalise on the economic potential of Sabah's multicultural heritage through tourism. The commodification of the *Magavau* ceremony as part of the 'Aki Nabalu' musical resonates with what Kirshenblatt-Gimblett (2004: 61) considers to be the 'metacultural production' of intangible cultural heritage:

> Persistence in old life ways may not be economically viable and may well be inconsistent with economic development and with national ideologies, the valorisation of those life ways as heritage (and integration of heritage into economies of cultural tourism) is economically viable, consistent with economic development theory, and can be brought into line with national ideologies of cultural uniqueness and modernity.

Judeth John Baptist wrote the musical script for 'Aki Nabalu'. She traces her ancestry to the Kadazan people of the District of Penampang, although she grew up among the Lotud people in the District of Tuaran. As the Head of the Research and Resource Section at the Sabah State Museum, Judeth John Baptist is a specialist on the Indigenous cultures of Sabah, having spent over 30 years collaborating with local Indigenous people on the documentation of their cultural heritage. She played a crucial role in the establishment of the Sabah State Museum's Heritage Village, an open-air museum complex comprising over 23 life-size 'traditional' houses, and constructed by the respective local community groups using their own construction methods and materials. This process was documented by the Sabah State Museum. Over the course of her life, she has played a positive brokerage role in promoting the preservation of Sabah's Indigenous cultural heritage by mediating and translating between the cultural authorities and local Indigenous people. She has, over time, earned much respect and trust from local Indigenous people for her work in preserving and promoting their cultural heritage. This was immensely useful during my fieldwork in Sabah, where I was able to draw on Judeth John Baptist's extensive networks and goodwill with local Indigenous people to carry out my research. In particular, many local Indigenous people whom I met were happy to support my research on learning that Judeth John Baptist was my research sponsor.

In writing the script for 'Aki Nabalu', Judeth John Baptist emphasised how she had preserved the integrity of the ritual practices by ensuring no or minimal interference to their sequence as decided by ritual specialists and local villagers, as she said:

> We identify the ethnic groups through advice from different people, such as the Village Headman or the District Headman or the Local Assemblyman. I do a very thorough research, and always emphasise the people who really know in-depth about their cultures related to whatever programmes I do. This matters because otherwise, it will have a lot of unnecessary *campur-campur* (mixing), and I don't like that. This is an opportunity and a venue for local communities to showcase their cultures on stage. And I emphasise whenever we do the

performance on stage, I always say that you don't change whatever choreography they've done because it's their cultures, and they should be the masters of their own cultures, so you must not tamper with anything. I don't want you to tamper with the music, dance, or movement, and even the costume. To me, we always emphasise the sensitivity of these people and their cultures. These people's cultures need to be highlighted and respected.

The *Magavau* ceremony (Figure 5.4) was also selected to represent Malaysia at a regional conference organised by the Southeast Asian Regional Centre for Archaeology and Fine Arts (SEAMEO SPAFA) in Bangkok from 11 to 14 May 2015, on the spiritual dimensions of rice culture in Southeast Asia. Malaysia's participation was coordinated by Judeth John Baptist, who organised the delegation of performers and spoke about the ritual as a museum expert. As there were slight variations in the *Magavau* rituals that were performed by different Kadazan community groups, she consulted with several senior *bobohizans* to work out a sequence of that would suitably represent Sabah's cultural heritage within the timeframe assigned for the performance at the conference. Given the time constraints, only important segments of the *Magavau* ceremony were staged, and the customary *sumazau* dance was incorporated to facilitate audience participation and as a climax to the staged performance. As Judeth John Baptist said of the 20-minute performance:

> I discussed with the senior *bobohizans* to work out the ritual performance. We took certain parts of the ritual, because we could not do

Figure 5.4 The *Magavau* ceremony staged for the SEAMEO SPAFA conference in Bangkok in 2015. Photograph: SEAMEO SPAFA.

the whole ritual. It's impossible. We mainly included the climaxes of the ritual. For one segment, we were supposed to put a live chicken, and a coconut palm leaf, on top of the *sarong* (local tube cloth) used to cover the people. The live chicken represents symbolically the action of bringing the spirits of the people to their bodies. We didn't use the live chicken at the performance, but we explained this to the audience.

In the staging of the *Magavau* ceremony for the 'Aki Nabalu' musical and the SEAMEO SPAFA conference, Judeth John Baptist played a key broker-age role in mediating and translating between the local Kadazan ritual spe-cialists and cultural agencies to compile a version of the *Magavau* ceremony that was not only endorsed as an 'authentic' representation of it by the local Kadazan people but also perceived to be 'authentic' by the audiences. Al-though the *Magavau* ceremonies performed at the 'Aki Nabalu' musical and the SEAMEO SPAFA conference were deemed 'authentic' in this way, they were nonetheless still staged encounters mediated by different stakeholders and bounded up with issues of ownership, power to define it, and audience expectations. As a broker coordinating these staged performances, Judeth John Baptist holds significant authority in determining the representation of the ceremony during these staged performances, although she chooses to respect the perspectives of the Indigenous ritual specialists who 'own' these cultural practices and work with them in a constructive way to promote their cultural heritage.

In tourism studies, it is often argued that the staging of cultural prac-tices for tourism leads to cultural commoditisation when they are marketed for economic gain. Greenwood (1989), in his study of the Alarde ritual in Fuenterrabia, Spain, argues that tourism has drained the 350-year-old fes-tival of its cultural meanings for the local community. Similarly, Errington and Gewertz (1989: 51) have observed that the Chambri people of Papua New Guinea have altered their patterns of authority and re-valued their customs so as to include tourists in their initiation rituals, prompting them to ask whether the Chambri have understood 'that if they continued to sell their initiations (and perhaps other ceremonies) as tourist attractions, they would themselves no longer find them convincing and effective'. Humanis-tic geographers such as Relph (1976) and Tuan (1977) argue that the com-modification of heritage leads to the museumification and Disneyfication of Indigenous cultural heritage, as customary houses are converted into mere empty shells devoid of a sense of place and their associated humanistic attributes. The process of museumification also dehumanises Indigenous people by turning them into spectacles in a 'human zoo' to be viewed by tourists (Dellios 2002). Such analyses, however, fail to recognise authentic-ity as a mediated experience among different stakeholders and the underly-ing politics of representation.

By placing the authority and onus on the local Indigenous people to de-cide for themselves what constitutes an 'authentic' representation of their ritual practices, Judeth John Baptist appears to resist the commodification of these cultural practices through the process of staging and safeguarding them from auto-exoticism. By extending the authority to the Indigenous people to decide for themselves, she also appears to resist the formation of a culture of dependency between her as the broker and the Indigenous people as the 'owners' of the cultural heritage. This allows cultural heritage to emerge as an instrument for Indigenous self-determination and empowerment. Nevertheless, the differences between the staged performances of the *Magavau* ceremony for the musical and the conference demonstrate how each performance, even though it may be performed and coordinated by the same people, constitutes its own process of mediation and negotiation between the different stakeholders to conform with the expectations for each occasion (Theodossopoulos 2011).

Towards the end of my fieldwork, I asked an apprentice *bobohizan*, who is based at the Monsopiad Cultural Village, Adam Gontusan, if he could perform a ritual ceremony at the cultural village. I offered to sponsor the ceremony as a way of showing my gratitude to the spirits in the area. It would also provide me with an opportunity to document a small appeasement ritual. Aged around 30 years old, Adam Gontusan is the youngest *bobohizan* in Sabah. Since 2012, he has been undergoing training with a senior *bobohizan* to become an initiated specialist of Kadazan rituals. He had been a dancer and a narrator at the Monsopiad Cultural Village before taking on his current role as a residential *bobohizan* at the site.

While Adam Gontusan has been praised by some Kadazan elders for his willingness to undertake the arduous *bobohizan* apprenticeship, he has also been criticised for his unconventional approach (Chan 2016). He is, however, an immensely popular *bobohizan*, and many villagers have engaged his services to meet their ritual needs, especially in removing malignant spirits and conducting exorcisms (Chan 2016). Adam Gontusan laments the challenges of learning the craft, as many *bobohizans* are getting old, and they no longer remember the rituals since they do not perform them regularly. There are also limited opportunities to participate in or observe ritual ceremonies, as it is prohibitively expensive to conduct rituals in Sabah today.

Faced with the immense difficulty of learning the craft from senior *bobohizans*, Adam Gontusan relies on his ingenuity to make the best from what is available. He frequently engages his familiar spirit or *divato* in Kadazan language, which lives in his *komburongo*, to guide him in his rituals. The *komburongo* is an item of ritual paraphernalia, made of bunches of sacred ginger pieces strung together, which is used to communicate and summon the familiar spirit that will take over and possess the body of the *bobohizan* during a trance. As Adam Gontusan has said:

> The *divato* is the familiar spirit that can do many things. When the *bobohizans* perform the ritual, they ask their *divatos*, who live inside the *komburongo*, to assist them and to support them during the rituals.

When the *divato* is awake, you can smell an orangey smell from the *komburongo*. You can ask the *divato* to help you do many things, like curing a person. The *divato* will tell the *bobohizan* what she needs to do.

After consulting with the spirits in the area through his *divato*, Adam Gontusan set the date for the ritual ceremony, the afternoon of Saturday, 14 June 2015 (Figure 5.5). It would comprise a few rituals from the *Magavau* ceremony, namely the *Modsuung*, the *Modsuut*, and the *Magampah*. The *Modsuut* and *Magampah* rituals, which would normally last at least one full day and include animal sacrifices, were condensed into a three-hour segment with no animal sacrifice. I later learned that some cultural taboos associated with these rituals were also not observed. For example, a *Magampah* ritual would usually involve placing a live chicken on a *sarong* that is used to cover the seated participants, symbolising the bringing of the spirits of the people to their bodies through the conduit of the live chicken. But instead, Adam Gontusan swept the *sarong* with a coconut palm leaf.

This ritual ceremony appeared to have been drawn from the *Magavau* ceremony that was staged at the SEAMEO SPAFA conference that Adam Gontusan had participated in, which alludes to how apprentice *bobohizans* have drawn upon staged cultural performances as inspiration in reinventing their ritual practices, but which also raises questions of infringement of intellectual property rights (see Geismar 2005, 2013). This also shows how contemporary ritual practices evolve over time, incorporating innovations introduced through the touristic staging of culture. At the same time, the ritual ceremony appears to have acquired 'performative authenticity'

Figure 5.5 Two *bobohizans*, Adam Gontusan and Kudut, conducting the *Modsuung* ritual at the Monsopiad Cultural Village. Photograph: Author.

(Zhu 2012) through Adam Gontusan's embodied practice. As he has said of his ritual practice:

> When I start the ritual and enter the world of the spirits, I am no longer aware of what I am saying, and those around me have to listen in order to hear what conversations are taking place. It is also during chants that my third eye is opened and I can see spirits.
>
> (Chan 2016)

Adam Gontusan's practices as an apprentice *bobohizan* demonstrate that ritual tradition is a construction involving 'a selective representation of the past, fashioned in the present, responsive to contemporary priorities and agendas, and politically instrumental' (Linnekin 1992: 251). It can acquire 'performative authenticity' (Zhu 2012) through, for example, Adam Gontusan's' embodied practices. This also attests to the multifaceted and ever-evolving manifestations of cultural representations that are constructed and mediated by different stakeholders, depending on the context and interpretation (Harrison 2013).

The transformation of the *Magavau* ceremony from a ritual practised in the fields to a staged performance conducted at festivals and celebrations can be considered part of a broader renaissance of Indigenous cultural heritage in Sabah that has been unfolding since the 1980s, in tandem with the emergence of the Indigenous rights movement in Malaysia. Projects for Awareness and Community Organisations in Sabah (PACOS Trust), Sabah's largest Indigenous NGO, is behind the Indigenous cultural renaissance in Sabah, with its Executive Director, Anne Lasimbang, playing a brokerage role in encouraging the practice of cultural heritage among the Indigenous people in Sabah. Anne Lasimbang comes from an influential family in Sabah and her siblings have taken up significant leadership roles across several human rights and Indigenous NGOs locally in Malaysia and regionally in Asia. Her sister, Jannie Lasimbang, who founded PACOS Trust with Colin Nicholas, is currently the Chairperson of the Sabah branch of Malaysia's largest anti-government coalition, BERSIH. BERSIH is an acronym for the Coalition for Clean and Fair Elections, which also means 'clean' in Malay. It is a coalition of NGOs, political parties, and civic society groups, seeking to reform the current electoral system in Malaysia to ensure free and fair elections. Jannie Lasimbang is also the President of the Asian Indigenous People's Pact (AIPP), a pan-Asian NGO that advocates for the rights of the Indigenous people in Asia. Anne Lasimbang's other sister, Rita, Lasimbang founded the aforementioned KLF to protect, promote, and revive Indigenous languages and cultural heritage in Sabah.

Concerned with the social injustices facing Indigenous people in Malaysia and inspired by the Christian social justice movement, Anne Lasimbang came to be involved as a student activist while studying at the National University of Malaysia in the 1980s. When I interviewed her, she recalled her early forays into Indigenous activism and how the UN's Declaration of the International Decade for the World's Indigenous People raised the level of Indigenous consciousness in Malaysia:

> When we first started, we were student activists. There was no consciousness of 'Indigenous' as how we understand 'Indigenous' today. We were just conscious about our rights, the environment and the social injustices around us. The word 'Indigenous' was not there yet. It was when the United Nations had the International Decade for the World's Indigenous People, that we began to talk and look at ourselves, and really look at what we have, what we are losing, then that consciousness became more systematic. With the declaration, people from different parts of the world came together, and began to talk about the different issues that Indigenous people are facing, especially those losing their lands, losing their cultures, losing their languages. Then they suddenly see, oh, it is not just me, but the other communities too are facing the same issues. From then on, there is that wave of consciousness. Now, with the younger generation, there is more consciousness that we have the *Belia Orang Asal* (Young Indigenous People), so they are prouder of their identities.

With the rise in Indigenous consciousness among the Indigenous people in Sabah, cultural practices, costumes, and languages that were previously regarded as signifying their inferior, backward, and underdeveloped status have been re-appropriated as positive resources. Such performances of Indigenous cultural heritage have come to be drawn upon as sources of self-knowledge and self-identity in pursuing the goals of Indigenous rights and self-determination. As Anne Lasimbang said:

> I remember when I was a kid in primary school, we were all in English medium schools. That was a time when you felt that you didn't even want to speak your language, you were quite ashamed of the food that you eat, you were seen as backward. Some people even told us: 'You should start eating from plates, not from leaves.' But now, people want to have the leaves because the leaves are better. Because it is organic, back to the basics. I was once even questioned at a conference: 'What do you want? You want to become a doctor, or you want to wear loin cloths?' I really remember that one because somebody pointed out to me: 'You are showing backwardness.' But I answered: 'Oh well, when I feel like I want to wear loin cloths, I will wear the loin cloths. I shouldn't feel uncomfortable in it.' That is the consciousness in the past that Indigenous culture is associated with being backward, but now, people appreciate their Indigenous culture because it gives that unique identity.

By alluding to the wearing of loin cloth and eating from leaves, Anne Lasimbang is engaged in a staged performance of her cultural identity as an

Indigenous person, evoking the Western ideological imagination of primitivism and exoticism, which has now taken on a positive connotation, as a visual symbol for asserting her Indigenous identity. However, as the question posed to Anne Lasimbang demonstrates, with regard to whether she prefers to be a doctor or an Indigenous person, such strategic essentialism consciously maintains the construction of difference between Indigenous and non-Indigenous people, recasting the former as backward and undeveloped. This contradictory dualism, as discussed by Kallen (2015), puts their interests at odds with the development agenda and may compromise their options for Indigenous advocacy.

Through the programmes of PACOS Trust, Anne Lasimbang plays a crucial brokerage role, mediating and translating between the vernacular world of the Indigenous people of Sabah and transnational Indigenous activism circles to advance Indigenous advocacy and activism in the region. She facilitates the performance of Indigeneity and Indigenous cultural heritage in Sabah, by drawing extensively on the environmental agenda at PACOS Trust to position them as 'ecologically noble savages' (Redford 1990), imbued with cultural wisdom and integrity, and in possession of politically significant claims to Indigenous self-determination and empowerment. The PACOS Trust runs an organic café that sources its ingredients from a large community nursery that grows native plant species, located within its premises. The community nursery provides a marketplace for Indigenous villagers to buy seedlings of Indigenous plants for planting in their own villages. The promotion of Indigenous ways of cultivation and the planting of native plants can be conceived of as a staged performance by Indigenous people to portray themselves as having strong conservationist ethics and using environmental resources in ways that are non-destructive, sustainable, and mindful of the effects on the future generations (Conklin and Graham 1995; Hames 2007). By encouraging the performance of their Indigeneity and Indigenous cultural heritage through adopting environmentally friendly practices, PACOS Trust is signalling that Indigenous people take responsible stewardship towards their environment, lending further weight to their customary claims on their ancestral lands, territories, and resources.

Although native customary rights were already recognised during the British colonial administration of North Borneo, and later instituted in the post-colonial state legislations of Sabah, vast tracts of ancestral lands currently occupied by Indigenous people are still not registered as such due to many historical and contemporary issues such as the slow processing of land rights applications, inaccurate land surveys and inspections, and poor records of lands and territories claimed under native customary rights by the government authorities (SUHAKAM 2013; Leonie et al. 2015). Under the Torrens land system inherited from the British colonial period, lands without registered titles automatically belong to the state and are classified as state lands (Idrus 2010). Therefore, Indigenous people must prove their native status by demonstrating the continued practice of their customs and traditions or *adat*, to reclaim these state lands.

The Malaysian Forestry Department (2015: 30), in their certification manual for the regulation of sustainable timber extraction practices in Malaysia, defines *adat* as the 'accepted norms and customs that govern the lives of Indigenous communities, which include their way of life, basic values, systems of belief, codes of conduct, manners, conventions, agricultural and cultural practices according to which Indigenous societies are ordered'. This definition of *adat*, which has been adopted by the national legislation on native customary rights, embraces an essentialised formulation of Indigeneity based on 'an antiquated anthropological notion of 'the "authentic" or whole Indigenous subject, framed and referenced by mythic time and complex kinship' (Wolfe 1999: 197 quoted in Birrell 2009: 222). It has motivated Indigenous people in Sabah to revive or (re)invent their cultural practices to meet this essentialised formula in order to make native customary claims to their ancestral lands, territories, and resources.

One Indigenous group in Sabah, which has legally gained native customary rights to extract timber from the nearby forest reserves for domestic use as a result of reviving or (re)inventing their *adat*, is the Orang Sungai living in Kampung Balat Kinabatangan, in the District of Sandakan. Under the Sabah Forest Enactment Act of 1968,[7] Indigenous people have 'conceded privilege' or rights that native customary users or occupiers had to extract resources from forest reserves owned by the state (SUHAKAM 2013). Due to the active Islamisation of Indigenous people by the Malaysian government, many Orang Sungai had converted to Islam by the 1990s and began to wear Malay costumes. As a result, they gradually lost the knowledge and skills to weave their 'traditional' costumes. It is generally only older members of the Orang Sungai community that still speak their native language.

Through the encouragement of the PACOS Trust, the Orang Sungai have revived or (re)invented their weaving practices. Anne Lasimbang, who first met the Orang Sungai when PACOS Trust was running a training workshop in the area in the 1990s, recalled:

> When we arrived, we asked them: 'Do you have a traditional costume?' They couldn't find. They were all wearing the Malay one without the *tudong* (headdress). But one of the old people said: 'Yah, we have', and they took it out. There were also like the gongs for the dances, but only one or two could play the musical instruments. Then they started to learn to make their costumes and play the musical instruments through knowledge exchanges with other Indigenous groups in Sabah from whom they learn to revive their cultural heritage. And why is it important? Because their village is in this forest reserve, for them to be recognised as a community within that forest reserve, that they are not coming from Indonesia. Many of the people there are Bugis from Indonesia who go and occupy land. So how do they prove that they are

natives? So, they have to show their costumes, they have to revive their costumes. The Forestry department now recognises the village, so they can continue to extract resources from the forest reserve.

Although the Indigenous people seem to have acquired new cultural practices through these exchanges, the adoption of these cultural practices is deliberately framed as a form of cultural revivalism, implying that these cultural practices had once existed but were later lost. This is arguably a form of strategic self-instrumentalisation of Indigenous cultural heritage, performed by the Indigenous people to conform with the autochthonic and essentialist formulation of Indigeneity embraced in the legal rhetoric of and the transnational discourse on Indigenous activism and advocacy.

Anne Lasimbang underscored the importance of cultural heritage for Indigenous activism:

> Now that we have a lot of cases of land grabbing in our own territories, suddenly cultural heritage is very important, and how do you prove that? The courts will ask you to prove why do you say it is native lands? Why do you say it is native customary rights? So you say it belongs to my community. *Sungai* (River)? So what is the *Sungai* in the community that makes you think you are Indigenous? So you have to show all in court. You have to produce evidence on how people are getting married, their boats, their clothes, how they farm, anything on culture to prove. We shouldn't be proving, but now, we have to go to courts to prove that this is a form of native customary rights, so cultural heritage now becomes very important. It's not just identity for the person, but in terms of asserting their territories. But people last time think it's not important. People think that they go to work, they get something to eat, enough. Now that in the world, more people want to grab your land, you need to prove, you need to speak the language, you need to practise your culture. If you can't show, they ask, so you are a Malay? So now, it's very important.

The revival or (re)invention of weaving practices amongst the Orang Sungai to meet the criteria for claiming native customary rights, and hence the rights to extract resources from the forest reserves of Sabah, demonstrates how an essentialised conceptualisation of Indigenous cultural heritage is being adopted as a political assertion of native customary rights, a phenomenon that has also been observed among the Semai and Temiar people in Peninsular Malaysia (Subramaniam and Edo 2016). This renaissance or (re)invention of *adat* can also be conceived of as a staged performance of cultural heritage for the consumption of the Malaysian state. In particular, this involves the staging of certain aspects of cultural practice to meet essentialised definitions of *adat* as stipulated in Malaysian statutes and regulations, in order to stake claims to ancestral lands, territories, and resources. Unlike the unpremeditated staging of cultural practices in the vernacular lives of Indigenous people in the uncommodified *Mohlukas* ritual, *Magavau* ritual, and *Hari Moyang* celebrations, the performance of Indigenous cultural practices here seems to have a deliberate objective to mobilise and assert native customary rights.

As the legal concept of native title acknowledges an autochthonic and primordial notion of Indigeneity, this has led to the spatialisation of culture, since Indigenous people need to demonstrate their continued practice of their cultural heritage in order to claim native customary rights (Bunnell and Nah 2004; Merlan 2007; Birrell 2009; Porter 2010; Cooke 2013). Cultural mapping, a community-based instrument for collecting, recording, and locating information of both tangible and intangible cultural expressions and its distribution within a certain territory, has emerged as an important political tool for connecting Indigenous identities with their places (UNESCO 2009). Since 1994, the Borneo Project, an American organisation based in Berkeley, California, has offered funding, equipment, and training for the development of participatory mapping efforts among the Indigenous people in Sarawak and Sabah (Lasimbang 2004a). From using simple compasses with hand-plotted maps in the early days, the Indigenous people in Sabah now rely on sophisticated GPS equipment and mapping software to produce geographically accurate maps, which are frequently accepted by the courts as important evidence for claims to their native customary rights.

Cultural mapping has been instrumentalised by Indigenous people to demarcate and stake claims to ancestral territories and resources, protect Indigenous rights, promote management of biodiversity, preserve diversity, and mediate conflicts to seek resolution (Orlove 1991; Peluso 1995; Fox 2002; Bauer 2009; Taylor 2013; Bell 2014, 2016). It allows Indigenous people to demarcate their customary landmarks, ancestors' graves, and other culturally significant features, producing and reifying their histories and cultural heritage spatially, so that these can be mobilised as evidence demonstrating their continued practice of cultural heritage. This enables Indigenous people to meet the essentialised notion of Indigeneity as stipulated in the legal statutes and state regulations, enabling them to strategically instrumentalise their cultural heritage to protect their ancestral resources from encroachment or to contest encroachment of these resources by inscribing local meanings onto these lands and territories.

Cultural mapping technologies such as GIS (Geographic Information System) are increasingly adopted as a tool of governance for governments to exert oversight and control over Indigenous people and their territories (Palmer and Rundstrom 2013; Bryan and Woods 2015). Yet, these technologies can also be mobilised to contest and negotiate official interpretations of histories and places. Through counter mapping, Indigenous people can re-inscribe local knowledge in place, thus promoting community empowerment and social justice (Minkin et al. 2014; Bell 2015; Duxbury et al.

2015). Cultural mapping is thus perceived as a political tool that is susceptible to instrumentalisation by powerful actors, which can, in turn, create new power dynamics or reinforce existing power relations (Bauer 2009; Bell 2015; Duxbury 2015; Freitas 2016).

The PACOS Trust has initiated the 'Identity Markers' project to encourage Indigenous people in Sabah to document their cultural heritage, with plans for the materials collected to be incorporated into the local curriculum taught in community learning centres. As Anne Lasimbang explained:

> We hold community workshops, and we talk about identity markers. What is it that identifies us as Indigenous people? And they will do the usual thing, set out their food, so we will write food, their dance, so we will write dance, their language and so on, so they've a long list of cultural identity markers. So if you say it's your food, what is it that you want to document? We work with youths, children and mothers. We want to develop books and curriculum that we can use to teach children, so that means the curriculum does not come from us. They have identified or clarified their cultural identity markers. They are the ones who list them down, so we develop the curriculum for them based on their lists. They say in ten years' time, they want their dances to be good. They want their dances to be taught to the kids, to the youths, so we do a curriculum for learning the dances. With the dances, we need the music and musical instruments. So how do you teach that? So these become the curriculum as well. And stories, we ask them to start recording all these stories. Hopefully, it is a long process. But they have started, and we will slowly help them put those into books. Later on, they will record songs and lullabies.

The 'Identity Markers' project presents an example of how NGOs and their brokers encourage the self-identification and performance of Indigenous cultural heritage, setting in motion a process that produces and reifies staged performances of Indigenous cultural heritage as ontological, rather than acknowledging their invented nature and dynamic subjectivities. Unlike the active staging and production of Indigenous cultural heritage for different political, economic, and social agendas at the cultural villages – one that perpetuate a culture of dependency that marginalises Indigenous people – Indigenous NGOs actively stage and reify Indigenous cultural heritage with the goal of preserving the heritage and asserting Indigenous rights. In so doing, they promote Indigenous self-determination and empowerment.

To facilitate knowledge sharing and capacity-building on issues facing Indigenous people in Sabah, the PACOS Trust organises thrice-yearly tactical meetings for them at its headquarters in the District of Penampang. I had the opportunity to observe a two-day tactical meeting held at the PACOS Trust in June 2015. At this meeting, Anne Lasimbang engaged the assistance of her sister Rita Lasimbang from KLF to conduct a workshop on documenting and publishing community stories. PACOS Trust regularly conducts other workshops on the documentation of different aspects of Indigenous cultural heritage such as native languages, folktales and legends, food recipes, costumes, games, handicrafts, songs and dances, as well as ritual practices. Indigenous people are also encouraged to organise events at their villages for the staging of their culture and customs.

These tactical meetings offer insights into the workings of PACOS Trust and other Indigenous NGOs, especially with respect to how these Indigenous brokers mobilise Indigenous people in the self-identification and performance of their cultural heritage. This process can also be conceived of as a systematic mode for making and (re)making regimes of truth about Indigeneity and Indigenous cultural heritage, leading to the production or reinvention of Indigenous cultural heritage that is then spread through the network of Indigenous NGOs that form the transnational Indigenous rights movement.

A regular component of the tactical meetings is for each village to share the different events and activities they have organised in the preceding months, classified by economic, social, and cultural programmes. The sharing session prompts friendly competition between the different Indigenous villages, as each seeks to outdo the others in terms of the scale and volume of programmes they organise. At the same time, it offers an avenue for the Indigenous people from different villages to exchange ideas and capacities, which also opens up opportunities for collaboration. Importantly, it also functions as a forum for airing grievances and sharing ideas on dealing with problems. PACOS Trust regularly arranges for videos of their recent rallies to be screened at these tactical meetings, accompanied by talks from Anne Lasimbang and other protesters sharing their personal experiences and urging the participants not to be afraid to stand up for their rights. This sharing of experiences galvanises a collective identity and resistance against the marginalisation and dispossession faced by the Indigenous community.

In setting up these tactical meetings, PACOS Trust mobilises a collective identity forged by the circulation of a set of ideas about rights and recognition coalescing around concepts of anti-discrimination and self-determination that help to define what it means to be an Indigenous person. This collective identity and common set of interests help Indigenous people strategically position themselves within a kind of 'tribal slot', rendering it as a useful political tool for Indigenous activism and advocacy (Trouillot 1991; Li 2000; Barnard 2006). The work of PACOS Trust thus demonstrates how Indigenous cultural heritage has been instrumentalised, particularly through the positive brokerage of Indigenous activists such as Anne Lasimbang, for Indigenous self-determination and empowerment, fulfilling the ethos lauded in the 'culture for development' discourse.

Frictions, tensions, and issues

At the Monsopiad Cultural Village, a source of tension between the founders of the site and the direct descendants of Monsopiad, who own the artefacts, arose from the representation of some aspects of the Village's cultural heritage, which led to 'heritage dissonance' (Tunbridge and Ashworth 1996). A key attraction that has been subjected to multiple interpretations is a menhir, known as *Gintutun Do Mohoing* (Figure 5.6), which means the 'contemplation of people who die without children' (Phelan 1997). Menhirs are believed to be sacred in Sabah and each is said to have a spirit residing in them that must be appeased regularly with blood sacrifices and ritual chanting. According to published sources and oral historical accounts by Wildy Moujing, his ancestor erected the *Gintutun Do Mohoing*, measuring about two metres in height, to commemorate the memory of his brother Tuza'ai, a former Village Headman, and his wife Sunduai who died without children (Phelan 2001). Although there was no record of when the menhir was brought from Pulau Sulug to its current location at the Monsopiad Cultural Village, there was documentary evidence to show that it had been appeased with the blood of sacrificed animals during the *Magang* ceremony conducted by the Moujing family in 1974 (Phelan 1997, 2001).

While the *Gintutun Do Mohoing* was erected to commemorate a childless couple, it has fulfilled other ritual functions. It was believed that when local warriors arrived home from successful headhunting expeditions, they would place each human skull in a bamboo structure, known as a *bangkaha*, which was erected around the menhir, to allow the hair, flesh, and skin to decay before the skull was brought home to be installed in the house

Figure 5.6 The *Gintutun Do Mohoing* menhir at the Monsopiad Cultural Village. Photograph: Author.

(Phelan 2001). Based on another oral account, it is claimed that a man named Binut from Tuaran was sacrificed on this menhir to seal the agreement of peace between the villagers of Kampung Kuai-Kadazon and the villagers of Kampung Kurai, between which there had been deep enmity for many generations (Phelan 2001). According to this account, Binut was tied to the menhir and the villagers from both villages cut him until he died from pain and the excessive loss of blood (Phelan 2001).

Although the *Gintutun Do Mohoing* is thought to predate the time of Monsopiad, the founders of the Monsopiad Cultural Village present a different narrative during the guided tour at the site. According to the tour script:

> About 300 years ago, during the era of Monsopiad, a deadly plague afflicted Kampung Kuai-Kadazon during which many people died. A *Moginakan* ritual was conducted, during which a *bohungkitas* ascended to the spiritual world to consult with the spirits. An agreement was reached, whereby one of the spirits residing in the spiritual world, known as Gintutun, decided to descend to the human world and reside in a menhir to be installed by the villagers of Kampung Kuai-Kadazon. The task landed on Monsopiad to lead a delegation of warriors and seven *bobohizans* to Pulau Gaya, an offshore island, to bring back a menhir. After identifying a suitable menhir, the *bobohizans* summoned forces from the spiritual world to assist in the transport of the menhir back to the village, after which a grand ritual lasting seven days and seven nights and involving the sacrifice of seven buffaloes, seven pigs, seven roosters, and seven goats was carried out to install the menhir, with the victims of the plague buried at the site of the menhir. The menhir is known as 'Monsopiad's monolith' and serves as the guardian of the human skulls in the cultural village.

The tour narrative appears to have been crafted by the founders of the Monsopiad Cultural Village, who seek to associate Monsopiad with the menhir to present a coherent narrative about the artefacts in the cultural village. This serves as an example of how brokers have invented narratives to meet the expectations of tourists searching for authenticity and demonstrates how the commodification process can lead to heritage dissonance. Nevertheless, the Indigenous people who work at the Monsopiad Cultural Village are also complicit in presenting this tour narrative to tourists, suggesting that they have willingly conformed to their expected roles in order to receive benefits from the Monsopiad Cultural Village (Doolittle 2004). This can be conceptualised as a form of 'customised authenticity' (Wang 2007) between the tour operators and their visitors. The direct descendants of Monsopiad did not agree with the tour narrative presented at the Monsopiad Cultural Village, demonstrating how the owners' lack of agency and authority in representing their own heritage renders it susceptible to alternative and ultimately dissonant representations by brokers.

The direct descendants of Monsopiad have repeatedly objected to the relocation of a slab-like menhir of about 96 cm in height and 49 cm in width widely believed to be Monsopiad's tombstone, largely on account of the ritual prohibitions attached to its movement. The menhir has lines and a series of triangles cut into it, forming a series of diamond-shaped figures (Phelan 1997). Dousia Moujing (the caretaker for the human skulls) believes that these carvings were made by Monsopiad himself, who intended it to be used as his tombstone (Phelan 1997). The menhir currently stands on a small hill overlooking Kampung Kurai and Kampung Kuai-Kadazon. When the Monsopiad Cultural Village was established in 1996, the proposal to relocate the menhir to the site was briefly considered by the direct descendants of Monsopiad, as it could become a highlight of the Monsopiad Cultural Village by providing further 'evidence' of the existence of Monsopiad. However, upon consultation with the spirits through the *bobohizans*, the descendents decided against relocating the menhir. The spirits advised that the menhir was too powerful to be moved. Although the General Manager employed at the site during the time I was conducting fieldwork was keen for the menhir to be relocated to the Monsopiad Cultural Village, this continued to be met with resistance from the direct descendants of Monsopiad, who claimed that they would need to consult the spirits and hold an elaborate ritual for the relocation, which would be prohibitively expensive. Here, Indigenous people have held back on the commodification of certain aspects of their cultural heritage for apparently 'genuine' cultural reasons, safeguarding their cultural heritage from alienation and auto-exoticism.

Conclusion

The Monsopiad Cultural Village, which was founded by a British entrepreneur and his Kadazan wife as a tourist attraction to capitalise on the benefits of cultural tourism, has come to be entangled in a complex web of tensions and local politics. The Monsopiad Cultural Village, which extends significant authority to its founders as key brokers, reinforces a structural relationship that marginalises local Indigenous workers at the village. In particular, the founders, who have both 'insider' and 'outsider' allegiances, appear to derive a significant portion of the revenue from the site and have the final say over the representation of cultural heritage within it. This structural relationship appears to be endorsed by the local Kadazan elites who own the lands and artefacts on which the Monsopiad Cultural Village is based. In this chapter, I demonstrate how such community-based cultural projects entrench a culture of dependency that leads to the marginalisation of some members of the Indigenous community in the hands of others. By showing how people with Indigenous ancestry may not always act in the best interests of other Indigenous people, I complicate the typical representation of Indigenous communities in the museological literature that conceptualises Indigenous communities as a collective whole with a common agenda and social allegiance. This, I argue, affects the workings of the community-based cultural projects, which may fulfil or compromise the needs of the local communities they intend to serve.

The Monsopiad Cultural Village functions as an institutionalised form of 'primitivist tourism' (Stasch 2015), drawing upon the historical construction of Indigenous people of Borneo as backward, undeveloped, and uncivilised people for tourist consumption, which continues to shape contemporary tourists' imaginaries about them. Rather than rejecting the headhunting heritage as a symbol of their backwardness and barbarism, the Indigenous Kadazan people are actively embracing this essentialised self-portrayal as 'primitive people' and 'exotic savages' for the assertion of their Indigenous identity. They are willing to be exoticised in order to capitalise on this commodification for their own ends. There are also instances where they resist the commodification and exoticisation of their cultural heritage by stipulating the practice of certain ritual observances and holding back on the commodification of some aspects of their cultural heritage such as the relocation of what is allegedly Monsopiad's tombstone. This case study therefore makes an important contribution to Indigenous museology in the Southeast Asian context, by demonstrating how Indigenous museums are sites of contestations and negotiations where different agendas are played out, rather than sites promoting the development of Indigenous communities.

While modernisation has led to a decline in the practice of the *Magavau* ceremony since the 1970s, it has undergone a revival in the last decade as it is transformed into a staged performance. The transformation of the *Magavau* ceremony into a staged performance is negotiated by different stakeholders and mediated by Indigenous brokers such as Rita Lasimbang and Judeth John Baptist, who give the ownership and authority on the representation of the cultural heritage to the Indigenous communities. Each staged performance also constitutes its own 'negotiation of expectations' (Theodossopoulos 2011) between the different stakeholders, to conform to what is deemed appropriate for each occasion. The staged *Magavau* ceremony is, in turn, embodied and embraced by the local Indigenous people as a symbol of self-representation and cultural identity, thus acquiring 'emergent authenticity' (Cohen 1988), but it has also been appropriated by apprentice *bobohizans* to reinvent their ritual practices. Indigenous people in different parts of Sabah are also engaging in the revival of their cultural heritage, encouraged by the strategic brokerage of NGOs such as PACOS Trust, to assert their native customary rights to land, territories, and resources. The different stakeholders are embroiled in a complex and dynamic web of power relations and identity politics, producing complex outcomes for the Indigenous people. This chapter thus develops a critical approach on the concept of heritage instrumentalisation by examining the interwoven power relations and politics in the making and transformation of heritage.

Notes

1 Some materials used in this chapter have been published in Cai (2018).
2 A menhir is a tall, vertical standing stone, often man-made, that is widely found across Africa, Asia, and Europe.
3 A head feast is probably a ritual ceremony to appease the human skulls.
4 See Lingenfelter (1990), Regis (1993), Pugh-Kitingan and John Baptist (2009), Sirom and Topin (2017) for information on Indigenous cosmologies in Sabah.
5 *Modsuut* is an Indigenous consultation process with the spiritual world to seek advice on unresolved matters after all other avenues to seek resolution have been exhausted.
6 'Aki Nabalu' means the resting place of the ancestors, with 'aki' meaning grandfather, which is an address of respect for elders and 'Nabalu' meaning coffin for the dead. 'Aki Nabalu' can be taken to mean Mount Kinabalu, Southeast Asia's highest peak at 4,095 metres, which is located in Sabah. The Indigenous communities that live on Mount Kinabalu and its foothills as well as those living within sight of the mountain believe that it is the final resting place of departed souls.
7 Section 41 of the Forest Enactment Act 1968 on the preservation of native rights:

> 'Subject to any provisions of the rules prohibiting or regulating the cutting or removal of any specified form of forest produce or prohibiting or regulating the cutting or removal of all or any forest produce in any specified locality, nothing in this Enactment shall be deemed to prohibit the cutting and removal from State land which is not for the time being in the lawful occupation of some person or, with the permission of the owner thereof, from alienated land, by any native of any timber, *attap* or other forest produce which may be necessary
>
> a for the construction or repair of a dwelling-house for the abode of himself and his family;
> b for the construction of fences and temporary huts on any land lawfully occupied by him;
> c for the construction or repair of native boats;
> d for the upkeep of his fishing stakes and landing places;
> e for fire-wood to be consumed for his domestic purposes; or
> f for the construction and upkeep of clinics, schools, community halls, places of worship, bridges and any work for the common benefit of the native inhabitants of his kampung'.

6 The big man as arbitrator of heritage

Introduction[1]

The Linangkit Cultural Village (Figure 6.1) is an example of a community-initiated and managed cultural project that serves different agendas simultaneously. A powerful broker took centre-stage, marshalling the resources to support the financial sustainability of the Linangkit Cultural Village, entrenching a working relationship that was difficult to replace after his sudden demise. The case study of the Linangkit Cultural Village highlights the fragility of the structure of such community-based cultural projects which renders them susceptible to strategic mobilisation by different stakeholders and the prominent roles brokers play in determining the success or failure of such projects. I argue that such community-based cultural projects often come to perpetuate a culture of dependency between the brokers managing

Figure 6.1 The Lotud longhouse with the exhibition galleries at the Linangkit Cultural Village. The Linangkit Cultural Village is sited in Kampung Selupoh in the District of Tuaran in the eastern Malaysian state of Sabah. Photograph: Author.

these projects and the local communities whose cultural heritage is represented in these projects due to the unequal power relationships among the different stakeholders, complicating the 'culture for development' discourse widely promoted by UNESCO, national governments, and museum institutions.

The ritual cleansing of Mount Kinabalu to appease the angered mountain guardians after the 2015 earthquake highlights an occasion where Indigenous people actively hold back from the commodification of their cultural heritage, demonstrating how Indigenous people have agency over the transformation of their cultural heritage, even as they are actively mobilising their cultural heritage to negotiate their place and position within contemporary Malaysia. During calamitous moments such as the Mount Kinabalu earthquake, Indigenous people turn to their ritual practices to appease the spirits and restore the balance between the spiritual and physical worlds, demonstrating their continued faith in the ritual efficacy of their cultural heritage. In this instance, cultural heritage is instrumentalised to serve altruistic needs of the local communities. By examining how the Indigenous communities resist and negotiate the commodification of their cultural heritage through these cleansing rituals, this chapter applies a critical approach to the understanding of heritage instrumentalisation.

The Lotud is a subgroup of the Indigenous Dusunic people, residing mainly in the District of Tuaran on the west coast of Sabah. Numbering around 20,000 people, they can be divided into three groups: the Suang Lotud on the plains around Kampung Marabahai near Tuaran Township, the Lotud Sarayoh around Kampung Bantayan and further inland into the hills and highlands, and the Suang Olung on the coast around Kampung Olung (Cai and John Baptist 2016). The Lotud speak a distinct language and differentiate themselves from other Indigenous subgroups in Sabah through their food, costume, craft, music, belief system, and ritual practices.

The Linangkit Cultural Village, located in Kampung Selupoh in the District of Tuaran, was set up in 2007 by the Jilan family, a prominent Lotud family with extensive political and business connections. Designed to display and preserve Lotud cultural heritage, the Linangkit Cultural Village, which was closed for renovations in late 2013 for the construction of a new community hall, re-opened to tourists in July 2015 when I began my fieldwork. The Linangkit Cultural Village has several buildings on site, which include a Lotud longhouse, which doubles up as an exhibition gallery narrating the cultural heritage of the Lotud people, an eatery selling roast chicken, a small convenience shop, and other facilities including the aforementioned, newly constructed community hall. The site offers a cultural package at a charge of RM 85 (£16) per person that includes a guided tour of the exhibition gallery, detailed explanations of Lotud rituals and customs, and a river cruise, as well as cultural dances performed by the local Lotud villagers.

The Lotud longhouse, which encompasses the exhibition gallery, is partitioned into three separate rooms. The first room features a kitchen with a wooden stove, together with the Jilan family's heirlooms of eight *Pusaka* (heirloom) jars, known locally as *gusi*, which are customarily handed down from one generation to the next, as well as photographs of the last *Mangahau* ritual ceremony, which was conducted for the *gusi* in 2002. *Gusi* are mainly large stoneware glazed jars imported from China from as early as the fifteenth century or made by Chinese potters who migrated to mainland Southeast Asia or the Borneo coast thereafter (Rutter 1922; Harrisson 1986). They are primarily passed down by inheritance and are believed to have spiritual or magical powers (Rutter 1922; Harrisson 1986; Césard 2014). *Gusi* are greatly sought after by Indigenous people in Borneo as symbols of prestige and social status (Césard 2014). The *Mangahau* ceremony is a form of jar worship conducted by the Lotud people for blessing the spirits of the *gusi* and driving out evil (Rutter 1922). The second room features life-size mannequins of two Lotud high priestesses, known as *tantagas*, dressed in their ritual specialist costumes, alongside displays of their ritual paraphernalia. The third room features a Lotud bedroom, including a wooden bed decorated for a Lotud wedding ceremony, and life-size mannequins of a couple dressed in their Lotud marriage costumes. It also has on display several sets of Lotud costumes, which tourists are invited to try on for photo-taking opportunities.

The Linangkit Cultural Village was founded by the Jilan family, under the leadership of the late Datuk Patrick Jilan, who was also the Deputy Chairman of the Board of Trustees of Sabah Parks until his sudden death in May 2016. In an interview I conducted with him in August 2015, Datuk Patrick said of his motivation to establish the Linangkit Cultural Village:

> The objective is to preserve the culture of Lotud. The Lotud is a very small ethnic group, so if we don't protect the Lotud culture, that'll be finished, and the world will never see it again. The world will never know what Lotud is. Even now, the older generation don't encourage their sons and daughters to speak in their Lotud dialect. If we lose our culture and our dialect, and we only know our race is Lotud, it's no use already. That's why we set up the Linangkit Cultural Village to keep the Lotud culture alive. We want the world to know what's Lotud culture, dialect, food, and music.

The Linangkit Cultural Village was set up with an initial investment of RM 530,000 (£100,000) raised from within the Jilan family to construct a complex of buildings, including the Lotud longhouse, on their customary lands in Kampung Selupoh. Datuk Patrick spoke of his family's efforts to establish the Linangkit Cultural Village.

> Some put in RM 100,000 (£19,000), some put in RM 50,000 (£9,500). These are our own savings from the Jilan family. Initially, we invested

about RM 300,000 (£57,000), but the construction cost us another RM 230,000 (£43,000), so we invested about RM 530,000 (£100,000) altogether between 2007 and 2010. It's the Jilan family running it as a family business which helps to sustain it. We believe in the unity of the family, the strength of the family, the solidarity of the family to make the revenues and investment sustainable.

The Linangkit Cultural Village is managed as part of a variety of small business ventures owned by the Jilan family located within the compounds of the cultural village. These include an eatery, convenience store, a catering and event management business, a cultural troupe, and a small business tailoring Lotud costumes. The new community hall also provides an additional source of revenue for the family business, as it can be leased by local villagers, institutions, and corporations for a nominal fee to conduct corporate and community events, such as award-giving ceremonies and weddings, as well as for sporting activities such as badminton. As part of their catering and event management business, the Jilan family also has on offer packages for Lotud-themed weddings that include the rental of a wooden bed for the groom and bride decorated for a Lotud bride and groom. The exhibits are owned and curated by members of the Jilan family, then under the directive of Datuk Patrick in consultation with the village elders of Kampung Selupoh.

The revenues from the business ventures are injected back into the maintenance of the longhouse and its compounds, keeping the Linangkit Cultural Village financially sustainable. In addition, the staff working for the business ventures also maintain the exhibition gallery and run the cultural packages offered to tourists. It operates on a lean business model with two permanent staff managing day-to-day site operations and some of the business ventures, as well as a team of young people from the nearby Lotud villages who can be engaged as dancers, musicians, and helpers on a casual basis when demand arises.

Prior to its expansion in 2013, the Linangkit Cultural Village hosted around 150–200 tourists monthly. Due to its business model of supporting the upkeep of the exhibition gallery with a range of business ventures, the Linangkit Cultural Village does not rely solely on its admission revenue to sustain its operations. Datuk Patrick explained the business model:

> It's just sustainable and manageable. We don't care about the profit. Our profit margin is very small, but the most important thing is our goal. Our main objective is to preserve the Lotud culture, and the food, music, and everyday lives of the Lotud community.

Contexts, personalities, and interests

Datuk Patrick was extremely well-connected in the political circles of Sabah and drew on his wide political connections and influence for the development of the Linangkit Cultural Village. After working in the Entertainment and Radio Section of the Department of Broadcasting Malaysia, Sabah for a number of years in the 1970s, Datuk Patrick joined politics in the 1980s and became the Chairman of Sabah Sports Board after his political party, Parti Bersatu Sabah (PSB) or the United Sabah Party, came into power (*The Daily Express*, 6 May 2016). In 2007, he was appointed the Deputy Chairman of the Board of Trustees of Sabah Parks, a position he held until his death in May 2016 (Tee 2016). Datuk Patrick was an active member of the United Sabah Dusun Association (USDA), and a brother-in-law of Deputy State Assembly Speaker, Datuk Dr Johnson Tee (*The Daily Express*, 6 May 2016). In 2013, he was honoured as Panglima Gemilang Darjah Kinabalu (PGDK), or Commander of the Order of Kinabalu, which carried the title of Datuk for his services rendered to the Sabah State (Tee 2016).

When I interviewed him, Datuk Patrick cited education as principle mission of the Linangkit Cultural Village, as he identified the lack of interest among Lotud youths as the key challenge in preserving the Lotud cultural heritage. He hoped to encourage the younger generation to learn about their cultural heritage by convincing them that Lotud culture, especially Lotud music and dance, could improve their future employability. He drew on the instrumental value of culture to make a case for learning about Lotud cultural heritage. As he explained:

> The participation of Lotud youth is really needed to sustain our cultural heritage. Out of 100 Lotud youths, there are maybe 10 who are interested to learn about the music and dance, but they can only sustain their interests for 1 month, and then they disappear. So, we try to educate them. We pursue this idea that tradition is business. They are our main target for the *Bojumbak* festival, the Lotud music and dance festival. We consider tradition as business, so that this will help the youths make up their minds about learning their cultural heritage because it can be a profession in the future.

To this end, the Linangkit Cultural Village plays an active role in promoting Lotud cultural heritage among the local villagers, especially Lotud youths. For example, the Linangkit Cultural Village previously organised Sunday workshops for children from the nearby Lotud villages to learn about their cultural heritage. Datuk Patrick spoke of these workshops:

> From 2007 to 2008, during the school holidays, as well as some weekends, we get the older villagers to come to the cultural village to teach the young people about Lotud culture, about the Linangkit embroidery, dialect, music, and dance. We want to create the atmosphere that the young people will feel the culture, the dance, the music, so that when they grow up and get married, they know how to teach their children about Lotud culture. When they are in universities or go overseas, they can also tell their friends what Lotud culture is like, to keep our culture alive.

The Linangkit Cultural Village regularly hosts students from universities in Malaysia and abroad to promote Lotud cultural heritage to national and international audiences, as well as to capitalise on the economic potential of cultural heritage by providing casual employment for the local villagers, who are engaged as helpers and instructors to host the students and to teach them about Lotud cultural practices. In 2013, the Linangkit Cultural Village hosted a two-week cultural programme for students from Deakin University, Australia to learn about Linangkit embroidery and the Lotud dialect (Sario 2013).

The Linangkit Cultural Village appears to be well-integrated into the village life of Kampung Selupoh. Datuk Patrick's sister, Margaret Jilan, is the Village Headwoman of Kampung Selupoh, and has a duty of care over the local Lotud villagers, especially over *adat* (customs) matters. As such, the Linangkit Cultural Village regularly supports the hosting of communal activities and ritual ceremonies during the festive seasons by providing venue and other in-kind sponsorship such as ritual paraphernalia and consumables. Margaret uses its compounds as a venue to conduct discussions with villagers from Kampung Selupoh. The Linangkit Cultural Village is also a gathering place for a group of local youths, some of whom work at the site on a casual basis and hang out within the compounds to play football or use the small gym on-site. Since its re-opening in July 2015, the Linangkit Cultural Village has also running free yoga classes at the community hall every week, which is well-attended by the local Lotud villagers.

Seen in this light, the Linangkit Cultural Village can be conceptualised as an Indigenous museum that is intricately engaged with the needs of the local villagers. It promotes community cohesion by providing a platform for local villagers to come together for communal activities and ritual ceremonies. It also draws upon Lotud cultural heritage 'as a source of authority and power' (Stanley 2007: 16) to help locals cope with rapid urbanisation and modernisation by offering opportunities for work, as well as to learn about their cultural heritage. This will not only inculcate in them a sense of pride for their Indigenous culture and identity but also improve their future employability.

The name of the Linangkit Cultural Village 'Linangkit' is derived from a term used to describe a panel of dense fabric produced by the needle-weaving technique (Figure 6.2) that is practised by several Indigenous groups living in the western and northern regions of Sabah (Lasimbang and Moo-Tan 1997; Regis 2007). Sometimes called 'tapestry weaving' or 'needle weaving', the Linangkit technique uses a needle and thread to create a system of tiny intricately connected identical knots to form a dense fabric of colourful motifs, which are used on the costumes of several Indigenous groups in Sabah, particularly amongst the Dusun, Iranun, Bajau, Lotud, and Rungus people (Regis 2007). The Linangkit technique is similar to the European technique of 'tatting' or 'frivolité', although Linangkit weaving uses only a needle and thread to form a panel of dense strong fabric with

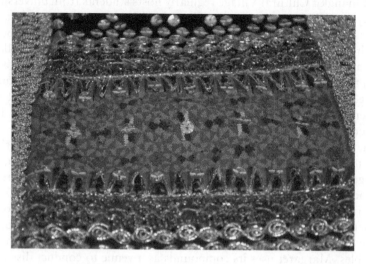

Figure 6.2 A Lotud motif on a Lotud costume made with the Linangkit needle-weaving technique. Photograph: Author.

high durability, while the European techniques of tatting and frivolité involve the use of a small bobbin to create a lace-like fabric (Lasimbang and Moo-Tan 1997). The Linangkit technique is used to embellish the black Lotud costumes with geometric motifs, usually a repeating pattern with crosses in the middle, known to be inspired by watermelon seeds, and sewn predominantly in colours of orange and red, which are generally associated with the Lotud people (Lasimbang and Moo-Tan 1997).

While the Linangkit technique is not unique to the Lotud people, and therefore cannot be solely claimed as a Lotud cultural practice, it has been adopted as an icon synonymous with the Lotud identity for branding purposes. As Datuk Patrick explained, inferring a desire to differentiate the Lotud ethnic group from the terminology 'Kadazandusun', which has been used to denote all Dusunic groups in Sabah, including the Lotud:

'Linangkit' is synonymous of 'Lotud'. Other ethnic groups also have Linangkit but they don't call it Linangkit, so the Lotud is the only ethnic group that calls this weaving technique 'Linangkit'. So that's why we make use of the term 'Linangkit'. Here, people know that 'Linangkit' means Lotud. We don't have to call our cultural village 'Lotud Cultural Village'. 'Linangkit' sounds much better, more commercial. And people know 'Linangkit' much better than they know 'Lotud'. People know about the Kadazan, but this is mainly for people from the Penampang District. We're Lotud, we don't consider ourselves as Kadazan.

The Linangkit Cultural Village thus serves as a vehicle for the Lotud people to assert the uniqueness of their cultural identity in relation to the Malay-Muslims and other Indigenous subgroups in Sabah.

While the Linangkit technique is hailed as the pride of Lotud people, since around a decade ago, it has gradually been replaced by cross-stitch as a way of embellishing Lotud costumes, as the Linangkit technique is difficult to master, and the geometric motifs made using the Linangkit technique are time-consuming to produce. According to Yatie, a worker at the cultural village:

> The cross-stitch method of doing Linangkit is known as modern Linangkit or replica Linangkit. It was invented as an easier replacement about ten years ago, when the local communities become too lazy to do the original Linangkit and the eye-sights of the old women become too poor to cope with the embroidery. Good eyesight is needed for the intricate works of the real Linangkit embroidery.

Due to these factors, geometric motifs made using the Linangkit technique are becoming a rarity and they are now highly valued among the Lotud people as material possessions and as family heirlooms. This has also led to a substantial increase in their market price over the last decade. Many Lotud families no longer make the Lotud costumes themselves but are turning to the market to purchase their Lotud costumes, leading to the growth of a lucrative market for Linangkit embroidery. The naming of the Linangkit Cultural Village after the Linangkit embroidery seems to be a form of strategic instrumentalisation by Datuk Patrick to capitalise on the market recognition of and appreciation for Linangkit embroidery in Sabah in order to enhance awareness of the Linangkit Cultural Village and the Lotud people.

In 2013, the Jilan family received a grant of RM 1.5 million (£283,000) from the Sabah State Government to construct a community hall (Figure 6.3) beside the Lotud longhouse, in exchange for transferring the ownership of the 1 acre of land on which the Linangkit Cultural Village sits to the State Government. This plot of land is relatively small, nested within a larger plot of ancestral lands owned by the Jilan family. Datuk Patrick spoke of the family's success in lobbying the government for the award of the grant:

> The government has seen what we have done. We've performed better in their eyes, based on what they've heard and what they've seen on TV. I did explain to the government, if you don't help, we are equivalent to endangered species, ethnic group wise. The government is very good, very proactive, especially our assemblymen like Panglima Hajiji. They are very supportive of us, having seen what we've done from 2007 to 2013. We give the government the land, but in return, we are appointed to do the management because the government experience is that,

Figure 6.3 The newly constructed community hall funded by the Sabah State Government at the premises of the Linangkit Cultural Village. Photograph: Author.

according to some government officials, if they just give a community, say RM 2 million (£380,000), nobody will look after the building to completion. That will be a white elephant. It is a burden to the government, and of course, the people will always take all the materials. But this one, the government has appointed us to look after the community hall of the Lotud community. The accountability is there.

As part of the agreement for government investment in the Linangkit Cultural Village, the Jilan family relinquished the management rights to the Linangkit Cultural Village to Persatuan Komulakan Lotud Sabah, the Lotud Youth Association (KLOSA), with Peter Lintar, KLOSA's president, who is a distant relative of the Jilan family, appointed as its Chief Executive Officer. KLOSA, in turn, appointed the Jilan family to manage the Linangkit Cultural Village as a service provider. As Datuk Patrick spoke of the family decision to relinquish management rights to KLOSA:

It's much better that the younger generation, the Y-Generation, is doing the marketing and management. They know better about engagement in the age of Internet and Facebook, and it's an opportunity for them to learn. If the elderly people just control the cultural village, then it's no use for them. We try to build up a following for the Lotud culture by giving the younger generation a chance to do the management on their own. We will not interfere with their decision, but of course, the elderly people like us will tell them what the real culture is, so that they will not deviate from the original culture.

The Jilan family, especially Datuk Patrick, can be conceptualised as brokers for the Linangkit Cultural Village, mediating between the business world and the local village economy of Kampung Selupoh. In particular, Datuk Patrick drew upon the 'culture for development' rhetoric, positioning the Linangkit Cultural Village as a vehicle for the preservation of Lotud cultural heritage while capitalising on the potential of cultural tourism to develop the village economy and improve the livelihoods of local Lotud people by creating employment. Although Datuk Patrick emphasised the preservation of Lotud cultural heritage as his primary objective for setting up the Linangkit Cultural Village, it appears that the site has also been instrumentalised as a means to advance the business interests, extend the political influence, and elevate the social status of the Jilan family. This instrumentalisation is premised on the production and maintenance of cultural differences (c.f. Appadurai 1996) between the Lotud people and other Indigenous subgroups in Sabah.

As a broker, Datuk Patrick was also mediating and translating between state agencies and the local village economy of Kampung Selupoh to secure government funding for the building of a new community hall at the Linangkit Cultural Village. While he attributed the Sabah State Government's financial support for the Linangkit Cultural Village to his family's proven record of good management, it appears that it was his extensive political connections, especially his role as the Deputy Chairman of the Board of Trustees of Sabah Parks that helped him secure the government grant. In this case, the Linangkit Cultural Village may have served as a mechanism for facilitating the channelling of government funds to reward political allies, a form of money politics widely practiced in Sabah's political arena, especially in the timber logging industry (Reid 2009; Straumann 2014). A respondent who had known the Jilan family for many years said of the new community hall funded by the Sabah State Government: 'The new building [at Linangkit Cultural Village] which the government is funding probably costs three times more than its actual construction costs. These government contracts are all about politics'. Seen in this light, the complicated management arrangement following the award of the government grant, that is the transfer of the management right of the Linangkit Cultural Village to KLOSA, which was later contracted back to the Jilan family, as well as the transfer of the land on which the Linangkit Cultural Village sits to the government, can be conceived of as a strategy to prevent the Sabah State Government from being perceived as directly subsiding a private enterprise with public funds. The project also demonstrates Sabah State Government's support for its Indigenous people, and its endorsement of the 'culture for development' discourse that is widely promoted by international bodies such as UNESCO.

While the preservation of Lotud cultural heritage is frequently cited by the Jilan family as the primary motivator for the establishment of the Linangkit Cultural Village, it appears that Lotud culture has been mobilised to enhance the Jilan family's business interests, political influence, and social status. These agendas also align with the interests of other stakeholders, be it the local Lotud villagers who have been contracted to work at the cultural village, the tourists who wish to learn about the Lotud cultural heritage, or the Sabah State Government, which seeks to promote cultural tourism in Sabah. It also provides a platform for others to learn about Lotud cultural heritage while serving as a vehicle for asserting Indigenous Lotud identity. The Linangkit Cultural Village simultaneously fulfils multiple agendas for different stakeholders, who instrumentalise Lotud cultural heritage and the Linangkit Cultural Village for their own agendas and objectives. However, the arrangement seems to condone wider practices of money politics among the political elites in Sabah, a key issue underlying the incessant encroachment onto native customary lands and territories belonging to the Indigenous people in Sabah today.

Since the re-opening of the Linangkit Cultural Village to tourists in July 2015, and until his unexpected death, Datuk Patrick had been mulling over plans to expand his business interests by developing a homestay accommodation, based around the historical Lotud lifestyle, at the Linangkit Cultural Village on a plot of his family's ancestral land across a small river, having received some interest from tourists. He spoke about this long-term vision:

> Just imagine that we will market to the whole world, we want to go back to the basics: Year 1800 or Year 1900. Come to the Linangkit Cultural Village to experience life in the past. Our visitors will spend at least three days and two nights here, no lights, no telephone, no TV in a small hut which we plan to expand on our lands across the river. We have an old well there, where you can take water for your consumption; we will provide fishing nets, so that you can fish for your own food in the river, which you can cook in the hut over wood fire. In this way, you can experience life in the olden days. That's our plan, so hopefully it will be successful.

When I asked what he thought about accommodating the tourists within the Lotud longhouse, Datuk Patrick replied:

> Some western people want to experience sleeping with the sacred jars, but we have to consider the proposal, whether to allow them or not. I don't think we can allow this now. Our consideration is the respect for the jars. These jars are collected about 600 to 700 years ago by our ancestors and have been in circulation among our family since. We can't control what the people who stay there do with our jars. They can do a lot of things which may damage our jars. If the jars are damaged, we can't replace them.

While members of the Jilan family are open to instrumentalising their cultural heritage for tourism, they do value their family heirlooms, especially their *gusi*, and have reservations about potentially subjecting these material objects to damage or destruction. This suggests that aspects of Lotud heritage are still regarded as inalienable and have affective properties for Indigenous people, who desire to preserve them for posterity, even as they are instrumentalised for economic, political, and social objectives.

While Datuk Patrick regarded the *gusi* as family heirlooms that must be protected from damage and destruction, he did not believe in their spiritual powers. As he explained:

> For the question on how to appease the spirits of the Chinese jars, that one I don't understand, because I believe in prayers, and in our prayers, we believe that the spirits do not exist anymore. Different people, different views, different perceptions. Just like me, I believe that Jesus Christ is our God, and he will understand but we also don't deny those people who want to perform their way of worshipping. In Linangkit Cultural Village, the jars are blessed by priests with prayers. We have our Father to come over here to do the blessings.

Datuk Patrick's revelation was revealing, as it alluded to his lack of belief in the spiritual properties of the *gusi* owing to his conversion to Christianity. It seems that Datuk Patrick has become alienated from Indigenous Lotud spiritual beliefs and the efficacy of the Lotud ritual practices, although the material culture may still carry affective properties for him as family heirlooms. This suggests that different people have different levels of attachment to different aspects of their cultural heritage, which, in turn, has an impact on how different aspects of cultural heritage are valorised and practised by different members of a community.

Transformation, representation, and interpretation of culture

To officially mark the re-opening of the Linangkit Cultural Village to tourists, a *Mohlukas* ceremony was conducted from 15 to 22 August 2015 at the Lotud longhouse. Based on Lotud cultural beliefs, a newly constructed house must be cleansed through a *Mohlukas* ceremony to remove malignant spirits and other undesirable elements that may adversely affect the new occupants of the house, and to ensure a blessed life for its dwellers (Hashim 2007; Cai 2016). A *Mohlukas* ceremony, which typically takes place over a week, entails the continuous chanting of the *rinait* by the *tantagas* over several days and the ritual sacrifices of animals such as buffalos and chickens.

The *Mohlukas* ceremony was held to placate some members of the Jilan family who felt that it was important to perform the ceremony. As Datuk Patrick explained:

> The request came from my sister, Margaret, the Village Headwoman, and a few of the elders. It's also to provide people who have never seen the ceremony a chance to see it. It's our culture, but we don't believe in all these rituals. We are Christian. Because we don't want to have sour relationships amongst our families, so we just give money to perform the rituals. My brother and I bought the buffalo, and my sister also contributed something.

While Datuk Patrick did not believe in the ritual efficacy of the *Mohlukas* ceremony owing to his conversion to Christianity, he was willing to accommodate the request of his sister, Margaret, and the village elders, to host the ceremony at the Linangkit Cultural Village, and even to contribute financially. This attests to the process of mediation and negotiation between the different stakeholders regarding the staging of their ritual practices. Datuk Patrick's interest in the *Mohlukas* ceremony lay not in its affective properties or its ritual efficacy, but in documenting the process for posterity. As he elaborated:

> I don't believe in these rituals. Older people, yes. But what we have done for *Mohlukas* is really to do recordings, so that people like you can see what we are doing with the ritual. Then I said to our family, we just perform the rituals, we ask those people who can perform to do it. This will be the last recordings of the *Mohlukas*, and we can do a documentary of the occasion. But different people have different perceptions, especially people with no religion. They don't have religion, they don't worship gods, but they only believe that the rituals can help them. But as far as they are doing good, we will always support them. We don't insult them, we don't say your ritual is not true. We don't make our family relationships sour, so we just perform.

This also demonstrates the differential attitudes towards Indigenous beliefs and ritual practices among the Christian Lotud converts in Sabah. While some Lotud people such as Margaret and the village elders still believe in and practise their Indigenous rituals alongside their Christian beliefs, others, such as Datuk Patrick, reject these Indigenous beliefs and ritual practices in favour of a purely Christian doctrine. This, in turn, has an impact on the valorisation and treatment of different aspects of Lotud cultural practice among the different members of the Lotud community and resonates with what Chua (2012: 522) has described as the different 'shades and degrees' in the valorisation of Christianity among the Bidayuh people in Sarawak. She warns us against treating 'continuity and discontinuity as clear-cut, diametrically opposed categories' in understanding the process of conversion from animist religions to world religions.

To identify a suitable date for the *Mohlukas* ceremony, a *Monolibabou* ritual was conducted in the middle of the night of 15 July 2015 at the longhouse to seek guidance from the spirits for the *Mohlukas* ceremony (Figure 6.4). A *Monolibabou* ritual is part of a Lotud consultation process with the spiritual world on spiritual matters (Cai and John Baptist 2016). The *Monolibabou* ritual attracted the participation of many village elders from Kampung Selupoh. The wooden bed decorated for a Lotud wedding ceremony and mannequins of a Lotud wedding couple were temporarily removed from the exhibition gallery to make way for the ceremony. After a potluck dinner at the Linangkit Cultural Village prepared by a few village elders, the presiding spirit medium, known locally as *libabou*, Odun Sobinting (Puan Jumat Gumat), prepared the ritual paraphernalia, which included husked white rice grains and unhusked red rice grains placed in two separate woven trays, a special ceremonial sword called *lungkaris*, and a plate with seven rice balls, coconut oil, betel nuts, and sireh leaves sliced into seven portions, an uncooked egg, and *bahar*, the Lotud coconut wine. After her habitual puff of local tobacco, Odun Sobinting sat cross-legged facing a window in the dimly lit longhouse, covered her entire body with a *sarong* (local tube cloth), and started chanting softly while holding a string of beads.

After several hours of chanting, Odun Sobinting began to jerk violently and wave her hands frantically under the *sarong*. She started to

Figure 6.4 A spirit medium, *libabou*, in trance for the *Monolibabou* ritual conducted at the Linangkit Cultural Village. The *libabou*, covered by a purple *sarong*, is chanting softly while holding a string of beads. Photograph: Author.

talk in a low voice, as if she was having a conversation with someone. She then waved her hands again, as if she was bidding someone goodbye, before she sank back into her chanting. Over the course of the night, Odun Sobinting went in and out of trance, and communicated with several spirits, alternating between talking and chanting. During the *Monolibabou* ritual, the villagers received permission from the spirits to conduct the *Mohlukas* ceremony one month later, on 15 August 2015. The *Monolibabou* ritual can be conceptualised as a staged performance of Lotud cultural heritage, which is produced, performed, and negotiated through the mobilisation of a selection of ritual paraphernalia and the ritual performance of the *libabou* that conform with the expectations of the Lotud consultation process with the spiritual world. Specifically, the *libabou*'s ritual performance of chanting and establishing contact with spiritual beings, seeking their permission to conduct the *Mohlukas* ceremony, and waving them goodbye while going in and out of trance conformed with the manner of a Lotud consultation with the spiritual world as understood within the Indigenous Lotud cosmology. Coupled with the ritual paraphernalia, which served as markers to inscribe notions of Lotud 'authentic' ritual practices, the *libabou*'s ritual performance thus acquired 'performative authenticity' (Zhu 2012) and carried ritual efficacy for the villagers participating in the ritual.

The grand occasion finally arrived on 15 August 2015. The *Mohlukas* ceremony began at dawn with the ritual sacrifice of a buffalo by the riverbank near the Linangkit Cultural Village, as an offering to the spirits and the ancestors. The slaughtered buffalo was then covered with dried coconut leaves, which were burnt to char the skin, before it was cut up and cooked for the guests. According to Lotud beliefs, the head of the buffalo should be hung below the stairs of the longhouse while one of its legs is hung at the top of the longhouse (Hashim 2007). On this occasion, the head and the leg of the buffalo were not hung at the longhouse but were cooked for the feast. As Datuk Patrick explained:

> In the past, the purpose of hanging the buffalo head is because we don't have a freezer to preserve the meat, so we hang them at the longhouse for the blood to drip dry, so that there's something to eat the following day. But this time, it's different, it's modern day. So, we ask the family members to cook it, we shouldn't waste food.

This serves as an example of how Lotud ritual practices continue to evolve over time, as the local villagers rationalise their cultural practices in response to modernisation. This demonstrates how adaptations to contemporary circumstances are made to the *Mohlukas* ceremony that may deviate from the ritual accuracies of the past and attests to the multifaceted, dynamic, and ever-evolving manifestations of cultural representations that are socially constructed by different stakeholders, according to context and interpretation (Graham et al. 2000; Harrison 2013).

It was a very busy morning for the Lotud villagers of Kampung Selupoh, as they worked together like a big family to prepare the dishes for the grand feast of buffalo meat that would mark the commencement of the *Mohlukas* ceremony. There was *Sup Tarajun* (a Lotud buffalo meat soup made with lemongrass and other local spices), curried buffalo meat, grilled buffalo meat, and stewed buffalo meat, and the longhouse was soon infused with mouth-watering fragrances. The kitchen display at the longhouse was converted into a working kitchen, as the local villagers cooked the buffalo meat over the wooden stove, and two other gas stoves temporarily installed for the occasion, alongside the *gusi* and the exhibit displays. On this occasion, the exhibition gallery in the longhouse was converted into a community space, with the wooden bed decorated for a Lotud wedding ceremony and mannequins of a Lotud couple temporarily removed to make way for conducting the ritual blessing for the Linangkit Cultural Village. The use of the exhibition gallery and its objects for the *Mohlukas* ceremony demonstrates a different manner of contemplating the museum's contents. The emphasis on the role of the museum in transmitting cultural heritage, rather than in displaying objects, resembles the characteristics of Indigenous museums and Indigenous curation, as suggested by Kreps (2003) and Stanley (2007).

While the buffalo meat was being cooked for the grand feast, some local villagers were busy hanging up the colourful panels of appliqued cloth with distinctive geometric motifs, known as the *lalavangan*, along the walls of the third room in the longhouse. The ceiling of the room was also decorated with strips of colourful fabrics known as *sandai*. Mats and pillows were laid on the floor for the *tantagas* who would be conducting the *Mohlukas* ceremony over the week. The second room, in which mannequins of two Lotud *tantagas* and their ritual paraphernalia were displayed, was temporarily cordoned off with a big curtain to secure the ritual paraphernalia from theft during the ceremony. As Datuk Patrick explained:

> We cover the museum's showcase with materials during the ritual. We didn't want to show them, because they're small items that we can put in the pocket. That's not only damage, but we may lose items. But for the sleepover, rituals and eating in the longhouse, we're not worried about it.

Although the most valuable items in the longhouse were the *gusi*, which cost thousands of RM each at their current market values, they were left where they were in the working kitchen, as the members of the Jilan family confidently told me that no one would dare to steal them. The Lotud people believe that these *gusi* have spirits that will punish anyone who disturbs them. This demonstrates how ritual prohibitions and cultural taboos can serve as an Indigenous method of safeguarding Indigenous cultural heritage

(Kreps 2014). That said, such cultural taboos will likely have limited influence on others who do not believe in their ritual efficacy.

It was a grand occasion and many guests were invited to attend the start of the *Mohlukas* ceremony. As noon approached, six *tantagas* from the Sub-district of Tamparuli in the District of Tuaran, headed by chief *tantagas*, Odun Badin, arrived at the longhouse, as did the guests, where they were treated to a sumptuous meal of buffalo meat dishes and *bahar*. The guests included the District Officer of Tuaran, the District Cultural Head of Tuaran, the village heads of other nearby Lotud villages, as well as families and friends of the Jilan family, who served as witnesses to the ceremony. The local elites and community leaders were invited to sit together around a group of shared dishes to symbolise the invitation extended to the spirits to partake in the merry-making of the *Mohlukas* ceremony (Figure 6.5).

Ritual ceremonies can be viewed as a status symbol in Sabah, as they are expensive to organise and perform. Patronised by local elites and community leaders, they also provide an important platform for building political connections. The *Mohlukas* ceremony served as an opportunity for the Jilan family to demonstrate their wealth and enhance their social prestige. The ceremony, which had been staged by the Lotud *tantagas* and the village elders mainly to bless the Linangkit Cultural Village, had thus been mobilised by local elites and community leaders for political networking. The Lotud villagers participated in the ritual ceremony as an occasion for communal gathering and for the assertion of their social identity and cultural pride.

Figure 6.5 The local elites and community leaders sat together around a group of shared dishes to symbolise the invitation extended to the spirits to partake in the merry-making of the *Mohlukas* ceremony held at the Linangkit Cultural Village. Photograph: Author.

Although Datuk Patrick did not believe in the ritual efficacy of the *Mohlukas* ceremony, there was much political and social capital to be gained by the Jilan family for hosting the ceremony. The ceremony also carried other instrumental values for Datuk Patrick, such as signifying his support for his sister as the Village Headwoman and his respect for the village elders, gaining the trust and support from the local villagers of Kampung Selupoh, demonstrating to the state agencies that he had made good of the government funding for the new community hall, and, importantly, signalling his sincerity about preserving the Lotud cultural heritage, all of which would contribute indirectly to enhancing his business interests, political influence, and social status within Sabah society. Presumably, Datuk Patrick's lack of belief in the Indigenous ritual practices might have made it easier for him to instrumentalise his cultural heritage for economic, political, and social ends. This demonstrates that the *Mohlukas* ceremony can simultaneously serve different agendas and objectives of different stakeholders, as they may not conflict with one another.

The ritual began with a village elder singing the *moninjau* song to mark the commencement of the *Mohlukas* ceremony, in a ritual named *Mogkawangan*. After sprinkling some *bahar* around the longhouse, the *tantagas* sat down in the gallery decorated with *lalavangan* and *sandai*, and started chanting the *rinait*. The Lotud *rinait* consist of long ritual chants and prayers. They form a unique genre of poetic oral tradition, constituted of paired lines with the same meanings, the first in vernacular language and the second in ritual language. The Lotud *rinait* recount the Lotud creation of the world, the legends of the Lotud deities, the genesis of rice, prescriptions for moral living, and other cultural aspects of Lotud cultural life. The *rinait* can be recited with loud chanting or soft whispering, depending on the local contexts (Pugh-Kitingan and John Baptist 2009). Various sections of the Lotud *rinait* were narrated by the *tantagas* throughout the week-long ceremony.

The longhouse was filled with the laughter and chattering of the guests, who would occasionally break into a loud cheer. Even as the guests took their leave in the evening, the *tantagas* continued chanting throughout the night. The chanting carried on for four days and nights, during which some *tantagas* and villagers stayed in the longhouse. On the second day, a chicken was ritually sacrificed to the spirits. The elaborate ritual featured a variety of paraphernalia such as the offerings of unhusked red rice grains and husked white rice grains placed into separate trays, a *lungkaris*, the *komburongoh*, a chain of metal plates known as *sindavang*, and a bowl of cooked rice with a fish tail placed in it. After prayers were recited by the *tantagas*, the chicken was slaughtered outside the longhouse, where its blood was left to flow onto the floor so that the spirits could receive the sacrifice. The inedible parts of the chicken were later buried along the riverbank, while its meat was cooked with *bambangan*, the local wild mango, in a soup that was later served to the local villagers.

Figure 6.6 The *tantagas* jingling their *sindavang* during the *Mohlukas* ceremony conducted in the garden. Photograph: Author.

On the third day, a second chicken was ritually sacrificed in a similar manner, and a chick was sacrificed and buried at the base of the longhouse. The *tantagas* recited prayers with the live chick outside the longhouse, before it was killed and buried together with a bowl of cooked rice and a fish tail placed in a coconut husk (Figure 6.6). On the fourth day, one more chick was sacrificed and buried at the longhouse, while another chick was sacrificed and buried near the riverbank to appease the river spirits for the safety of the local villagers who use the river.

The ceremony broke for a day of rest, before continuing with a second ritual called the *Monumbul* on the sixth day. Dressed in their Lotud ritual costumes that included a gold-plated headband called *siwot*, the two *tantagas* presiding over the ritual recited the *rinait* to give blessings to the house, accompanied by music from two Lotud musical instruments, namely the gong and *gantang*. They were also jingling their *sindavang*, contributing to a beautiful symphony of music through the evening, as they coordinated their chanting in a rhythmic tone. The ritual music served as a channel to communicate with the spirits. One *tangatas* chanted inside the longhouse, while another *tantagas* took her place at the verandah of the longhouse, before they adjourned to the riverbank to continue the chanting. As a mark of respect to the spirits on that day, the *tantagas* refrained from consuming meat, as well as cultivated fruits and vegetables.

The culmination of the *Mohlukas* ceremony took place on the eighth day, after another day of rest, in a ritual known as the *Monolinsim*, to appease the spirits of the river and to chase away evil spirits to prevent mishaps in the river. A wooden structure was erected, and the presiding *tantagas*, who was also a *libabou*, conducted a *modsuut* to communicate with the spirits in trance. As the *tantagas* chanted, with her body covered in a *sarong*, her familiar spirit was sent to establish communication with the spirits of the river, as well as other spirits involved in the *Mohlukas* ceremony to confirm if they had received the ritual offerings made by the local villagers. The week-long *Mohlukas* ceremony ended with the ritual sacrifice of another chicken along the riverbank, which was later cooked and served to the participants of the ceremony.

While the first day of the *Mohlukas* ceremony was presided over by at least seven *tantagas* and attended by over a hundred guests, the rest of the ceremony was usually performed by only one or two *tantagas*, who were supported by a handful of three to four village elders, including Margaret, the Village Headwoman. As I was conducting fieldwork at the Linangkit Cultural Village during the *Mohlukas* ceremony, I inevitably became the person undertaking the documentation of the ceremony for the Jilan family. I was with the *tantagas* and village elders at the Linangkit Cultural Village throughout the ceremony, and I documented most of the ceremony through photography and audio-visual recordings, which were later passed on to the Jilan family for their records. My presence at the *Mohlukas* ceremony certainly impacted on the manner in which the ritual was carried out, as the *tantagas* performed the ritual with a serious demeanour when they were being filmed but adopted a more relaxed attitude when my video camera was not in operation.

As one of the village elders participating in the ceremony was a Muslim convert, the slaughter of the chickens used in the ritual sacrifice was performed by this Muslim villager while reciting verses from the Quran, after the *tantagas* had recited the relevant *rinait* for the sacrifice. However, the inclusion of the Muslim prayers did not seem to affect the ritual efficacy of the *Mohlukas* ceremony, and no one commented or seemed to mind consuming the food that had been blessed by the Muslim prayers. This alludes to another mediation and negotiation among the *tantagas* and village elders at the *Mohlukas* ceremony to accommodate the different religious needs of the ceremony participants, attesting to the multifaceted and dynamic manifestations of the *Mohlukas* ceremony as a cultural representation that is socially and culturally constructed and mediated by different stakeholders (Harrison 2013).

While the *Monolinsim* ritual marked the official finale of the *Mohlukas* ceremony, for Datuk Patrick and his immediate family, it was the private Christian ceremony conducted at the Linangkit Cultural Village on the following day that marked the conclusion of the ceremony. As he recounted:

> When we set up the cultural village in 2007, we did some Christian prayers to bless the place, and after completion, we did the housewarming and the blessing. We also did the prayers and blessings when we put in the Chinese jars. This time, after they completed the *Mohlukas* ceremony on Saturday, we performed our beliefs, and did the full Christian

prayers on Sunday. We didn't want the bad spirits here, so we cleansed the place with our Christian prayers. We depend on God. So, we got a priest here, and blessed the place. It was a private affair.

When asked if it was intended to cleanse the spirits arising from the *Mohlukas* ceremony, Datuk Patrick clarified:

No, we don't mean that. It was not because of the *Mohlukas* rituals. If you understand, the bad spirits come to the world, much earlier than human beings. We believe in all that. We don't want to insult other religions, we respect them. No sour communication and relationship with the people, because those people still believe in all the ritual ways, let them go, we don't insult them. We're happy with the ceremony because all these rituals may not be performed anymore. They cost money, maybe, Peter spent RM 1,000 (£190) on the rice.

He added that Lotud ritual ceremonies were merely a commercial gimmick:

Maybe some of the communities, they did believe in the rituals, but for me, whatever rituals you perform, that's for commercial, because of tourism. The belief is no more.

Although there were earlier discussions on publicising the *Mohlukas* ceremony at the Linangkit Cultural Village as a tourism event on the Sabah Tourism Board's event calendar, this did not happen. Presumably, Datuk Patrick may have intended to market the *Mohlukas* ceremony as a tourism event but decided otherwise after discussions with his family members and the villagers of Kampung Selupoh. The decision to hold the *Mohlukas* ceremony at the Linangkit Cultural Village was mediated and negotiated by different stakeholders according to their different agendas. Some of the villagers, especially the *tantagas* and village elders, wanted to valorise the ceremony for the altruistic objective of appeasing the spirits and blessing the compounds of the Linangkit Cultural Village. This points to the uneven valorisation of Lotud ritual practices among the Lotud people, alluding to the problems of conceptualising the Lotud people as a collective community with a common agenda and a clear position on the management of their cultural heritage.

On this occasion, the *Mohlukas* ceremony held at the Linangkit Cultural Village was not staged for tourist consumption, but as a community event for the consumption of the local elites, community leaders, and the Lotud villagers. However, this did not prevent the different stakeholders from instrumentalising the ceremony for different agendas. For Datuk Patrick, it served as a vehicle to demonstrate the wealth and social prestige of the Jilan family, while offering a platform for political networking, thus extending his political and social capital. For the Lotud villagers, it served as an opportunity for communal gathering, and an opportunity to assert their social identity and cultural pride. For the *tantagas* and Lotud villagers who still believe in the ritual efficacy of the *Mohlukas* ceremony, it was a demonstration of their faith in their ritual beliefs and practices. This again demonstrates how different agendas and objectives of different stakeholders can co-exist for the community staging of the *Mohlukas* ceremony at the Linangkit Cultural Village.

Like the *Monolibabou* ritual, the week-long *Mohlukas* ceremony can be considered a staged performance of Lotud cultural practices mediated and negotiated by different stakeholders according to their expectations of what comprises an 'authentic' *Mohlukas* ceremony, which serves not only to appease the spirits but also to fulfil the myriad economic, political, and social objectives of the different stakeholders, be they members of the Jilan family, villagers of Kampung Selupoh, or the wider Lotud community, as well as other political and community leaders in Sabah. At times, certain segments of the ceremony were modified to accommodate the needs of some members of the community, such as the inclusion of Muslim prayers for the slaughter of the chickens used in the ritual sacrifice, which did not seem to affect the ritual efficacy of the *Mohlukas* ceremony for the *tantagas* and village elders. At other times, compromises were made to preserve the integrity of the *Mohlukas* ceremony, for example, by not publicising it as a tourism event.

Like the Kadazan *Magavau* ceremony, the *Mohlukas* ceremony has been transformed into a form of cultural performance for tourist consumption. It was one of the seven ritual ceremonies featured in the 'Aki Nabalu' musical performed during Sabah Fest 2014 cultural festival (see Chapter 5). In 2014, the same group of *tantagas* from the Sub-district of Tamparuli in the District of Tuaran performed a short segment of the *Mohlukas* ceremony, condensing a week-long ritual ceremony into a five-minute performance, demonstrating how Lotud ritual practices have also been transformed into a form of cultural performance to meet the needs of touristification and commercialisation. Their involvement was mediated by Judeth John Baptist from the Sabah State Museum, who has a close relationship with the *tantagas*. Judeth John Baptist grew up in the District of Tuaran and had previously sponsored the residency of a head *tantagas* at the Sabah State Museum to document the Lotud *rinait*.

As with the treatment of the Indigenous ritual practices for the 'Aki Nabalu' musical, Judeth John Baptist has sought to preserve the integrity of the ritual practices in the musical by ensuring no or minimal interference to the sequence of the rituals as decided by the ritual specialists and local villagers. Like the *Magavau* ceremony staged for the 'Aki Nabalu' musical, the staged *Mohlukas* ceremony featured a group of performers dressed in Lotud costumes setting up a miniature Lotud house on the stage as a prelude for the performance of the *Mohlukas* ritual by the *tantagas*. In the five-minute segment allocated for this ritual performance, the *tantagas* circled the miniature Lotud house several times as they jingled their *sindavang* and chanted the *Mohlukas rinait*, as a photograph of other paraphernalia used in the ritual was shown on a screen. It did not feature any of the ritual sacrifices made during the *Mohlukas* ceremony conducted at the Linangkit Cultural Village. The staged performance of the *Mohlukas* ceremony at the 'Aki Nabalu' musical constituted a 'front stage' where the week-long ceremony was shortened to a five-minute segment devoid of ritual paraphernalia and sacrifices for tourist consumption, against a 'back stage' of living vernacular cultural practices performed at the Linangkit Cultural Village for the villagers' own consumption, taking place out of the sight of tourists and starkly different from its performance on the 'front stage'. This demonstrates how the concept of authenticity is a mediated experience between various stakeholders and serves diverse objectives for different occasions.

Frictions, tensions, and issues

In August 2016, I returned to Tuaran to visit the Linangkit Cultural Village and my host families, as well as to pay my respects to the family of the late Datuk Patrick, who had died suddenly in May earlier that year. At the Linangkit Cultural Village, I ran into its Chief Executive Officer, Peter Lintar, who was at the cultural village for a meeting. My polite enquiries about how the Linangkit Cultural Village had been doing for the past year since my fieldwork had ended were quickly met with two solemn words: 'not good'. I was surprised at this revelation, but the situation soon became clear as I caught up with several of my research participants. Since the death of Datuk Patrick, their salary payments had become rather uncertain. Some of the revenue from the cultural packages and the rental of the community hall had gone missing. There had been a visible decline in visitor numbers. No activities were being planned, and hence, there was not much work to be done. The financial sustainability of the Linangkit Cultural Village seemed to have fallen rapidly and was under threat in the months following Datuk Patrick's death. While the Linangkit Cultural Village appeared to have been well-managed during my fieldwork from July to September 2015, it fell into disarray shortly after the passing of its principal broker. The viability of the Linangkit Cultural Village seemed to hinge almost entirely on Datuk Patrick, who managed the cultural village by mediating the different needs and demands of its stakeholders and marshalled resources to ensure smooth day-to-day operations and sustained development.

Although Peter had been appointed as the Chief Executive Officer of the Linangkit Cultural Village when it re-opened its doors to tourists in July 2015, the main authority of the cultural village appeared to have remained with Datuk Patrick. Peter faced continued difficulties and resistance in stepping into the role. The prevailing structure of the Linangkit Cultural Village served to extend the authority of the cultural village to a powerful broker, in this case Datuk Patrick, and entrench a working relationship that was difficult to replace after his death. In particular, Datuk Patrick had been able to command influence over his family members, who were managing other business ventures within the compounds of the Linangkit Cultural Village, and demand that they turn over their revenues to keep the family's entire business enterprise centred around the Linangkit Cultural Village. After Datuk Patrick's death, Peter, as a distant relative, seemed unable to command the authority that Datuk Patrick had wielded over members of the Jilan family. For the Linangkit Cultural Village to become financially sustainable again, it appeared that the power dynamics between the different stakeholders would need to be renegotiated to identify a powerful broker who could marshal the resources to support the financial sustainability of the Linangkit Cultural Village. This highlights the fragility of the structure of the Linangkit Cultural Village and other cultural villages like it, rendering them susceptible to strategic instrumentalisation, manipulation, and mobilisation by powerful stakeholders, who may facilitate or compromise the intended objectives of these cultural villages, depending on their intentions and the power relations among different stakeholders.

While I have shown how Indigenous people are sometimes complicit in the commodification of certain aspects of their Indigenous cultural heritage, there are occasions when Indigenous people hold back from the commodification of certain aspects of their practices. One example of the continued faith of Indigenous people in certain cultural practices is demonstrated by the ways in which, during calamitous moments, such as the 2015 Mount Kinabalu earthquake, Indigenous people seemed to turn to their ritual practices to appease the spirits and restore the balance between the spiritual and physical worlds. On 5 June 2015, an earthquake of 6.0 magnitude rattled the state of Sabah, with the epicentre near Mount Kinabalu, one of Southeast Asia's highest peaks, a UNESCO World Heritage Site and a popular climbing spot. The earthquake killed 18 mountain guides and climbers and stranded over a hundred climbers who were later rescued. Allegations soon emerged on social media that the earthquake had been caused by a group of 10 Western male and female tourists who had photographed themselves naked on the mountain. These photographs, which had been circulated the weekend before the earthquake struck, angered many residents who believed that Mount Kinabalu is sacred and should be treated with respect. They also believed that the earthquake had been caused by the actions of these tourists, which had angered the mountain's guardian spirits. When the photographs first emerged, a group of high priestesses from Sabah's Indigenous Dusunic groups warned that something bad would happen, and that a big ritual sacrifice would be needed to appease the angered guardian spirits.

Mount Kinabalu holds special significance for the Indigenous Dusunic groups in Sabah, who believe that the mountain is the spiritual resting place for the souls of the departed. They believe that the souls of their ancestors live on Mount Kinabalu. They also believe that when they die, their souls will travel upwards towards their creator in the sky. Due to their imperfect condition, their souls will rest on the peak of Mount Kinabalu and wait for emancipation. After the deadly earthquake on 5 June 2015, over a dozen ceremonies to cleanse the mountain were conducted by the high priestesses of different Dusunic groups living on Mount Kinabalu and its foothills, as well as those living within sight of the mountain. These included the *bobolian* priestesses of both the Dusun Tindal of the District of Kota Belud, and the Central Dusun of the District of Ranau. The Lotud *tantagas* from the District of Tuaran also took it upon themselves to conduct an appeasement ritual for Mount Kinabalu's guardian spirits on 16 June 2015 with the support and assistance of Sabah Native Court.

I was conducting fieldwork in Sabah when the Mount Kinabalu earthquake struck, and I was able to document the appeasement rituals conducted by the Lotud *tantagas* from the District of Tuaran with my research sponsor, Judeth John Baptist from the Sabah State Museum.[2] Although there was no precedent of a ritual for the appeasement of Mount Kinabalu, the *tantagas* felt that they had an obligation to restore the balance between its angry guardian spirits and the people of Sabah. The *tantagas* consulted with the spirits through two *Monolibabou* ritual ceremonies to seek guidance about what triggered the earthquake on Mount Kinabalu, and how the angry mountain guardians could be appeased (Figure 6.7). A *Monolibabou* ritual is part of a Lotud consultation process with the spiritual world on spiritual matters, which involves the *libabou* going into trance to establish communication with the spirits of the other world, to understand their concerns and seek their guidance on spiritual matters.

Figure 6.7 The *Monolibabou* ritual conducted by the Lotud ritual specialists on 13 June 2015. The *libabou* had her hands on her head, covered by a *sarong*, as she shook her head in trance. Photograph: Judeth John Baptist from Sabah State Museum.

I attended one of the *Monolibabou* ritual ceremonies conducted on the evening of 13 June 2015, and documented the ritual, which also attracted members of the local and foreign media and curious onlookers who were excited about the opportunity to observe the ritual communication with the spirits of the other world. The ceremony began in the evening, with speeches by the District Native Chief and the Village Headman. Due to the unexpected presence of foreign media and curious onlookers, all eager to document the ritual using their electronic equipment, the Village Headman requested everyone to not use flash photography and to reduce the level of noise they were making so as not to interfere with the ritual. The ceremony attracted much attention because the Native Court had announced the ceremony to the local newspapers. In this instance, the ritual ceremony practised at the 'back stage' came to be the 'front stage', as it was opened up for tourist consumption, voyeurism, and indeed my own academic documentation. Nonetheless, this did not seem to give way to cultural commodification, as the Indigenous people held control over their ritual practices, and tourists were asked to conform with the cultural expectations of these ritual ceremonies. This was another moment where the Indigenous people held back on the commodification of their Indigenous cultural practices, thus maintaining their ritual efficacy.

Through these consultations, the *tantagas* learnt that the mountain guardians were upset not only by the transgressions of climbers who 'behaved like animals' and performed sexual acts while on the mountain but also by the immoral behaviour of some villagers living in the mountain's foothills who had committed incest (Patrick 2015). As recounted by the familiar spirit of Odun Lumanjar, the presiding *libabou* for one of the consultations:

> [The mountain guardians] are angry about one man, tall and white who asked permission to climb but he had a wife who was also five months' pregnant. So the wife was prohibited to make the climb. They went home and maybe because their desire was not fulfilled, the child was stillborn. The man was not happy. They cremated the body and brought the ashes to the top of the mountain. There, they spread the ashes but they did not ask permission from the souls that reside there. The ashes fell into holes on the mountain. How can you take all the ashes out again?
>
> (Patrick 2015)

The Lotud people still observe the tradition of burying their dead and have a strong taboo against cremation. They viewed the alleged incident as deeply offensive to the mountain guardians of Mount Kinabalu. Sexual relations between father and daughter, as well as marriages between first cousins and siblings are considered as abominations and incur heavy penalties under local customary laws (Woolley 2006).

Regarding the tourists who posed nude on the mountain, the familiar spirit of Odun Sobinting, another presiding *libabou* for the consultation, said:

> [The mountain guardians] tried to tell the tourists that stripping nude is not allowed, but they cannot hear them. One cannot do bad things when climbing Mount Kinabalu, but now the taboos have been broken, there is a need to do a cleansing ritual. One cannot wait, and the ritual must be conducted quickly. It can be a sacrifice of rice grains and can be done at the village.

To the relief of the Lotud people, the guardians of Mount Kinabalu explained how they could resolve the situation. According to the familiar spirit of Odun Lumanjar, the Lotud villagers did not need to travel to Mount Kinabalu to conduct their appeasement ritual, and there would not be any animal sacrifice. As explained metaphorically by the familiar spirit of Odun Lumanjar:

> It is a long climb from the bottom to the top of the mountain. You should do it slowly, and I will guide you as long as you say the *rinait* correctly. You will need to chant this section of the *rinait*, moving from the bottom of Mount Kinabalu, going to different parts of the mountain, and eventually reaching the top. Because the mountain is huge, you can divide yourselves into smaller groups to cleanse the different parts of the mountain, until you reach the top. You will collect the impurities and dirt at the different geographical areas of the mountain, and roll them into a ball, and flush them out to the open sea, as you travel down the mountain. This will cleanse the mountain of the impurities that have accumulated there.

On 16 June 2015, the Lotud ritual specialists conducted a cleansing ritual, known as the *Tumabur*, to appease the guardians of Mount Kinabalu, which was also well-attended by foreign media and curious onlookers (Figure 6.8). After placing a few white stones to symbolise Mount Kinabalu on the ground, the *tantagas* and *libabou* began chanting, sometimes with the jingling of a piece of ritual paraphernalia made of a string of small bells that they used to summon the spirits. The *libabou* brandished a ceremonial sword in a dance movement called the *Rumantas* to clear their pathway to Mount Kinabalu, which looked as though they were clearing grass, as they scattered grains of uncooked rice on the ground as an offering. Every now and then, the two *libabou*, who had also participated in the *Monoli-babou* rituals, went into trance as they communicated with the guardians of Mount Kinabalu through their familiar spirits. Odin Badin, the head *tantagas*, periodically asked the two *libabou* to ascertain their locations on Mount Kinabalu so that the relevant sections of the *rinait* could be chanted

Figure 6.8 The *tantagas* (right) and *libabou* (left) in trance for the *Tumabur* ritual ceremony. Photograph: Author.

according to the geographical areas of the mountain the familiar spirits were surveying. As explained by *tantagas* Inan Jarambah, who participated in the ritual:

> In our culture, during the ritual, we would first go up the mountain and then we will travel to meet the sun, the moon, the stars, the sky and then go back to the mountain, to the valley, the river and at last, to the sea.
>
> (Patrick and Majantim 2015)

The ritual lasted five hours, excluding an hour-long lunch break, ending with the presentation of a gong, a ceremonial sword, and a necklace to the District Native Chief, the Village Headman, and the Kadazandusun Cultural Association's (KDCA) Executive Secretary, to symbolise the ritual offering and compensation to the guardians of Mount Kinabalu and the departed souls that reside on the mountain. The *tantagas* then offered food to the familiar spirits that had helped them in the spiritual journey to Mount Kinabalu for the *Tumabur* ritual. The presentation of these offerings completed the ritual. The *Tumabur* ceremony can also be conceived as a staged performance, by which the 'back stage' became the 'front stage', as the Lotud ritual ceremony, which was staged for the appeasement of the spirits, came to be appropriated by tourists and onlookers as an 'authentic' cultural practice. However, the ritual specialists did not make any special provision to accommodate these onlookers, demonstrating an instance of Indigenous agency and resistance, and it seemed that the presence of tourists and onlookers did not affect the ritual efficacy.

During the *Tumabur* ritual ceremony, news arrived that a major flood in the foothills of Mount Kinabalu had triggered flows of wood, rocks, boulders, mud, and debris down the mountain. The mud washed away houses and damaged the bridges that provided access to these villages, forcing the evacuation of more than 1,000 people living at Kampung Mesilau on the eastern side of the mountain and Kampung Kiau in the District of Ranau on the western side (*The Straits Times*, 16 June 2015). Uprooted trees and rocks from the floods choked the Liwagu and Mesilau Rivers on Mount Kinabalu, creating dams of floating debris that could result in even more damage to the villages along its banks should they cause the rivers to overflow (*The Straits Times*, 19 June 2015).

The *tantagas* and *libabou* who conducted the *Monolibabou* and *Tumabur* rituals surmised that these events were the result of the ritual cleansing of Mount Kinabalu. The floods and mudflows flushed out impurities on the sacred mountain and sent them to the sea, restoring the balance on the mountain, which had been overheated. Additional cleansing ceremonies were conducted by a Dusunic group in Ranau on 27 June 2015 and by the KDCA on 7 July 2015, both at the villages located on the foothills and slopes of Mount Kinabalu, followed by a dozen more conducted by other Dusunic groups in Sabah. Since the completion of these appeasement ceremonies, the balance of Mount Kinabalu appears to have been restored and life for those living around the mountain had gradually returned to its former state. The Mount Kinabalu appeasement rituals show deep-seated beliefs in the efficacy of ritual practices to neutralise calamities.

Conclusion

The Linangkit Cultural Village, established to preserve the Lotud cultural heritage, has been instrumentalised by a politically influential broker, the late Datuk Patrick Jilan, to advance different social, political, and economic agendas. Datuk Patrick drew upon the 'culture for development' discourse, positioning the Linangkit Cultural Village as a vehicle for the preservation of Lotud cultural heritage to capitalise on the economic potential of cultural tourism and to create employment for the local Lotud villagers, so as to advance his business interests, extend his political influence, and elevate the social status of the Jilan family. However, the Linangkit Cultural Village fell almost immediately into disarray after his unexpected death. This demonstrates how the prevailing structure of the cultural village, which serves to extend authority to a powerful broker, in this case Datuk Patrick, and entrench a working relationship around him, makes his replacement difficult. My purpose of this chapter is to bring attention to the fragility of the prevailing structure of the Linangkit Cultural Village or other community-based cultural projects like it, which seem to render them susceptible to strategic instrumentalisation by powerful stakeholders, who may facilitate or compromise the intended objectives of the cultural village, depending on their intentions and the power relations between different stakeholders.

Although Datuk Patrick did not believe in the Lotud beliefs and ritual practices owing to his conversion to Christianity, and felt alienated from some aspects of Lotud cultural heritage, he nonetheless agreed to host the *Mohlukas* ceremony to bless the compounds of the Linangkit Cultural Village and to remove malignant spirits and other undesirable elements. The *Mohlukas* ceremony was also simultaneously instrumentalised by different stakeholders to serve their different agendas, such as asserting Lotud cultural identity, demonstrating wealth and social status, and providing opportunities for social gathering and political networking, which did not seem to conflict with one another. After the *Mohlukas* ceremony, Datuk Patrick conducted a Christian prayer ceremony to bless the compounds of the Linangkit Cultural Village, alluding to the uneven valorisation of Lotud ritual practices among the Lotud people. More broadly, it demonstrates that cultural heritage need not be evenly valorised and can, therefore, serve different agendas simultaneously.

The ritual cleansing of Mount Kinabalu in the aftermath of the 2015 earthquake shows that Indigenous people turn to their cultural beliefs and ritual practices to appease the spirits and restore the balance between the spiritual and physical worlds, attesting to their continued faith in the ritual efficacy of their cultural practices to neutralise crisis during calamitous times. Nonetheless, the *Monolibabou* and *Tumabur* ritual ceremonies have attracted much media attention so much so that the ritual practices on the 'back stage' have moved to the 'front stage', open for outsiders' consumption. However, this does not seem to give way to cultural commodification, as the Indigenous people have held control over their ritual practices, exercising an active resistance to the commodification and alienation process. Indigenous people thus still have control and agency over their cultural heritage, even as they mobilise their cultural heritage to negotiate the contemporary realities of modernisation and urbanisation. By examining how the Indigenous communities resist and negotiate the commodification of their cultural heritage, this chapter shows how concept of heritage instrumentalisation is interwoven with power politics of brokerage and representation.

Notes

1 Some materials used in this chapter have been published in Cai and John Baptist (2016) and Cai (2018).
2 See Cai and John Baptist (2016) for details of the appeasement rituals.

7 Conclusion

This book examines the politics of heritage-making in Malaysia, exploring the boom in Indigenous cultural villages in both East and Peninsular Malaysia in the last three decades. Focusing on four Indigenous cultural villages in Malaysia as case studies – the Mah Meri Cultural Village and Orang Seletar Cultural Centre in Peninsular Malaysia, and the Monsopiad Cultural Village and Linangkit Cultural Village in East Malaysia – my research has revealed that Indigenous people often lack full agency over the management of these sites and the representation of their cultural heritage, complicating the predominant academic and museological discourse on the positive and transformative role of culture in development. Rather, these Indigenous cultural villages are beset with issues of brokerage, contestation, and negotiation over the representation of cultural heritage, and conflicting motivations with regard to the instrumentalisation of the cultural heritage. These factors bring into question their capacity to contribute to greater Indigenous self-determination and the community empowerment of the Indigenous people they purport to represent.

Although these Indigenous cultural villages are mostly established with the objective to capitalise on the economic potential of cultural tourism and thereby facilitate the socio-economic development of the Indigenous people they claim to represent, they often come to be controlled by powerful brokers, be they ethnic outsiders or members of local Indigenous communities. This entrenches a structural relationship that breeds Indigenous people's reliance on these broker figures. Brokers often control and manipulate these cultural villages that they themselves economically and socially benefit from, rendering the Indigenous people to a subordinate position by cultivating and perpetuating a culture of dependency between the brokers and the Indigenous people. Building on these lines of enquiry, the research set out in this book has focused on understanding the complex economic, political, and social dynamics at play at these Indigenous cultural villages. I have investigated how and why certain Indigenous cultural practices are staged and commodified for tourist consumption, while other aspects are held back, and explored the roles and motivations of different stakeholders in this heritage-making process.

At the Mah Meri Cultural Village, there is a tense relationship between the ethnic Malay broker who is responsible for the Cultural Village, and the Mah Meri villagers whose cultural heritage it represents. Although there were plans to hand the site over to the villagers to run as a community-owned project after an initial three-year start-up period, in 2014, but up. until 2020, the Mah Meri Cultural Village remains under the management of the broker, much to the dismay of the Mah Meri villagers. While the broker appears to be earning a decent income from the enterprise, the villagers have been relegated to lowly paid casual workers. At the same time, the broker presents himself as an advocate of the Mah Meri villagers and as an expert on their culture, based on the 'ethnographic capital' (Steinmetz 2008) he has accumulated over the 13 years of interacting with the villagers. He also adopts a paternalistic attitude with regard to the Mah Meri workers, conceptualising them as underdeveloped Malays and Malay subjects with limited capacities to cope with the outside world. Hence, they need his assistance and protection. This perception is rooted in the historical construction of Indigenous people as the primitive Other. What has been couched in terms of a capacity-building project for the Mah Meri villagers appears to have, instead, cultivated and perpetuated a culture of dependency between the broker and the Mah Meri villagers. Due to the politics of brokerage, such Indigenous cultural villages serve to perpetuate the continued marginalisation of Indigenous people in contemporary Malaysia.

Similar to the Mah Meri Cultural Village, the Monsopiad Cultural Village has also come to be managed and controlled by key brokers. The founders hold the management rights, which reinforces a structural relationship that marginalises the Indigenous workers at the site. The founders, a British entrepreneur and his Kadazan wife (a distant cousin of the direct descendants of Monsopiad who own the lands and artefacts upon which the Cultural Village is based), are simultaneously perceived as 'insiders', on the account of the wife's familial relations with the direct descendants of Monsopiad, and as 'outsiders' due to the British entrepreneur's foreign nationality and ethnicity. This blurs the simplistic distinction between 'insiders' and 'outsiders' in relation to the politics of brokerage. The unequal structural relationship appears also to be endorsed by the direct descendants of Monsopiad, the land-owning Indigenous elites. They possess the power to change the situation by repossessing the lands and artefacts and run the Cultural Village themselves as rental incomes have not been paid on time but have chosen instead not to interfere. Rather, these Indigenous elites rely on the founders to manage and operate the site, cultivating a culture of dependency on the brokers, as they seek to capitalise on the Monsopiad Cultural Village for their own personal gain. This problematises the assumption that ethnic insiders will necessarily act in the interests of their fellow Indigenous people and demonstrates the multiple allegiances and agendas within the Indigenous communities, which may be in conflict, complicating the idealised representation of these communities as harmonious and unified wholes in much of the museological literature.

At the Orang Seletar Cultural Centre, which has been established as an alternative means of livelihood for the Indigenous Orang Seletar people in the face of diminishing fish stocks, the villagers have come to rely on external brokers, particularly a Malaysian Chinese environmental educator, Wong Yun Yun, to realise the opportunities offered by cultural tourism. Although the Orang Seletar Cultural Centre is wholly owned and managed by the local villagers, its workings still cultivate a culture of dependency between the external brokers and the Indigenous beneficiaries. While Wong intended that the eco-tourism tours would dispel the exoticisation of the Orang Seletar as primitive people, by staging their 'essentialised past' on at the Orang Seletar Cultural Centre alongside their 'dynamic present', manifested in their everyday, lived experiences, the historical construction of the Orang Seletar people as the 'primitive Other' is nonetheless still mobilised as a 'hook' for enticing tourists on these tours. Touristic imaginaries of the Orang Seletar people, based on their historical construction as exotic, backward, and uncivilised, are being mobilised here, but also complicated. The Orang Seletar villagers are thus subjected to the constraints of 'intractable double binds' (Clifford 2013), as they have to be exoticised as the 'primitive Other' in order to enjoy the benefits of tourism.

The Orang Seletar Cultural Centre and the village of Kampung Sungai Temon, within which the Centre is situated, are under the threat of eviction, as the villagers do not possess legal land titles to the village. During the ongoing lawsuit against the private landowners, property developers, and state agencies of the Danga Bay waterfront development, who encroached on their customary lands and waters, they were assisted by a non-Indigenous Orang Asli rights activist and a team of pro-bono lawyers from the Malaysian Bar Council. Together they played positive brokerage roles by mediating and translating a selective body of historical literature and oral accounts of the Orang Seletar's customs and cultural practices into the legal terminology used within court proceedings, in order to facilitate the assertion of the villagers' native customary claims. While the recognition of native titles and proprietary rights in and to native lands within Malaysian law offers a channel for Indigenous people to redress their historical marginalisation and dispossession by instrumentalising an essentialised notion of their Indigenous culture to assert their native claims, this still places them in a subaltern position, as they will be subjected to the non-Indigenous governing logic of the Malaysian judiciary system.

At the Linangkit Cultural Village, in which the cultural heritage of the Indigenous Lotud people is displayed, the sustainability of the site rests on a single powerful internal broker, the late Datuk Patrick Jilan – a Lotud community leader who was able to mediate between the needs of the different stakeholders and wield significant power over them in order to marshal resources to sustain the Linangkit Cultural Village. Specifically, he was able to persuade his family members, who run businesses at the Linangkit Cultural Village, to hand over some of their revenues to support the site operations. His sudden death thrusted the Linangkit Cultural Village into disarray, as his successor has been unable to step into this role and command that the stakeholders continue to financially support the site. The Linangkit Cultural Village, thus, highlights the structural fragility of these cultural villages, which cultivates a culture of dependency on certain powerful brokers and renders them susceptible to strategic instrumentalisation by the brokers, who may facilitate or compromise their sustainable development depending on the outcomes of power interplays, and, indeed, their continued involvement.

Rather than promote the self-determination and empowerment of the Indigenous people, these cultural villages perpetuate the continued marginalisation of Indigenous people in the predominantly Malay-Muslim Malaysian society by entrenching a culture of dependency. However, the Indigenous people are not passive victims, but are actively contesting and negotiating their marginalised positions by collaborating with brokers when it is in their interests to do so or by adopting various covert and overt strategies of resistance when their agendas conflict with those of the brokers. Nonetheless, their positions are considerably weakened due to a lack of collective voice, as Indigenous people do not constitute a homogeneous community but are made up of individuals with different agendas and allegiances. This alludes to Ferguson's (1994) argument that the 'development' apparatus (here extended to include 'culture for development' initiatives) serves to entrench existing cultural structures and social actors, expanding bureaucratic powers rather than alleviating the poverty of marginalised people.

In contrast with the brokers at the Mah Meri Cultural Village and the Monsopiad Cultural Village, the activists advocating for Indigenous rights in Malaysia, such as Colin Nicholas from Center for Orang Asli Concerns (COAC) and Anne Lasimbang from Projects for Awareness and Community Organisations in Sabah (PACOS Trust), play more positive brokerage roles by mediating between the local politics of Indigenous people in Malaysia and the broader transnational Indigenous rights movement, drawing upon a strategic essentialism of Indigeneity and Indigenous cultural heritage to facilitate Indigenous self-determination and empowerment. Their instrumentalisation of Indigeneity and Indigenous cultural heritage operates differently from the brokers at the Indigenous cultural villages. At a local level, these Indigenous activists seek to shape the agendas of Indigenous people through persuasion and forging collaborations, giving them the autonomy to decide for themselves which aspects of their cultural practices ought to be valorised, thus instilling in them a sense of empowerment. At a broader level, they serve to perpetuate an established norm for the systematic production of regimes of truth about Indigeneity and Indigenous cultural heritage that appear to be spread through the network of Indigenous NGOs forming the transnational Indigenous rights movement. These activists also derive 'ethnographical capital' (Steinmetz 2008) from their brokerage through their cultivating of a positive professional reputation, which can, in turn, enhance the power and influence of their brokerage.

At these Indigenous cultural villages, there is a deliberate transformation of certain aspects of Indigenous cultural practice into commodified cultural heritage for tourist consumption. This has the potential to 'give away' these practices, which are transformed into staged performances. Due to the unequal power relations between the brokers and the Indigenous people entrenched in the structural relationship of the cultural villages, the Indigenous people often lack the full agency to determine the representation of their own cultural heritage at the cultural villages. However, the Indigenous people are not passive onlookers to the commodification of their cultural heritage; they also hold back some aspects of their cultural practices from the staging process, thus safeguarding them from commodification and alienation. The Indigenous cultural villages thus emerge as staged arenas, where certain aspects of Indigenous cultural heritage are transformed for tourism consumption, through a process of contestation and negotiation by different stakeholders, including self-representations by the Indigenous people themselves, to conform with tourist imaginaries of Indigenous people based on their historically constructed stereotypes as the exotic, primitive Other. However, as noted earlier, this constitutes a 'double-bind' (Kallen 2015), as the Indigenous people have to be exoticised as primitive, backward, and undeveloped to enjoy the benefits of these cultural projects, compromising their Indigenous advocacy and activism.

At the Mah Meri Cultural Village, the Mah Meri villagers become willing accomplices to the exoticisation and commodification of their cultural heritage on some occasions. They actively capitalise on the self-essentialisation of their primitive personas for their own benefit, especially in the commodification of their wedding ceremony in the Mah Meri Cultural Village, and in the promotion of Mah Meri woodcarving as an Indigenous craft handed down for generations. In other instances, they hold back on the commodification of their cultural heritage, safeguarding it from alienation, such as keeping their *Hari Moyang* celebrations 'off stage' from tourists even though they continue to face pressures to open up their 'back stage' to tourists. Nonetheless, their positions are considerably weakened by their lack of a collective voice, since the Mah Meri community is a heterogeneous group made up of individuals with different interests and agendas. While the Mah Meri people have largely been successful in presenting their cultural heritage, this has rendered their heritage susceptible to appropriation, both by other Indigenous groups seeking to instrumentalise their own cultural practices for their own agendas and by filmmakers or other entrepreneurs for their personal gain. This appropriation by others not only raises questions of infringement of intellectual property rights but may also cast the Mah Meri people in a negative light to outsiders.

At the Orang Seletar Cultural Centre, the Orang Seletar villagers strategically mobilise an essentialised formulation of Indigeneity and Indigenous cultural heritage based on autochthony and primordiality, to assert their native customary claims. During the ongoing lawsuit, the Orang Seletar villagers staged their historical connections to their customary lands and waters for the benefit of the judge, who was brought on a tour of the Orang Seletar Cultural Centre and culturally significant geographical landmarks to assert their long connection with the lands and territories. The Orang Seletar villagers also wore 'traditional' headdresses at the court hearings to stage their cultural identities, alluding to the myth of Indigenous people as environmentally minded 'ecological noble savages' (Redford 1990) who seek sustainable use of natural resources, in contrast with the wanton exploitation of the environment by capitalist interests, represented here by the plaintiffs. The court proceedings served as an arena in which complex power relations over the control of the Orang Seletar customary lands and waters were played out between the different stakeholders, as lawyers and witnesses on each opposing side strategically mobilised a corpus of state apparatus as well as representations of Indigeneity and Indigenous cultural heritage to stake their respective claims.

At the Monsopiad Cultural Village, a collection of human skulls believed to have been captured by Monsopiad is exoticised for tourist consumption. Rather than rejecting this heritage as a symbol of backwardness and barbarism, the Indigenous Kadazan people have re-appropriated headhunting as a way to assert their Indigenous identity in Malay-Muslim society. This staged performance of Kadazan headhunting heritage also conforms to tourists' imaginaries of the exotic, primitive Indigenous people of Borneo and embodies the Indigenous people's self-essentialisation melded into the tourists' imaginaries (Salazar and Graburn 2015). At the same time, the direct descendants of Monsopiad request that tourists complete a rite of respect to the skulls, which can be construed as a 'customised authenticity' (Wang 2007), but also offers an arena for Indigenous people to resist the commodification and alienation of their cultural practices.

The *Magavau* ceremony, which until around 30 years ago was practised in the rice fields for the appeasement of the rice spirits during the harvest season, has been staged as a cultural performance at major state and private celebrations in the last five years, and in the 'Aki Nabalu' musical for the Sabah Fest 2014 cultural festival, as a symbol of Kadazan cultural identity. A full day ritual ceremony, previously conducted by a group of *bobohizans*, is now condensed into a cultural performance not lasting more than 20 minutes, staged by a group of *bobohizans* and non-*bobohizans* who have learned the *Magavau* sequence and chants. This represents what Kirshenblatt-Gimblett (2004) describes as a 'metacultural production' of cultural heritage. Each touristic staging nonetheless constitutes its own 'negotiation of expectations' (Theodossopoulos 2011) among the different stakeholders, even though they may be performed by the same group of *bobohizans* and coordinated by the same broker. These staged performances may, in turn, serve as an inspiration for apprentice *bobohizans* to reinvent contemporary Kadazan ritual practices, alluding to the multifaceted, ever-evolving, and dynamic nature of cultural representations, while raising questions of intellectual property rights infringement.

At the Linangkit Cultural Village, the performance of the *Mohlukas* ceremony to initiate the re-opening of the Cultural Village to tourists at the completion of a new community hall sheds light onto how a ritual ceremony can simultaneously serve the multiple agendas and interests of different stakeholders. While the late Datuk Patrick did not believe in the ritual efficacy of the *Mohlukas* ceremony due to his Christian beliefs, he supported its performance at the Linangkit Cultural Village, as it carried other instrumental values for him, such as offering a platform for him to network with political elites and community leaders, symbolised his support for his sister who is the Village Headwoman, and signalled that he had made good of the government funding for the Linangkit Cultural Village, all of which contributed to the expansion of his business interests, political influence, and social status within Sabah society. Nevertheless, the late Datuk Patrick's intentions did not seem to have affected the beliefs of the Lotud *tantagas* and village elders in the efficacy of the *Mohlukas* ceremony, alluding to the uneven valorisation of Lotud ritual practices among the Lotud people and the problems of construing Lotud community as a unified whole with a common position on the management of their cultural heritage.

While Indigenous people often appear to be willing accomplices in the commodification of their cultural practices, on occasion they actively resist this commodification. Cultural taboos and ritual prohibition establish limits on and serve as a self-imposed deterrence against the instrumentalisation of certain kinds of cultural heritage. The cultural taboos surrounding the treatment of human skulls and *gusi*, as well as ritual prohibitions on the relocation of Monsopiad's tombstone, are examples of how Indigenous people practise resistance on account of their continued beliefs in the ritual efficacy of these artefacts. At times of disaster, such as the 2015 Mount Kinabalu earthquake, Indigenous people also turn to their ritual practices to appease the spirits and restore the balance between the natural and spiritual worlds. This attests to their faith in their ritual beliefs and practices. Nevertheless, there is pressure to open up this 'back stage' for the consumption of outsiders', which is, in turn, resisted by Indigenous people. Such examples allude to the constant contestation and negotiation between different stakeholders over the representation of Indigenous cultural practices.

By critically examining the impact of culture on development practices and encounters as manifested in the four Indigenous cultural villages in Malaysia, this book has explored the complexities inherent in adopting the 'culture for development' discourse as a developmental strategy. Opportunities for self-representation and self-determination can become dominated by the politics of brokerage, which can, in turn, facilitate or compromise the intended outcomes. In particular, it brings into question the effectiveness of current neoliberal approaches to development which seek to decentralise developmental aid provision through intermediary agencies and entrepreneurs. It challenges idealised notions of 'Indigenous communities' as unified and harmonious entities by showing how Indigenous cultures are actively forged, struggled over and negotiated by different stakeholders depending on their agendas and allegiances. It also critiques the dominant literature on the roles of Indigenous museums as arenas of Indigenous engagement and empowerment. Rather, it argues that Indigenous museums may be better understood as sites of negotiation and contestation, where complex objectives and agendas among different stakeholders are played out, producing variegated outcomes for the Indigenous people. The case studies presented here shed light on how Indigenous museology and the 'culture for development' discourse play out amidst the complex politics between different ethnic groups in Malaysia's highly heterogeneous ethnic, linguistic, and religious context, which has relevance for the wider 'developing' world, especially in Asia or in countries that have undergone decolonisation from the Western colonial powers since the 1960s and 1970s.

Resonating with Ferguson's (1994) observation that developmental projects that work through social actors and cultural structures have tended to expand the bureaucratic power of the state rather than alleviating the poverty of its intended recipients, this book evidences that a reliance on intermediary brokers to deliver developmental objectives can cultivate and perpetuate cultures of dependency between these brokers and the intended beneficiary communities. It thus calls for reconsideration of how the wider discourse on 'culture for development' can be operationalised by UNESCO, international aid agencies, national governments, and museum institutions, without reproducing the cultures of dependency that lead to the continued or further marginalisation of their intended beneficiaries.

Rejecting the economistic perspectives on development, Sen (1999) suggests that the main objective of development intervention is to expand the freedom of the beneficiary communities to lead the kinds of lives they value. Appadurai's (2013) reframing of development intervention as being directed to fostering people's 'capacity to aspire' can perhaps offer some insights into how marginalised groups can reclaim the freedom to determine their own futures by defining their own terms of recognition. Building on these arguments, Basu and Modest (2015: 15) suggest that the true value of culture lies in its intrinsic capacity to help beneficiary communities determine their own 'meanings, values and uses' of their own pasts, and the use of these pasts to build their own futures. However, the freedom of beneficiary communities to instrumentalise culture and heritage on their own terms is complicated by the politics of brokerage, as the case studies presented here have demonstrated, which can facilitate or compromise the intended developmental outcomes. My research also shows that the concept of culture, and particularly Indigeneity, can impose certain limitations on economic, political, and social development, as much as it can be instrumentalised to facilitate development, constituting a form of contradictory dualism.

A starting point for UNESCO, international aid agencies, national governments, and museum institutions wishing to adopt 'culture for development' as a developmental strategy is to recognise the impacts of brokerage and the contradictory dualism of culture, and particularly Indigeneity, on developmental initiatives. This will open up opportunities for refining the implementation of development initiatives to better achieve their intended outcomes of improving the well-being of marginalised groups. First, external agencies can facilitate the development and incorporation of a set of mechanisms that offer safeguards against unethical practices, which may be introduced through the brokerage process, as well as mitigate the negative implications of culture's 'double-bind' (Kallen 2015) characteristics, so that these initiatives can achieve the goal of truly championing self-determination and empowerment among the marginalised communities. Second, there is a need to reach for more sophisticated understandings of local power dynamics within marginalised communities. This can help us focus on examining the process of consensus production to promote efforts seeking to favour a change in the terms of recognition for the marginalised groups, as well as to help these groups understand their capacities for self-determination and cultivate their own voices for empowerment (Appadurai 2013).

Bibliography

Abram, S. Waldren, J. and Macleod, D. eds. 1997. *Tourists and tourism: identifying with people and places.* Oxford: Berg.

Adams, K.M. 1984. Come to Tana Toraja, "Land of the heavenly kings" travel agents as brokers in ethnicity. *Annals of Tourism Research.* 11: 469–485.

Adams, K.M. 1997. Touting touristic "primadonas"; tourism, ethnicity, and national integration in Sulawesi, Indonesia. In: *Tourism, ethnicity, and the state in Asian and Pacific societies.* Picard, M. and Wood, R.E. eds. pp. 155–180. Honolulu: University of Hawai'i Press.

Adams, K.M. 2003. Museum/City/Nation: negotiating identities in urban museums in Indonesia and Singapore. In: *Theorizing the Southeast Asian city as text: urban landscapes, cultural documents, and interpretative experiences.* Goh, R.B.H. and Yeoh, B.S.A. eds. pp. 135–158. Singapore: World Scientific Publishing Co. Pte. Ltd.

Aiken, S.R. and Leigh, C.H. 2011a. In the way of development: indigenous land-rights issues in Malaysia. *Geographical Review.* 101: 471–496.

Aiken, S.R. and Leigh, C.H. 2011b. Seeking redress in the courts: indigenous land rights and judicial decisions in Malaysia. *Modern Asian Studies.* 45: 825–875.

Ali, M. 2002. Singapore's Orang Seletar, Orang Kallang, and Orang Selat: the last settlements. In: *Tribal communities in the Malay world: historical, cultural, and social perspectives.* Benjamin, G. and Chou, C. eds. pp. 273–291. Singapore: Institute of Southeast Asian Studies.

Altbach, P.G. and Hassan, S.M. eds. 1996. *The muse of modernity: essays on culture as development in Africa.* Trenton, NJ: Africa World Press.

Amazing Borneo Tours. n.d. *Monsopiad's head hunter's tour.* Brochure of Package Tours. Sabah: Amazing Borneo Tours and Events Sdn. Bhd.

Amit, V. and Rapport, N. 2002. *The trouble with community: anthropological reflections on movement, identity and collectivity.* London: Pluto Press.

Anaya, S.J. 2008. Reparations for neglect of indigenous land rights at the intersection of domestic and international law – the Maya cases in the Supreme Court of Belize. In: *Reparations for indigenous peoples: international and comparative perspectives.* Lenzerini, F. ed. pp. 567–604. Oxford: Oxford University Press.

Andaya, B. and Andaya, L.Y. 2001. *A history of Malaysia.* 2nd ed. Basingstoke: Palgrave.

Andaya, L.Y. 2008. *Leaves of the same tree: trade and ethnicity in the Straits of Melaka.* Honolulu: University of Hawai'i Press.

Anderson, B. 1991. *Imagined communities: reflections on the origins and spread of nationalism.* 2nd ed. London: Verso.

Appadurai, A. 1986. *The social life of things: commodities in cultural perspective.* Cambridge, MA: Cambridge University Press.

Appadurai, A. 1996. *Modernity at large: cultural dimensions of globalisation.* London: University of Minnesota Press.

Appadurai, A. 2013. The capacity to aspire: culture and the terms of recognition. In: *The future as cultural fact: essays on the global condition.* pp. 179–195. London: Verso.

Ariffin, J. 2014. *My personal journey in observing the dynamic Iskandar Malaysia and its forgotten sea gypsies: economic development contradictions and cultural change.* Kuala Lumpur: International Research Institute for Economic Progress and Social Well-being.

Asch, M. and Samson, M. 2004. Comments: on the return of the native. *Current Anthropology.* 45(2): 261–262.

Asian Indigenous Peoples Pact (AIPP). 2016. *Who we are.* Retrieved on 20 October 2016 from World Wide Web: http://aippnet.org/about-us/

Athayde, S. 2014. Introduction: indigenous peoples, dams and resistance. *Tipiti: Journal of the Society for the Anthropology of Lowland South America.* 12(2): 80–92.

Baird, M.F. 2013. 'The breath of the mountain is my heart': indigenous cultural landscapes and the politics of heritage. *International Journal of Heritage Studies.* 19(4): 327–340.

Barnard, A. 2006. Kalahari revisionism, Vienna and the 'indigenous peoples' debate. *Social Anthropology.* 14(1): 1–16.

Bassett, K. 1993. Urban cultural strategies and urban regeneration: a case study and critique. *Environment and Planning A.* 25: 1773–1788.

Basu, P. and Damodaran, V. 2015. Colonial histories of heritage: legislative migrations and the politics of preservation. *Past and Present.* 223(Suppl. 10): 239–270.

Basu, P. and Modest, W. eds. 2015. *Museums, heritage and international development.* New York and London: Routledge.

Baud, M. and Rutten, R. eds. 2004. *Popular intellectuals and social movements: framing protest in Asia, Africa, and Latin America.* Cambridge: Cambridge University Press.

Bauer, K. 2009. On the politics and the possibilities of participatory mapping and GIS: using spatial technologies to study common property and land use change among pastoralists in Central Tibet. *Cultural Geographies.* 16: 229–252.

Bauman, G. 1996. *Contesting culture: discourses of identity in multi-ethnic.* London and Cambridge, MA: Cambridge University Press.

Bell, J.A. 2014. The veracity of form: transforming knowledges and their forms in the Purari Delta of Papua New Guinea. In: *Museum as process: translating local and global knowledges.* Silverman, R.A. ed. pp. 105–122. London and New York: Routledge.

Bell, J.A. 2016. Dystopian realities and archival dreams in the Purari Delta of Papua New Guinea. *Social Anthropology.* 24(1): 20–35.

Benjamin, G. 2014. *Temiar religion, 1964–2012: enchantment, disenchantment and re-enchantment in Malaysia's uplands.* Singapore: NUS Press.

Bennett, T., Cameron, F., Dias, N., Dibley, B., Harrison, R., Jacknis, I. and McCarthy, C. 2017. *Collecting, ordering, governing: anthropology, museums, and liberal government.* Durham, NC and London: Duke University Press.

Bergmeister, F.M. 2015. Shaping Southeast Asia: tracing tourism imaginaries in guidebooks and travel blogs. *ASEAS – Austrian Journal of South-East Asian Studies.* 8(2): 203–208.

Bertrand, J. 2011. 'Indigenous peoples' rights' as a strategy of ethnic accommodation: contrasting experiences of Cordillerans and Papuans in the Philippines and Indonesia. *Ethnic and Racial Studies.* 34(5): 850–869.

Beteille, A. 1998. The idea of indigenous people. *Current Anthropology.* 39(2): 187–192.

Bhatt, R.K. 2018. Guidelines for foreigners buying a house in Malaysia. *iproperty. com.my,* 18 April. Retrieved on 2 July 2019 from World Wide Web: https://www. iproperty.com.my/guides/guidelines-for-foreigners-buying-a-house-in-malaysia/

Bianchini, F. 1991. Urban renaissance? The arts and the urban regeneration process. In: *Tackling the inner cities: the 1980s reviewed, prospects for the 1990s.* MacGregor, S. and Pimlott, B. eds. pp. 215–250. Oxford: Clarendon Press.

Bianchini, F. and Parkinson, M. eds. 1993. *Cultural policy and economic regeneration: the West European experience.* Manchester: Manchester University Press.

Birrell, K. 2009. Indigeneity: before and beyond the law. *Studies in Law, Politics, and Society.* 51: 219–258.

Blaser, M., de Costa, R., McGregor, D. and Coleman, W.D. eds. 2010. *Indigenous peoples and autonomy: insights for a global age.* Vancouver: UBC Press.

Blood, E.D. 1990. The Lotud. In: *Social organization of Sabah societies.* Lingenfelter, S.G. ed. pp. 63–90. Kota Kinabalu: Department of Sabah Museum and State Archives.

Bock, C. 1881. *The head-hunters of Borneo: a narrative of travel up the Mahakkam and down the Barito, also, journeyings in Sumatra.* London: S. Low, Marston, Searle and Rivington.

Bottomley, G. 1991. Culture, ethnicity, and the politics/poetics of representation. *Diaspora: A Journal of Transnational Studies.* 1(3): 303–320.

Bouquet, M. 2012. *Museums: a visual anthropology.* Oxford and New York: Berg.

Britton, S. 1991. Tourism, capital, and place: towards a critical geography of tourism. *Environment and Planning D: Society and Space.* 9: 451–478.

Brosius, J.R. 1997a. Endangered forest, endangered people: environmentalist representations of indigenous knowledge. *Human Ecology.* 25(1): 47–69.

Brosius, J.R. 1997b. Prior transcripts, divergent paths: resistance and acquiescence to logging in Sarawak, East Malaysia. *Comparative Studies in Society and History.* 39(3): 468–510.

Brosius, J.R. 1999. Analyses and interventions: anthropological engagements with environmentalism. *Current Anthropology.* 40(3): 277–309.

Brosius, J.R. 2003. Voices for the Borneo rain forest: writing the history of an environmental campaign. In: *Nature in the Global South: Environmental projects in South and Southeast Asia.* Greenough, P. and Tsing, A.L., eds. pp. 319–346. Durham and London: Duke University Press.

Brulotte, R.L. 2012. *Between art and artefact: archaeological replicas and cultural production in Oaxaca, Mexico.* Austin: University of Texas Press.

Bryan, J. 2009. Where would we be without them? Knowledge, space and power in Indigenous politics. *Futures.* 41: 24–32.

Bryan, J. and Woods, D. 2015. *Weaponizing maps: Indigenous peoples and counterinsurgency in the Americas.* New York: Guildford Press.

Bunnell, T. and Nah, A.M. 2004. Counter-global cases for place: contesting displacement in globalising Kuala Lumpur Metropolitan area. *Urban Studies.* 41(12): 2447–2467.

Bunten, A. 2008. Sharing culture or shelling out? Developing the commodified persona in heritage industry. *American Ethnologist.* 35(3): 380–395.

Bunting, C. 2008. What instrumentalism? A public perception of value. *Cultural Trends*. 17(4): 323–328.

Cai, Y. 2016. Mohlukas: a housewarming ceremony at the Linangkit cultural village. *Sabah Malaysian Borneo*. 180: 10–13.

Cai, Y. 2017. Performing cultures, negotiating identities: the cultural politics of Indigenous cultural villages in West Malaysia. In: *Citizens, civil society and heritage-making in Asia*. Hsiao, H.H.M., Hui, Y.F. and Peycam, P. eds. pp. 114–136. Singapore: Institute of Southeast Asian Studies – Yusof Ishak Institute.

Cai, Y. 2018. Between tradition and modernity: the ritual politics of Indigenous cultural heritage in urbanising Sabah, East Malaysia. In: *Routledge handbook of urbanisation in Southeast Asia*. Padawangi, R. ed. pp. 179–190. London and New York: Routledge.

Cai, Y. and John Baptist, J. 2016. Cleansing the sacred mountain in the aftermath of the 2015 Mount Kinabalu earthquake. *Journal of the Malaysian Branch of the Royal Asiatic Society*. 89(310): 61–78.

Calligaro, O. 2013. *Negotiating Europe: EU promotion of Europeanness since the 1950s*. New York: Springer.

Canessa, A. 2012. Gender, indigeneity, and the performance of authenticity in Latin American tourism. *Latin American Perspectives*. 39: 109–115.

Carey, I. 1976. *Orang Asli: the aboriginal tribes of Peninsular Malaysia*. New York: Oxford University Press.

Carnwath, J.D. and Brown, A.S. 2014. *Understanding the value and impacts of cultural experiences: a literature review*. Manchester: Arts Council England. Retrieved on 21 May 2020 from World Wide Web: https://www.artscouncil.org. uk/sites/default/files/download-file/Understanding_the_Value_and_Impacts_of_Cultural_Experiences.pdf

Césard, N. 2014. Heirlooms and marriage payments. *Indonesia and the Malay World*. 42(122): 62–87.

Chan, C.S.C. 2012. Heterogeneity in the musical acquisition of Orang Asli children from the Mah Meri and Semai groups. *Malaysian Music Journal*. 1(2): 1–19.

Chan, J. 2016. Bobohizans: the shamans of Sabah teeter between old and new worlds. *Malay Mail Online*, 8 June. Retrieved on 27 July 2017 from World Wide Web: https://www.malaymail.com/news/life/2016/06/08/bobohizans-the-shamans-of-sabah-teeter-between-old-and-new-worlds/1136825

Chhabra, D., Healy, R. and Sills, E. 2003. Staged authenticity and heritage tourism. *Annals of Tourism Research*. 30(3): 702–719.

Chowdhury, N. 2012. The odd couple: Singapore and Malaysia team up on development zone. *Time Magazine*, 8 July. Retrieved on 2 May 2018 from World Wide Web: http://world.time.com/2012/07/08/the-odd-couple-singapore-and-malaysia-team-up-on-development-zone/

Chua, L. 2012. Conversion, continuity, and moral dilemmas among Christian Bidayuhs in Malaysian Borneo. *American Ethnologist*. 39(3): 511–526.

Clifford, J. 2001. Indigenous articulations. *The Contemporary Pacific*. 13(2): 467–490.

Clifford, J. 2013. *Returns: becoming indigenous in the twenty-first century*. London: Harvard University Press.

Clifford, K. 1998. *The predicament of culture: twentieth century ethnography literature and art*. Cambridge, MA: Harvard University Press.

COAC. 2011. *The river must flow*. Retrieved on 20 January 2017 from World Wide Web: https://www.youtube.com/watch?v=Y7QnpJPbXBc

COAC. 2014a. *Court battle against big time developers continues over ancestral territories.* Retrieved on 30 January 2017 from World Wide Web: https://www.facebook.com/notes/707485839295345/

COAC. 2014b. *Mah Meri from Carey Island arrested for defending ancestral grave.* Retrieved on 16 January 2015 from World Wide Web: https://m.facebook.com/notes/jaringan-orang-asal-semalaysia-joas/breaking-news-mah-meri-from-carey-island-arrested-for-defending-ancestral-grave/852932591414418/

COAC. 2016. *Malaysia: decision for the Orang Seletar case set for 27 October 2016.* Retrieved on 30 January 2017 from World Wide Web: http://iphrdefenders.net/malaysia-decision-orang-seletar-case-set-27-october-2016/

Cohen, E. 1988. Authenticity and commoditization in tourism. *Annals of Tourism Research.* 15(3): 271–386.

Cohen, E. 2008. Southeast Asian ethnic tourism in a changing world. *Asian Anthropology.* 7(1): 25–56.

Cohen, E. 2016. Ethnic tourism in mainland Southeast Asia: the state of the art. *Tourism Recreation Research.* 41(3): 232–245.

Cohn, B.S. 1996. *Colonialism and its forms of knowledge: the British in India.* Princeton, NJ: Princeton University Press.

Coles, A. 2008. Instrumental death of a reductionist. *Cultural Trends.* 17(4): 329–334.

Conklin, B.A. 1997. Body paint, feathers, and VCRs: aesthetics and authenticity in Amazonian activism. *American Ethnologist.* 24(7): 711–737.

Conklin, B.A. and Graham, L.R. 1995. The shifting middle ground: Amazon Indians and eco-politics. *American Anthropologist.* 97(4): 695–710.

Cooke, F.M. 2013. Constructing rights: indigenous peoples at the public hearings of the national inquiry into customary rights to land in Sabah, Malaysia. *Sojourn: Journal of Social Issues in Southeast Asia.* 28(3): 512–537.

Corntassel, J.J. 2003. Who is indigenous? 'Peoplehood' and ethnonationalist approaches to rearticulating indigenous identity. *Nationalism and Ethnic Politics.* 9(1): 75–100.

Country Garden. n.d. *Our development.* Retrieved on 30 January 2017 from World Wide Web: https://countrygardendangabay.com.my/

Crampton, A. 2003. The art of nation-building: (re)presenting political transition at the South African national gallery. *Cultural Geographies.* 10: 218–242.

Crang, M. 1999. Nation, region and homeland: history and tradition in Dalarna, Sweden. *Ecumene.* 6(4): 447–470.

Cresswell, T. 1996. *In place/out of place.* Minneapolis: University of Minnesota Press.

Crewe, E. and Harrison, E. 1998. *Whose development? An ethnography of aid.* London and New York: Zed Books Ltd.

Crick, M. 1989. Representations of sun, sex, sights, savings and servility: international tourism in the social sciences. *Annual Review of Anthropology.* 18: 307–344.

Crooke, E. 2008. *Museums and community: ideas, issues and challenges.* London and New York: Routledge.

Crossick, G. and Kaszynska, P. 2016. *Understanding the value of arts and culture: the AHRC cultural value project.* Swindon: Arts and Humanities Research Council. Retrieved on 7 July 2017 from World Wide Web: http://www.ahrc.ac.uk/documents/publications/cultural-value-project-final-report/

Datla, K.S. 2015. The origins of indirect rule in India: Hyderabad and the British imperial order. *Law and History Review*. 33(2): 321–350.

Davies, C.A. 2008. *Reflexive ethnography: a guide to researching selves and others*. 2nd ed. London and New York: Routledge.

de Costa, R. 2006. *A higher authority: indigenous transnationalism and Australia*. Sydney: University of New South Wales Press.

Dellios, P. 2002. The museumification of the village: cultural subversion in the 21st Century. *Culture Mandala: The Bulletin of the Centre for East-West Cultural and Economic Studies*. 5(1): Article 4. Retrieved on 14 June 2017 from the World Wide Web: http://epublications.bond.edu.au/cgi/viewcontent.cgi?article=1082&context=cm

Deloria, P. 1998. *Playing Indian*. New Haven, CT: Yale University Press.

Dentan, R.K., Endicott, K., Gomes, A.G. and Hooker, M.B. 1997. *Malaysia and the "Original People": A case study of the impact of development on Indigenous peoples*. Boston, MA: Allyn and Bacon.

Denton, K. 2014. *Exhibiting the past: Historical memory and the politics of museums in postsocialist China*. Honolulu: University of Hawaii Press.

Dewdney, A., Dibosa, D. and Walsh, V. 2013. *Post critical museology: theory and practice in the art museum*. London and New York: Routledge.

Diagle, M. 2016. Awawenitakik: the spatial politics of recognition and relational geographies of Indigenous self-determination. *Canadian Geographer*. 60(2): 259–269.

Dirks, N.B. 2008. *The scandal of empire: India and the creation of imperial Britain*. Cambridge, MA: Belknap Imprint, Harvard University Press.

Domhoff, G.W. 2003. *Senoi dream theory: myth, scientific method, and the Dreamwork movement*. Retrieved on 14 July 2017 from World Wide Web: http://dreamresearch.net/Library/senoi.html

Doolittle, A.A. 2004. Resources, ideologies, and nationalism: the politics of development in Malaysia. In: *Development brokers and translators: the ethnography of aid and agencies*. Lewis, D. and Mosse, D. eds. pp. 51–74. West Hartford, CT: Kumarian Press Inc.

Douglas, B. 2008. Climate to crania: science and the racialization of human difference. In: *Foreign bodies: Oceania and the science of race 1750–1940*. Douglas, B. and Ballard, C. eds. pp. 33–96. Canberra: The Australian National University Press.

Dove, M.R. 2006. Indigenous people and environmental politics. *Annual Review of Anthropology*. 35: 191–208.

Duxbury, N. 2015. Positioning cultural mapping in local planning and development contexts: an introduction. *Culture and Local Governance*. 5(1–2): 1–7. Retrieved on 14 August 2017 from the World Wide Web: https://uottawa.scholarsportal.info/ojs/index.php/clg-cgl/article/view/1437

Duxbury, N., Garrett-Petts, W.F. and MacLennan, D. eds. 2015. *Cultural mapping as cultural inquiry*. New York: Routledge.

Dwyer, C. 1999. Contradictions of community: questions of identity for young British Muslim women. *Environment and Planning A*. 31: 53–68.

Dwyer, C. and Jackson, P. 2003. Commodifying difference: selling EASTern fashion. *Environment and Planning A*. 21: 269–291.Eight Malaysia Plan. 2000. *Eight Malaysia Plan (2001–2005)*. Kuala Lumpur: Government Printers.

Ellingson, T. 2001. *The myth of the noble savage*. Berkeley: University of California Press.

Endicott, K. ed. 2015. *Malaysia's "original people": past, present and future of the Orang Asli.* Singapore: NUS Press.

Eoe, S.M. and Swadling, P. eds. 1991. *Museums and cultural centres in the Pacific.* Port Moresby: Papua New Guinea National Museum.

Erb, M. 2007. Adat revivalism in western Flores: culture, religion, and land. In: *The revival of tradition in Indonesian politics: the deployment of adat from colonialism to indigenism.* Davidson, J. and Henley, D. eds. pp. 247–274. London and New York: Routledge.

Errington, F. and Gewertz, D. 1989. Tourism and Anthropology in a Post-Modern World. *Oceania.* 60(1): 37–54.

Escobar, A. 1995. *Encountering development: the making and unmaking of the third world.* Princeton, NJ: Princeton University Press.

Evans, I.H.N. 1922. *Among primitive peoples in Borneo: a description of the lives, habits and customs of the piratical head-hunters of North Borneo, with an account of interesting objects of prehistoric antiquity discovered in the island.* London: Seeley.

Evans, I.H.N. 1923. *Studies in religion, folk-lore, and custom in British North Borneo and the Malay Peninsula.* Cambridge: Cambridge University Press.

Evans, I.H.N. 1927. *Papers on the ethnology and archaeology of the Malay Peninsula.* Cambridge: Cambridge University Press.

Evans, I.H.N. 1937. *The Negritos of Malaya.* London: Routledge.

Evans, I.H.N. 1953. *The religion of the Tempusuk Dusuns of North Borneo.* Cambridge: Cambridge University Press.

Fabian, J. 1983. *Time and the other: how anthropology makes its object.* New York: Columbia University Press.

Feldman-Bianco, B. 1999. Immigration, cultural contestations, and the reconfiguration of identities: the case of the female cultural brokers. *Journal of Latin American Anthropology.* 4(2): 126–141.

Ferguson, J. 1994. *The anti-politics machine: "development," depoliticization, and bureaucratic power in Lesotho.* Minneapolis and London: University of Minnesota Press.

Field, L.W. 2009. Four kinds of authenticity? regarding Nicaraguan pottery in Scandinavian museums, 2006–08. *American Ethnologist.* 36(3): 507–520.

Fiskesjo, M. 2015. Wa grotesque: headhunting theme parks and the Chinese nostalgia for primitive contemporaries. *Ethnos.* 80(4): 497–523.

Fonneland, T.A. 2013. Sami tourism and the signposting of spirituality. The case of Sami tour: a spiritual entrepreneur in the contemporary experience economy. *Acta Borealia.* 30(2): 190–208.

Forest People Programme. 2016. *Tongod villagers secure settlement of land claim with palm oil developer Genting Plantations.* Retrieved on 21 May 2020 from World Wide Web: https://www.forestpeoples.org/en/topics/palm-oil-rspo/news/2016/04/tongod-villagers-secure-settlement-land-claim-palm-oil-developer-g

Forni, S. 2017. Visual diplomacy: art circulation and iconoclashes in the kingdom of Bamun. In: *The inbetweenness of things.* Basu, P. ed. pp. 149–167. London: Bloomsbury Academic.

Forte, M.C. ed. 2010. *Indigenous cosmopolitans: transnational and transcultural indigeneity in the twenty-first century.* New York: Peter Lang.

Foster, R.F. 2001. *The Irish story: telling tales and making it up in Ireland.* London: The Penguin Press.

Fox, J. 2002. Siam mapped and mapping Cambodia: boundaries, sovereignty, and indigenous concepts of space. *Society of Natural Resources.* 15: 65–78.

Freitas, R. 2016. Cultural mapping as a developmental tool. *City, Culture and Society.* 7: 9–16.

Furley, O.W. 1971. Education and the chiefs in East Africa in the inter-war period. *Transafrican Journal of History.* 1(1): 60–83.

Furness, W.H. 1902. *The home-life of Borneo head-hunters: its festivals and folklore.* Philadelphia, PA: J.B. Lippincott Company.

Fyfe, G. and Ross, M. 1996. Decoding the visitor's gaze: rethinking museum visiting. In: *Theorizing museums: representing identity and diversity in a changing world.* MacDonald, S. and Fyfe, G. eds. pp. 127–152. Oxford: Blackwell Publishers.

Geismar, H. 2005. Copyright in context: carvings, carvers, and commodities in Vanuatu. *American Ethnologist.* 32(3): 437–459.

Geismar, H. 2013. *Treasured possessions: indigenous interventions into cultural and intellectual property.* Durham, NC and London: Duke University Press.

Gershon, I. 2006. When culture is not a system; why Samoan cultural brokers cannot do their job. *Ethnos.* 71(4): 533–558.

Ghosh, K. 2006. Between global flows and local dams: indigenousness, locality, and the transnational sphere in Jharkhand, India. *Cultural Anthropology.* 21(4): 501–534.

Gibson, L. and Pendlebury, J. eds. 2009. *Valuing historic environments.* Surrey: Ashgate Publishing Limited.

Gingging, F.A.M. 2007. "I lose my head in Borneo": tourism and the refashioning of the headhunting narrative in Sabah, Malaysia. *Cultural Analysis.* 6: 1–29.

Glass, A. 2006. From cultural salvage to brokerage: the mythologization of Mungo Martin and the emergence of northwest coast art. *Museum Anthropology.* 29(1): 20–43.

Goffman, E. 1959. *The presentation of the self in everyday life.* Garden City, NY: Doubleday.

Golding, V. and Modest, W. eds. 2015. *Museums and communities: curators, collections and collaborations.* London: Bloomsbury.

Gould, R.V. and Fernandez, R.M. 1989. Structures of mediation: a formal approach to brokerage in transaction networks. *Sociological Methodology.* 19: 89–126.

Graham, B., Ashworth, G.J. and Tunbridge, J.E. 2000. *A geography of heritage: power, culture and economy.* London: Arnold.

Graham, L.R. and Penny, H.G. 2014. *Performing Indigeneity: global histories and contemporary experiences.* Lincoln and London: University of Nebraska Press.

Gray, C. 2007. Commodification and instrumentality in cultural policy. *International Journal of Cultural Policy.* 13(2): 203–215.

Greenwood, D. 1989. Culture by the pound: an anthropological perspective on tourism as cultural commoditization. In: *Hosts and guests: the anthropology of tourism.* Smith, V.L. ed. 2nd ed. pp. 171–185. Philadelphia: University of Pennsylvania Press.

Gruber, J.W. 1970. Ethnographic salvage and the shaping of anthropology. *American Anthropologist.* 72(6): 1289–1299.

Grunewald, R. 2002. Tourism and cultural revival. *Annals of Tourism Research.* 29(4): 1004–1021.

Hale, C.R. 2006. Activist research v. cultural critique: indigenous land rights and the contradictions of politically engaged anthropology. *Cultural Anthropology.* 21(1): 96–102.

Hall, S. 1996. New ethnicities. In: *Stuart hall: critical dialogues in cultural studies.* Morley, D. and Chen, K.S. eds. pp. 441–449. London and New York: Routledge.

Hall, S. 1999. Un-settling 'the heritage', re-imagining the post-nation: whose heritage? *Third Text.* 13(49): 3–13.

Hall, T. and Robertson, I. 2001. Public art and urban regeneration: advocacy, claims and critical debates. *Landscape Research.* 26(1): 5–26.

Hames, R. 2007. The ecologically noble savage debate. *Annual Review of Anthropology.* 36: 177–190.

Harkin, M. 2003. Staged encounters: postmodern tourism and aboriginal people. *Ethnohistory.* 50(3): 575–585.

Harrison, L. and Huntington, S. eds. 2000. *Culture matters: how values shape human progress.* New York: Basic Books.

Harrison, R. ed. 2010. *Understanding the politics of heritage.* Manchester: Manchester University Press.

Harrison, R. 2013. *Heritage: critical approaches.* Abingdon and New York: Routledge.

Harrisson, B. 1986. *Pusaka: heirloom jars of Borneo.* Singapore: Oxford University Press.

Hashim, R. 2007. *Sabah traditional ethnic houses.* Kuala Lumpur: Department of Museum Malaysia.

Heibrum, J. and Gray, C.M. 2001. *The economics of art and culture.* 2nd ed. New York: Cambridge University Press.

Heinen, D. 2004. Comments: on the return of the native. *Current Anthropology.* 45(2): 262.

Hendry, J. 2002. Being ourselves for us: some transformative indigenous ideas of ethnographic display. *Journal of Museum Ethnography.* 14: 24–37.

Hendry, J. 2005. *Reclaiming culture: indigenous people and self-representation.* New York: Palgrave Macmillan.

Hinderaker, E. 1996. The 'four Indian kings' and the imaginative construction of the first British empire. *William and Mary Quarterly 3rd Series.* 53: 487–526.

Hinderaker, E. 2002. Translation and cultural brokerage. In: *A companion to American Indian History.* Deloria, P.J. and Salisbury, N. eds. pp. 357–375. Oxford: Blackwell Publishers Limited.

Hobsbawm, E. and Ranger, T. eds. 1983. *The invention of tradition.* Cambridge, MA: Cambridge University Press.

Hodgson, D.L. 2009. Becoming indigenous in Africa. *African Studies Review.* 52(3): 1–32.

Hoffstaedter, G. 2008. Representing culture in Malaysian cultural theme parks: tensions and contradictions. *Anthropological Forum.* 18: 139–160

Hohenstein, J. and Moussouri, T. 2018. *Museum learning: Theory and research as tools for enhancing practice.* London and New York: Routledge.

Holden, J. 2004. *Capturing cultural value: how culture has become a tool of government policy.* London: Demos. Retrieved on 7 July 2017 from World Wide Web: https://www.demos.co.uk/files/CapturingCulturalValue.pdf

Holden, J. 2006. *Cultural value and the crisis of legitimacy: why culture needs a democratic mandate.* London: Demos. Retrieved on 7 July 2017 from World Wide Web: https://www.demos.co.uk/files/Culturalvalueweb.pdf

Hose, C. and McDougall, W. 1912a. *The pagan tribes of Borneo, Volume I.* London: MacMillan and Co. Limited.

Hose, C. and McDougall, W. 1912b. *The pagan tribes of Borneo, Volume II.* London: MacMillan and Co. Limited.

Hoskins, J. ed. 1996. *Headhunting and the social imagination in Southeast Asia.* Stanford, CA: Stanford University Press.

Hudson, R. 1995. Making music work? Alternative regeneration strategies in a de-industrialised locality: the case of Derwentside. *Transactions, Institute of British Geographers.* 20: 460–473.

Idrus, R. 2010. From wards to citizens: indigenous rights and citizenship in Malaysia. *PoLAR: Political and Legal Anthropological Review.* 33(1): 89–108.

Inguanzo, I. and Wright, C. 2016. Indigenous movements in Southeast Asia: an analysis based on the concept of 'resonance'. *Asia-Pacific Social Science Review.* 16(1): 1–17.

Intrepid Travel. n.d. *Borneo tours and travel.* Retrieved on 29 June 2017 from World Wide Web: http://www.intrepidtravel.com/uk/borneo

IPHRD Network. 2017. *Malaysia: High Court grants the Orang Seletar rights to their customary lands and waters.* Retrieved on 10 July 2017 from World Wide Web: http://iphrdefenders.net/malaysia-high-court-grants-orang-seletar-rights-customary-lands-waters/

Iskandar Malaysia. 2016. *Our development plan.* Retrieved on 30 January 2017 from World Wide Web: http://iskandarmalaysia.com.my/our-development-plan/

Jabatan Kemajuan Orang Asli (JAKOA). 2016. *Pelan Strategik Jabatan Kemajuan Orang Asli: 2016-2020.* Retrieved on 21 May 2020 from World Wide Web: https://www.jakoa.gov.my/wp-content/uploads/2019/12/pelan-strategik-JAKOA.pdf

Jaringan Orang Asal SeMalaysia [Indigenous Peoples Network of Malaysia] (JOAS). n.d. *Background.* Retrieved on 21 May 2020 from World Wide Web: https://www.forestpeoples.org/en/partner/jaringan-orang-asal-semalaysia-joas-indigenous-peoples-network-malaysia

Jeyabalan, P. and Hutagalung, F. 2015. The effects of animal themed lessons on alphabet knowledge among the indigenous pre-schoolers in Pulau Carey, Malaysia. In: *The role of tourism in the hospitality and tourism industry.* Gaol, F.L. and Hutagalung, F. eds. pp. 69–76. Abingdon: Taylor and Francis Group.

Johnson, N.C. 1999. Framing the past: time, space and the politics of heritage tourism in Ireland. *Political Geography.* 18: 187–207.

Johor Bahru High Court. 2017. *Judgment Reason for Case No: 22NCVC-15806/2013.* Johor Bahru.

Jones, A. 1968. The Orang Asli: An outline of their progress in modern Malaya. *Journal of Southeast Asian History.* 9: 286–305.

Jones, S. 2008. Political ecology and land degradation: how does the land lie 21 years after Blaikie and Brookfield's Land Degradation and Society? *Geography Compass.* 2: 671–694.

Jumper, R.D.L. 1999. *Orang Asli now: the Orang Asli in the Malaysian political world.* New York: University Press of America, Inc.

Jung, C. 2003. The politics of indigenous identity: neoliberalism, cultural rights, and the Mexican Zapatistas. *Social Research.* 70(2): 433–462.

Kahin, G.M. 1947. The state of North Borneo 1881–1946. *The Journal of Asian Studies.* 7(1): 43–65.

Kallen, A. 2015. Hintang and the double-bind promise of development. In: *Museums, heritage and international development*. Basu, P. and Modest, W. eds. pp. 229–249. New York and London: Routledge.

Kaplan, F. 1994. ed. *Museums and the making of "ourselves": the role of objects in national identity*. Leicester: University of Leicester Press.

Karim, W.B. 1981. *Ma'Betisek concepts of living things*. Atlantic Highlands, NJ: The Athlone Press.

Karlsson, B.G. 2003. Anthropology and the 'indigenous' slot: claims to and debates about indigenous peoples' status in India. *Critique of Anthropology*. 23(4): 403–423.

Karp, I., Kreamer, C.M. and Lavine, S.D. eds. 1992. *Museums and communities: the politics of public culture*. Washington, DC and London: Smithsonian Institution Press.

Kenrick, J. and Lewis, J. 2004a. Indigenous peoples' rights and the politics of the term "indigenous." *Anthropology Today*. 20(2): 4–9.

Kenrick, J. and Lewis, J. 2004b. Comments: on the return of the native. *Current Anthropology*. 45(2): 263.

King, V.T. and Wilder, W.D. 2003. *An introduction to the modern anthropology of South-East Asia*. London: Routledge.

Kingsbury, B. 1998. "Indigenous peoples" in international law: a constructivist approach to the Asian controversy. *The American Journal of International Law*. 92(3): 414–457.

Kirsch, S. 2007. Indigenous movements and the risks of counter-globalisation: tracking the campaign against Papua New Guinea's OK Tedi mine. *American Ethnologist*. 34(2): 303–321.

Kirshenblatt-Gimblett, B. 2004. Intangible heritage as a metacultural production. *Museum International*. 56: 52–65.

KLF. 2005. *KLF golf 2005 souvenir book*. Kota Kinabalu: Kadazandusun Language Foundation.

Knell, J. and Taylor, M. 2011. *Arts funding, austerity and the big society: remaking the case for the arts*. London: Royal Society of Arts. Retrieved on 7 July 2017 from World Wide Web: https://www.thersa.org/globalassets/pdfs/reports/rsa-pamphlets-arts_funding_austerity_bigsociety.pdf

Koh, K.Y. and Hatten, T.S. 2002. The tourism entrepreneur. *International Journal of Hospitality and Tourism Administration*. 3(1): 21–48.

Koswanage, N. 2010. Oil palms threaten survival of Malaysia's tribal art. *Reuters*, 5 February. Retrieved on 27 June 2018 from World Wide Web: https://www.reuters.com/article/us-malaysia-tribe-art/oil-palms-threaten-survival-of-malaysias-tribal-arts-idUSTRE6140IP20100205

Kreps, C.F. 2003. *Liberating culture: cross-cultural perspectives on museums, curation, and heritage preservation*. London and New York: Routledge.

Kreps, C.F. 2007. The theoretical future of indigenous museums: concept and practice. In: *The future of indigenous museums: perspectives from the southwest Pacific*. Stanley, N. ed. pp. 223–234. Oxford: Berghahn.

Kreps, C.F. 2008. Appropriate museology in theory and practice. *Museum Management and Curatorship*. 23(1): 23–41.

Kreps, C.F. 2014. Thai monastery museums: contemporary expressions of ancient traditions. In: *Transforming knowledge orders: museums, collections and exhibitions*. Forster, L. ed. pp. 230–256. Cologne: Center for Advanced Studies.

Krohn, W.O. 1927. *In Borneo jungles: among the Dayak head-hunters.* NY: The Bobbs-Merrill Company.

Kuper, A. 1988. *The invention of primitive society: transformation of an illusion.* New York: Routledge.

Kuper, A. 2003. On the return of the native. *Current Anthropology.* 44(3): 389–395.

Kurin, R. 1997. *Reflections of a culture broker: a view from the Smithsonian.* Washington, DC and London: Smithsonian Institution Press.

Labadi, S. 2013. *UNESCO, cultural heritage and outstanding universal value.* Plymouth, MA: Alta Mira.

Labadi, S. ed. 2019. *The cultural turn in international aid.* London and New York: Routledge.

Labadi, S. and Gould, G.G. 2015. Sustainable development: heritage, community, economics. In: *Global heritage: a reader.* Meskell, L. ed. pp. 196–216. NJ: John Wiley and Sons.

Landorf, C. 2009. Managing for sustainable tourism: a review of six cultural World Heritage sites. *Journal of Sustainable Tourism.* 17: 53–70.

Lasimbang, A. 2004a. *Community mapping in Malaysia: the use of community maps in resources management and protecting rights over indigenous peoples' territory.* Paper presented to Regional Community Mapping Network Workshop, Diliman, Quezon City, Philippines, 8–10 December 2004. Retrieved on 16 February 2017 from World Wide Web: http://www.iapad.org/wp-content/uploads/2015/07/pacos.pdf

Lasimbang, R. 2004b. *To promote the Kadazandusun languages of Sabah.* Retrieved on 17 July 2017 from World Wide Web: http://www.accu.or.jp/appreb/09/pdf34-2/34-2P010-012.pdf

Lasimbang, R. and Moo-Tan, S. 1997. *An introduction to the traditional costumes of Sabah.* Kota Kinabalu: Natural History Publications and Department of Sabah Museum.

Leary, J. 1995. *Violence and the dream people: the Orang Asli in the Malayan emergency, 1948–1960.* Athens: Ohio University Center for International Studies.

Leonie, A., Lasimbang, J., Jonas, H. and Mansul, B. 2015. *Red and raw: indigenous rights in Malaysia and the law.* Donggongon, Sabah: Jaringan Orang Asal Semalaysia (Indigenous Peoples Network of Malaysia).

Lewis, D. and Mosse, D. eds. 2006. *Development brokers and translators: the ethnography of aid and agencies.* West Hartford, CT: Kumarian Press Inc.

Li, T.M. 2000. Articulating indigenous identity in Indonesia: resource politics and the tribal slot. *Comparative Studies in Society and History.* 42: 149–179.

Lin, R. 2016. Mah Meri carvers do it with spirit. *The Star Online,* 2 February. Retrieved on 21 May 2020 from World Wide Web: https://www.thestar.com.my/lifestyle/star2.com-video/2016/02/02/mah-meri-carvers-do-it-with-spirit

Lindquist, J. 2015. Anthropology of brokers and brokerage. In: *International Encyclopedia of the social & behavioral sciences.* Wright, J.D. ed. 2nd ed. Amsterdam: Elsevier.

Lingenfelter, S.G. ed. 1990. *Social organization of Sabah societies.* Kota Kinabalu: Department of Sabah Museum and State Archives.

Linnekin, J. 1983. Defining tradition: variations on the Hawaiian identity. *American Ethnologist.* 10: 241–252.

Linnekin, J. 1992. On the theory and politics of cultural construction in the Pacific. *Oceania*. 62: 249–263.

Lonetree, A. 2012. *Decolonizing museums: representing native America in national and tribal museums*. Chapel Hill: The University of North Carolina Press.

Low, S. 2003. Social sustainability: people, history, values. In: *Managing change: sustainable approaches to the conservation of the built environment*. Teutonico, J.M. and Matero, F. eds. pp. 47–64. Los Angeles, CA: Getty Conservation Institute.

Low, S.M. and Merry, S.E. 2010. Engaged anthropology: diversity and dilemmas. *Current Anthropology*. 51(S2): S203–S226.

Lowenthal, D. 1998. *The heritage crusade and the spoils of history*. Cambridge, MA: Cambridge University Press.

Lu, T.L.D. 2013. *Museums in China: power, politics and identities*. London and New York: Routledge.

Luke, T.W. 2002. *Museum politics: power plays at the exhibition*. Minneapolis: University of Minnesota Press.

Lumley, R. 1988. *The museum time machine: putting cultures on display*. London and New York: Routledge.

Luping, H.J. 2009. *Indigenous ethnic communities of Sabah: the Kadazandusun*. Kuala Lumpur: Ministry of Information, Communications and Culture Malaysia.

Lynch, G. 2011. Becoming indigenous in the pursuit of justice: the African Commission on human and peoples' rights and the Endorois. *African Affairs*. 111(442): 24–45.

MacCannell, D. 1973. Staged authenticity: arrangements of social space in tourist settings. *American Journal of Sociology*. 73(3): 589–603.

MacCannell, D. 1992. *Empty meeting grounds: the tourist papers*. London: Routledge.

Macdonald, S. 2006a. Expanding museum studies: an introduction. In: *A companion to museum studies*. MacDonald, S. ed. pp. 1–12. Hoboken, NJ: Blackwell Publishing Ltd.

Macdonald, S. 2006b. Mediating heritage: tour guides at the former Nazi party rally grounds, Nuremburg. *Tourist Studies*. 6: 119–138.

MacDonald, S. and Fyfe, G. eds. 1996. *Theorizing museums: representing identity and diversity in a changing world*. Oxford: Blackwell Publishers.

Majikol, E. and Majikol, S. 2000. *Monsopiad: the Kadazandusun warrior*. Kota Kinabalu: Kadazandusun Language Foundation.

Malaysian Forestry Department. 2015. *Malaysian criteria and indicators for Forest Management Certification [National Forest]*. Retrieved on 21 May 2020 from World Wide Web http://www.mtcc.com.my/wp-content/uploads/2015/02/MCI-Forest-Plantation.v2-16-Feb-2015.pdf

Mandelman, A. 2014. Unstrategic essentialism: material culture and Hawaiian articulations of indigeneity. *Social and Cultural Geography*. 15(2): 172–200.

Manickam, S.K. 2015. *Taming the wild: aborigines and racial knowledge in colonial Malaya*. Singapore: Asian Studies Association of Australia in association with NUS Press.

Marcus, G.E. 1995. Ethnography in/of the world system: the emergence of multi-sited ethnography. *Annual Review of Anthropology*. 24: 95–117.

Marstine, J. 2016. *Critical practice: artists, museums, ethics.* London and New York: Routledge.

Mason, A. 2010. Whither the historicities of Alutiiq heritage work are drifting. In: *Indigenous cosmopolitans: transnational and transcultural indigeneity in the twenty-first century.* Forte, M.C. ed. pp. 77–96. New York: Peter Lang.

Massey, D. 1994. A global sense of place. In: *Space, place and gender.* Massey, D. ed. pp. 146–156. Cambridge, MA: Polity Press.

McCarthy, C. 2007. *Exhibiting Maori: a history of colonial cultures of display.* Oxford and New York: Berg.

McCarthy, K.F, Ondaatje, E.H., Zakaras, L. and Brooks, A. 2004. *Gifts of the muse: reframing the debate about the benefits of the arts.* Santa Monica, CA: RAND Corporation. Retrieved on 7 July 2017 from World Wide Web: http://www.rand.org/content/dam/rand/pubs/monographs/2005/RAND_MG218.pdf

McCormack, F. 2011. Levels of indigeneity: the Maori and neoliberalism. *Journal of the Royal Anthropological Institute.* 17: 281–300.

McKean, P.F. 1976. Tourism, cultural change and cultural conservation in Bali. In: *Changing identities in modern Southeast Asia.* Banks, D.J. ed. pp. 237–248. Hague: Mouton.

Mead, S.M. 1983. Indigenous models of museums in Oceania. *Museum.* 138: 98–101.

Merlan, F. 2007. Indigeneity as relational identity: the construction of Australian land rights. In: *Indigenous experience today.* de la Cadena, M. and Starn, O. eds. pp. 125–149. New York and Oxford: Berg.

Merlan, F. 2009. Indigeneity: global and local. *Current Anthropology.* 50(3): 303–333.

Merrell, J. 1997. 'The cast of his countenance': reading Andrew Montour. In: *Through a glass darkly: reflections on personal identity in early America.* Hoffman, R., Sobel, M. and Teute, F.J. eds. pp. 13–39. Chapel Hill: University of North Carolina Press.

Merry, M. 1991. Malaysia and Brazil putting up resistance to 1992 Earth Summit. *Executive Intelligence Review.* 19(33): 10–11.

Merry, S.E. 2006. Transnational human rights and local activism: mapping the middle. *American Anthropologist.* 108(1): 38–51.

Metcalf, P. 2010. *The life of the longhouse: an archaeology of ethnicity.* Cambridge: Cambridge University Press.

Minkin, D., Whitelaw, G.S., McCarthy, D.D.P., and Tsuji, L.J.S. 2014. Cultural protection, empowerment and land use planning: identification of values in support of Fort Albany First Nation, Ontario, Canada, community based land use planning. *The Canadian Journal of Native Studies.* 34(1): 129–150.

Mitchell, D. 1995. There's no such thing as culture: towards a reconceptualization of the idea of culture in geography. *Transactions of the Institute of British Geographers.* 20(1): 102–116.

Moore, E. 2010. The Williams-Hunt collection, aerial photographs and cultural landscapes in Malaysia and Southeast Asia. *Sari: International Journal of Malay World Studies.* 27(2): 265–284.

Mowforth, M. and Munt, I. 2009. *Tourism and sustainability.* New York: Routledge.

N.A. 2012. Ministry to promote Mah Meri Cultural Village. *The Star Online,* 2 February. Retrieved on 8 May 2014 from World Wide Web: http://www.thestar.com.my/News/Nation/2012/02/02/Ministry-to-promote-Mah-Meri-cultural-village.aspx/

N.A. 2013. A never-ending policy. *The Economist*, 27 April. Retrieved on 21 May 2020 from World Wide Web: https://www.economist.com/briefing/2013/04/27/a-never-ending-policy

N.A. 2015. Sabah calls in army to clear river-choking debris. *The Straits Times Online*, 19 June 2015. Retrieved on 21 May 2020 from World Wide Web: https://www.straitstimes.com/asia/se-asia/sabah-calls-in-army-to-clear-river-choking-debris

N.A. 2015. Hundreds flee homes after Mount Kinabalu floods *The Straits Times Online*, 16 June 2015. Retrieved on 21 May 2020 from World Wide Web: https://www.straitstimes.com/asia/se-asia/hundreds-flee-homes-after-mount-kinabalu-floods

N.A. 2016. Sabah Parks Deputy Chairman dies. *The Daily Express*, 6 May 2016. Retrieved on 21 May 2020 from World Wide Web: http://dailyexpress.com.my/news.cfm?newsid=109465v

N.A. 2016. Spirit carvings of the Mah Meri Orang Asli. *The Star TV*, 3 February. Retrieved on 21 May 2020 from World Wide Web: https://www.thestartv.com/v/fcx-spirit-carvings-of-the-mah-meri-orang-asli

Nadasdy, P. 2005. Transcending the debate over the ecologically noble Indian: indigenous peoples and environmentalism. *Ethnohistory*. 52(2): 291–331.

Nah, A.M. 2003. Negotiating indigenous identity in postcolonial Malaysia: beyond being "not quite/not Malay." *Social Identities*. 9: 511–534.

Nah, A.M. 2008. Recognizing indigenous identity in postcolonial Malaysian law: rights and realities for the Orang Asli (aborigines) of Peninsular Malaysia. *Bijdragen tot de Taal-, Land- en Volkenkunde*. 164: 212–237.

Nicholas, C. 2000. *The Orang Asli and the contest for resources: indigenous politics, development and identity in Peninsular Malaysia*. Subang Jaya: Center for Orang Asli Concerns.

Nicholas, C. 2014. *Expert report on the history, presence and situation of the Seletar-Orang Asli in the Kampung Bakar Batu-Kampung Sungai Temon (Danga Bay) customary territory*. Presented to High Court of Malaya at Johor Bahru Case No. 22NCvC-158-06/2013.

Nicholas, C., Engi, J. and Teh, Y.P. 2010. *The Orang Asli and the UNDRIP: from rhetoric to recognition*. Subang Jaya: Center for Orang Asli Concerns.

Niezen, R. 2003. *The origins of indigenism: human rights and the politics of identity*. Berkeley: University of California Press.

Nordin, R. and Witbrodt, M.A. 2012. Self-determination of indigenous peoples: the case of the Orang Asli. *Asia Pacific Law Review*. 20: 189–210.

OECD/ICOM. 2018. *Culture and local development: maximising the impact: guide for local governments, communities and museums*. Paris: Organisation for Economic Co-operation and Development (OECD) and the International Council of Museums (ICOM). Retrieved on 21 May 2020 from World Wide Web: https://icom.museum/wp-content/uploads/2019/08/ICOM-OECD-GUIDE_EN_FINAL.pdf

OHCHR. 2013. *The United Nations Declaration on the Rights of Indigenous Peoples: A Manual for National Human Rights Institutions*. Switzerland, Geneva: Office of the United Nations High Commissioner for Human Rights (OHCHR). Retrieved on 27 December 2016 from World Wide Web: http://www.ohchr.org/Documents/Issues/IPeoples/UNDRIPManualForNHRIs.pdf

Omura, K. 2003. Comments: on the return of the native. *Current Anthropology*. 44(3): 395–396.

Onciul, B. 2015. *Museums, heritage and Indigenous voice: decolonising engagement*. London and New York: Routledge.

Orang Asli Museum. n.d.a. Brochure of Orang Asli museum. Gombak: National Orang Asli Museum.

Orang Asli Museum. n.d.b. Exhibition labels of Orang Asli museum. Gombak: National Orang Asli Museum.

Orlove, B.S. 1991. Mapping reeds and reading maps: the politics of representation in Lake Titicaca. *American Ethnologist.* 18(1): 235–273.

Osorio, S.G.C. and Best, G. 2015. A case study of culture brokers and their role in tourism management in the indigenous community of Taquile island in Puno, Peru. *International Journal of Tourism Research.* 17: 247–355.

Palmer, M. and Rundstrom, R. 2013. GIS, internal colonialism, and the U.S. Bureau of Indian Affairs. *Annals of the Association of American Geographers.* 103(5): 1142–1159.

Panelli, R. 2008. Social geographies: encounters with Indigenous and more-than-White/Anglo geographies. *Progress in Human Geography.* 32: 801–811.

Partners of Community Organizations in Sabah (PACOS) Trust. n.d. *Who are we.* Retrieved on 3 March 2016 from World Wide Web: http://pacostrust.com/about/who-are-we/

Patrick, T. 2015. All is not well on Mt Kinabalu. *The Daily Express Online,* 15 June 2015. Retrieved on 8 April 2017 from World Wide Web: http://www.dailyexpress.com.my/news.cfm?NewsID=100623

Patrick, T. and Majantim, R. 2015. First ritual to appease Mt Kinabalu guardians. *The Daily Express Online,* 17 June 2015. Retrieved on 8 April 2017 from World Wide Web: http://www.dailyexpress.com.my/news.cfm?NewsID=100693

Peace, A. 1998. Anthropology in the postmodern landscape: the importance of cultural brokers and their trade. *The Australian Journal of Anthropology.* 9(3): 274–284.

Pearce, D.G. 1992. Alternative tourism: concepts, classifications and questions. In: *Tourism alternatives: potentials and problems in the development of tourism.* Smith, V.L. and Eadington, W.R. eds. pp. 15 –30. Philadelphia: University of Pennsylvania Press.

Peers, L. 2007. *Playing ourselves: interpreting native histories at historic reconstructions.* Plymouth: Altamira Press.

Peers, L. and Brown, A.K. 2003. *Museums and source communities: a reader.* London and New York: Routledge.

Peluso, N.L. 1995. Whose woods are these? Counter-mapping forest territories in Kalimantan, Indonesia. *Antipode.* 27: 383–406.

Perley, B. 2014. Living traditions: a manifesto for critical Indigeneity. In: *Performing Indigeneity: global histories and contemporary experiences.* Graham, L.R. and Penny, H.G. eds. pp. 21–37. Lincoln and London: University of Nebraska Press.

Phelan, P.R. 1997. *Traditional stone and wood monuments of Sabah.* Kota Kinabalu: Centre for Borneo Studies.

Phelan, P.R. 2001. *Headhunting and the Magang ceremony in Sabah.* Kota Kinabalu: Natural History Publications (Borneo).

Porter, B.W. and Salazar, N.B. 2005. Heritage tourism, conflict, and the public interest: an introduction. *International Journal of Heritage Studies.* 11(5): 361–370.

Porter, L. 2010. *Unlearning the colonial cultures of planning.* Burlington, VT and Farnham: Ashgate.

Povinelli, E.A. 2011. The governance of the prior. *Interventions.* 13(1): 13–30.

Probojo, L. 2010. Ritual guardians versus civil servants as cultural brokers in the new order era. *Indonesia and the Malay World.* 38(110): 95–107.

Pugh-Kitingan, J. and John Baptist, J. 2009. Music for cleansing the universe-drumming and gong ensemble music in the Mamahui Pogun ceremonies of the Lotud Dusun of Tuaran, Sabah, Malaysia. *Borneo Research Bulletin.* 40: 249–276.

Radcliffe, S.A. ed. 2006. *Culture and development in a globalising world: geographies, actors, and paradigms.* London: Routledge.

Radcliffe, S.A. 2017. Geography and Indigeneity I: Indigeneity, coloniality and knowledge. *Progress in Human Geography.* 41(2): 220–229.

Radcliffe, S.A. 2018. Geography and Indigeneity II: critical geographies of Indigenous bodily politics. *Progress in Human Geography.* 42(3): 436–445.

Rahim, R. 2007. *Chita' Hae: culture, crafts and customs of the Hma' Meri in Kampung Sungai Bumbun, Pulau Carey.* Kuala Lumpur: Center for Orang Asli Concerns.

Rahnema, M. and Bawtree, V. eds. 1997. *The post-development reader.* London: Zed Books.

Ramos, A.R. 2003. Comments: on the return of the native. *Current Anthropology.* 44(3): 397–398.

Rata, E. 2002. The transformation of indigeneity. *Review (Fernand Braudel Center).* 25(2): 173–195.

Redford, K. 1990. The ecologically noble savage. *Orion Nature Quarterly.* 9(3): 25–29.

Regis, P. 1993. *Rice power and its magic: a brief introduction to the culture of rice in Sabah.* Kota Kinabalu: Department of Sabah Museum.

Regis, P. 2007. Textiles of Sabah. In: *The encyclopedia of Malaysia crafts and the visual arts.* Jamal, D.S.A. ed. pp. 66–67. Singapore: Editor Didier Millet.

Reid, A. 2009. *Imperial alchemy: nationalism and political identity in Southeast Asia.* Cambridge: Cambridge University Press.

Relph, E. 1976. *Place and placelessness.* London: Verso.

Robins, S. 2003. Comments: on the return of the native. *Current Anthropology.* 44(3): 398–399.

Roth, J. L. 1896a. *The natives of Sarawak and British North Borneo, Volume I.* London: Truslove and Hanson.

Roth, H.L. 1896b. *The natives of Sarawak and British North Borneo, Volume II.* London: Truslove and Hanson.

Rutter, O. 1922. *British North Borneo: an account of its history, resources and native tribes.* London: Constable and Company Limited.

Rutter, O. 1929. *The pagans of North Borneo.* London: Hutchinson and Co. (Publishers) Limited.

Sabah Museum. 2001. Highlights of Kaamatan. In: *Pesta Kaamatan 2001 souvenir booklet.* Said, N.J. and Charuruks, I.B. eds. pp. 28–29. Penampang: KDCA.

Sahlins, M. 1999. Two or three things that I know about culture. *The Journal of the Royal Anthropological Institute.* 5(3): 399–421.

Salazar, N.B. 2005. Tourism and glocalization "local" tour guiding. *Annals of Tourism Research.* 32(3): 628–646.

Salazar, N.B. 2007. Towards a global culture of heritage interpretation? Evidence of Indonesia and Tanzania. *Tourism Recreation Research.* 32(3): 23–30.

Salazar, N.B. 2009. Imaged or imagined? Cultural representations and the 'tourismification' of peoples and places. *Cahiers d'Etudes Africaines.* 49(193/194): 49–71.

Salazar, N.B. 2010. *Envisioning Eden: mobilising imaginaries in tourism and beyond.* New York and Oxford: Berghahn Books.

Salazar, N.B. 2012. Community-based cultural tourism: issues, threats and opportunities. *Journal of Sustainable Tourism.* 20: 9–22.

Salazar, N.B. 2013. Imagineering otherness: anthropological legacies in contemporary tourism. *Anthropological Quarterly.* 86(3): 669–696.

Salazar, N.B. and Graburn, N.H.H. eds. 2015. *Tourism imaginaries: anthropological approaches.* New York and Oxford: Berghahn Books.

Salazar, N.B. and Zhu, Y. 2015. Heritage and tourism. In: *Global heritage: a reader.* Meskell, L. ed. pp. 240–258. Somerset: John Wiley and Sons.

Samuels, K.L. 2015. Introduction: heritage as persuasion. In: *Heritage keywords: rhetoric and redescription in cultural heritage.* Samuels, K.F. and Rico, T. eds. pp. 3–28. Boulder: University Press of Colorado.

Sario, R. 2013. Australian university wants to preserve culture and language of Lotud folk. *The Star Online,* 2 January 2013. Retrieved on 21 May 2020 from World Wide Web: https://www.thestar.com.my/news/nation/2013/01/02/australian-university-wants-to-preserve-culture-and-language-of-lotud-folk

Saugestad, S. 2001. *The inconvenient indigenous: remote area development in Botswana, donor assistance and the first people of the Kalahari.* Uppsala: Nordiska Afrikainstitutet.

Saugestad, S. 2004. Comments: on the return of the native. *Current Anthropology.* 45(2): 263–264.

Schebesta, P. 1929. *Among the forest dwarfs of Malaya.* London: Hutchinson and Co. (Publishers) Limited.

Schech, S. and Haggis, J. 2000. *Culture and development: a critical introduction.* Oxford: Blackwell.

Schiller, A. 2001. Talking heads: capturing Dayak death-ways on films. *American Ethnologist.* 28(1): 32–55.

Schiller, A. 2007. Activism and identities in an east Kalimantan Dayak organization. *The Journal of Asian Studies.* 66: 63–95.

Scott, J.C. 1985. *Weapons of the weak: everyday forms of peasant resistance.* New Haven, CT: Yale University Press.

Scott, M.K. 2017. Mediating between Mayas and the art market: the traditional-yet-contemporary carved gourd vessel. In: *The inbetweenness of things.* Basu, P. ed. pp. 171–189. London: Bloomsbury Academic.

Sen, A. 1999. *Development as freedom.* Oxford: Oxford University Press.

Shahrum, B.Y. 1971. *Mah Meri Sculpture.* Kuala Lumpur: Department of Museums Malaysia.

Shelton, A. 2013. Critical museology: a manifesto. *Museum Worlds: Advances in Research.* 1: 7–23.

Simon, G.L. 2009. Geographies of mediation: market development and the rural broker in Maharashtra, India. *Political Geography.* 28: 197–207.

Simpson, M. 1996. *Making representations: museums in the post-colonial era.* London and New York: Routledge.

Singh, D.S.R. 2011. *The making of Sabah 1865–1941: the dynamics of indigenous society.* 3rd ed. Kota Kinabalu: Bahagian Kabinet dan Dasar.

Sirom, A. and Topin, B. 2017. *Kadazandusunoloji om Rinait.* Sabah: Kadazandusun Cultural Association.

Sivasothy, M. 2011. Orang Seletar: Johor's forgotten people. *The Business Station,* 24 August. Retrieved on 10 July 2017 from World Wide Web: http://www.bfm.my/orang-seletar-johors-forgotten-people.html

Skaria, A. 1997. Shades of wildness tribe, caste, and gender in western India. *The Journal of Asian Studies*. 56: 726–745.

Skeat, W.W. and Blagden, C.O. 1906a. *Pagan races of the Malay Peninsula, Volume I*. London: Macmillan and Company Limited.

Skeat, W.W. and Blagden, C.O. 1906b. *Pagan races of the Malay Peninsula, Volume II*. London: Macmillan and Company Limited.

Sleeper-Smith, S. ed. 2009. *Contesting knowledge: museums and indigenous perspectives*. Lincoln and London: University of Nebraska Press.

Smith, L. 2006. *Uses of heritage*. London and New York: Routledge.

Smith, V.L. 1989. Eskimo tourism: micro-models and marginal men. In: *Hosts and guests: the anthropology of tourism*. Smith, V.L. ed. 2nd ed. pp. 55–82. Philadelphia: University of Pennsylvania Press.

Sofield, T.H.B. 1993. Indigenous tourism development. *Annals of Tourism Research*. 20: 729–750.

Southall, A.W. 1970. The illusion of tribe. In: *The passing of tribal man in Africa*. Gutkind, P.C.W. ed. pp. 28–50. Leiden: E.J. Brill.

Spencer, V. 1997. Herder and nationalism: reclaiming the principle of cultural respect. *Australian Journal of Politics and History*. 43(1): 1–13.

Stahler-Sholk, R. 2007. Resisting neoliberal homogenization: The Zapatista autonomy movement. *Latin American Perspectives*. 34(2): 48–63.

Stanley, N. ed. 2007. *The future of indigenous museums: perspectives from the southwest Pacific*. Oxford: Berghahn.

Stasch, R. 2015. Introduction: double signs and intra-social heterogeneity in primitivist tourism encounters. *Ethnos*. 80(4): 433–447.

Steiner, C.B. 1994. *African art in transit*. Cambridge: Cambridge University Press.

Steinmetz, G. 2008. The colonial state as a social field: ethnographic capital and native policy in the German overseas empire before 1914. *American Sociological Review*. 73(4): 589–612.

Stoler A.L. 2016. *Duress: imperial durabilities in our times*. Durham, NC: NCL Duke University Press.

Stovel, K. and Shaw, L. 2012. Brokerage. *Annual Review of Sociology*. 38: 139–158.

Straumann, L. 2014. *Money logging: on the trails of the Asian timber mafia*. Basel: Bergli Books.

Su, D. 1995. Museums and museum philosophy in China. *Nordisk Museologi*. 2: 61–80.

Su, D. and An, L. 1998. China's first eco-museum – Soga Miao community Guizhou: The first test case of international ecomuseum concept in China. In: *Museology and globalisation (ICOM 19th General Assembly, Melbourne Australia, 1998)*. Young, L. ed. pp. 41–48. Canberra: University of Canberra.

Su, X. and Teo. P. 2009. *The politics of heritage tourism in China: a view from Lijiang*. London and New York: Routledge.

Subramaniam, Y. 2011. Rights denied: Orang Asli and rights to participate in decision-making in Malaysia. *Waikato Law Review*. 19(2): 52–73.

Subramaniam, Y. 2014. Affirmative action and the legal recognition of customary land rights in peninsular Malaysia: The Orang Asli experience. *Australian Indigenous Law Review*. 17(1): 103–122.

Subramanian, Y. and Edo. J. 2016. Common law customary land rights as a catalyst for the resurgence of Orang Asli shamanism in Peninsular Malaysia: some lessons from the Semai and Temiar peoples. *Shaman*. 24(1–2): 73–94.

SUHAKAM. 2013. *Report of the national inquiry into the land rights of indigenous peoples by Human Rights Commission of Malaysia.* Retrieved on 20 January 2017 from World Wide Web: http://nhri.ohchr.org/EN/Themes/BusinessHR/Business%20Womens%20and%20Childrens%20Rights/SUHAKAM%20BI%20FINAL.CD.pdf

Suzman, J. 2003. Comments: on the return of the native. *Current Anthropology.* 44(3): 399–400.

Szasz, M.C. 2001. *Between Indians and the white worlds: the cultural broker.* Norman: University of Oklahoma Press.

Tan, T. 2017. Orang Seletar win right to Johor land and compensation. *Free Malaysia Today,* 28 February. Retrieved on 11 July 2017 from World Wide Web: http://www.freemalaysiatoday.com/category/nation/2017/02/28/orang-seletar-win-right-to-johor-land-and-compensation/

Taylor, K. 2013. Cultural mapping: intangible values and engaging with communities with some reference to Asia. *The Historic Environment.* 4(1): 50–61.

Tee, D.J. 2016. Goodbye to my trusted friend. *The Borneo Post,* 15 May 2016. Retrieved on 19 July 2017 from World Wide Web: http://www.pressreader.com/malaysia/the-borneo-post-sabah/20160515/281840052889797

Theodossopoulos, D. 2011. Embera indigenous tourism and the world of expectations. In: *Great expectations: imagination and anticipation in tourism.* Skinner, J. and Theodossopoulos, D. eds. pp. 40–60. Oxford: Berghahn.

Theodossopoulos, D. 2013. Embera indigenous tourism and the trap of authenticity: beyond inauthenticity and invention. *Anthropological Quarterly.* 86(2): 397–425.

Theodossopoulos, D. 2015. Scorn or idealisation? Tourism imaginaries, exoticisation, and ambivalence in Embera indigenous tourism. In: *Tourism imaginaries: anthropological approaches.* Salazar, N.B. and Graburn, N.H.H. eds. pp. 57–79. New York and Oxford: Berghahn Books.

Thomas, N. 1991. *Entangled objects: exchange, material culture, and colonialism in the Pacific.* London: Harvard University Press.

Thornton, S. 2008. *Seven days in the art world.* London: Granta Books.

Tilley, C. 1997. Performing culture in the global village. *Critique of Anthropology.* 17(1): 67–89.

Torrence, R. and Clarke, A. 2011. "Suitable for decoration of halls and billiard rooms": finding indigenous agency in historic auction. In: *Unpacking the collection: networks of material and social agency in the museum.* Byrne, S., Clarke, A., Harrison, R. and Torrence, R. eds. pp. 29–54. New York: Springer.

Torrence, R. and Clarke, A. 2016. Excavating ethnographic collections: negotiations and cross-cultural exchange in Papua New Guinea. *World Archaeology.* 48(2): 181–195.

Toshihiro, N. 2009. *Living on the periphery: development and the Islamization of the Orang Asli.* Kyoto: Kyoto University Press.

Tregonning, K. 1958. *Under chartered company rule: North Borneo, 1881–1946.* Singapore: University of Malaya Press.

Trouillot, M. 1991. Anthropology and the savage slot: the poetics and politics of otherness. In: *Recapturing anthropology: working in the present.* Richard, G.F. ed. pp. 17–44. Sante Fe: School of American Research Press.

Tsing, A.L. 2005. *Friction: an ethnography of global connection.* Princeton, NJ: Princeton University Press.

Tuan, Y.F. 1977. *Space and place: the perspective of experience.* London: Edward Arnold (Publishers) Limited.

Tunbridge, J.E. and Ashworth, G.J. 1996. *Dissonant heritage: the management of the past as a resource in conflict.* Chichester: Wiley.

Turner, T. 2004. Comments: on the return of the native. *Current Anthropology.* 45(2): 264–265.

UNCSD. 2012. *The future we want: outcome document of the United Nations conference on sustainable development.* Paris: UNESCO Publishing. Retrieved on 28 June 2017 from World Wide Web: https://sustainabledevelopment.un.org/content/documents/733FutureWeWant.pdf

UNDRIP. 2007. *United Nations Declaration on the Rights of Indigenous Peoples.* New York: United Nations. Retrieved on 20 October 2016 from World Wide Web: http://www.un.org/esa/socdev/unpfii/documents/DRIPS_en.pdf

UNESCO. 1995. *Our creative diversity.* World Commission on Culture and Development. Paris: UNESCO Publishing. Retrieved on 28 June 2017 from World Wide Web: http://unesdoc.unesco.org/images/0010/001016/101651e.pdf

UNESCO. 2009. *Building critical awareness of cultural mapping: a workshop facilitation guide.* Paris: UNESCO Publishing. Retrieved on 14 August 2017 from the World Wide Web: http://unesdoc.unesco.org/images/0019/001903/190314e.pdf

UNESCO. 2010a. *The power of culture for development.* World Commission on Culture and Development. Paris: UNESCO Publishing. Retrieved on 21 May 2020 from World Wide Web: https://unesdoc.unesco.org/ark:/48223/pf0000189382

UNESCO. 2010b. *Community-based approach to museum development in Asia and the Pacific for culture and sustainable development.* Paris: UNESCO Publishing. Retrieved on 28 June 2017 from World Wide Web: http://unesdoc.unesco.org/images/0018/001899/189902e.pdf

UNESCO-Bangkok. n.d. *UNESCO - AHPADA seal of excellence for handicraft products in Southeast Asia.* Retrieved on 20 January 2017 from World Wide Web: http://www.unescobkk.org/culture/resources/unesco-bangkok-culture-in-the-news/seal-of-excellence/

Urry, J. 1990. *The tourist gaze.* London: Sage.

Urry, J. 1996. How societies remember the past. In: *Theorizing museums: representing identity and diversity in a changing world.* MacDonald, S. and Fyfe, G. eds. pp. 45–68. Oxford: Blackwell Publishers.

Urteaga-Crovetto, P. 2012. The broker state and the 'inevitability' of progress: The Camisea project and Indigenous peoples in Peru. In: *The politics of resource extraction: Indigenous peoples, multinational corporations, and the state.* Sawyer, S. and Gomez, E.T. eds. pp. 103–128. London and New York: Palgrave Macmillan.

Varutti, M. 2014. *Museums in China: the politics of representation after Mao.* Suffolk: Boydell & Brewer.

Vaughan, D.R. and Booth, P. 1989 The economic importance of tourism and the arts in Merseyside. *Journal of Cultural Economics.* 132: 21–34.

Velthuis, O. 2005. *Talking prices: symbolic meanings of prices on the market for contemporary art.* Princeton, NJ: Princeton University Press.

Vergo, P. ed. 1989. *The new museology.* London: Reaktion Books.

Vizenor, G. 1999. *Manifest manners: narratives on postindian survivance.* Lincoln and London: University of Nebraska Press.

Vizenor, G. 2007. *Literary chance: essays on native American survivance*. Valencia: Universitat de València.

Wagner, R. 1981. *The invention of culture: revised and expanded edition*. Chicago, IL: The University Press of Chicago.

Wang, Y. 2007. Customised authenticity begins at home. *Annals of Tourism Research*. 34(3): 789–804.

Watson, S. ed. 2007. *Museums and their communities*. London and New York: Routledge.

Weaver, D. 2010. Indigenous tourism stages and their implications for sustainability. *Journal of Sustainable Tourism*. 18(1): 43–60.

Weber, M. 1978. *Economy and society: an outline of interpretive sociology*. Berkeley: University of California Press.

Welsch, R.L. 2000. One time, one place, three collections: colonial processes and the shaping of some museum collections from German New Guinea. In: *Hunting the gatherers: ethnographic collectors, agents and agency in Melanesia, 1870s – 1930s*. O'Hanlon, M. and Welsch, R.L. eds. pp. 155–180. London and New York: Berghahn Books.

Werner, R. 1997. *Mah Meri*. Kuala Lumpur: University of Malaya Press.

Winter, T. 2013. Clarifying the critical in critical heritage studies. *International Journal of Heritage Studies*. 19(6): 532–545.

Witcomb, A. 2003. *Re-imagining the museum: beyond the mausoleum*. London and New York: Routledge.

Wong, T.K.D. 2009. Woolley and the codification of native customs in Sabah. *New Zealand Journal of Asian Studies*. 11(1): 87–105.

Wood, R.E. 1984. Ethnic tourism, the state, and cultural change in Southeast Asia. *Annals of Tourism Research*. 11: 353–374.

Woolley, G.C. 2006. *Tuaran adat: some customs of the Dusuns of Tuaran west coast residency, North Borneo*. Kota Kinabalu: Natural History Publications (Borneo).

Wyn, S. 1974. *My life with the headhunters*. New York: Doubleday and Co.

Wynne, D. 1992. *The culture industry: the arts in urban regeneration*. Aldershot: Avebury.

Yang, J., Ryan, C. and Zhang, L. 2014. The "culture broker" as performer: Tuva and Kazkhs "home visits" in Kanas, China. *Asia Pacific Journal of Tourism Research*. 19(5): 493–516.

Yap, S. 2011. Seletar's Cultural Heritage. *The Star Online*, 2 August. Retrieved on 21 May 2020 from World Wide Web: https://www.thestar.com.my/news/community/2011/08/02/seletars-cultural-heritage

Yarrow, T. 2008. Paired opposites: dualism in development and anthropology. *Critique of Anthropology*. 28(4): 426–445.

Yelvington, K.A., Goslin, N.G. and Arriaga, W. 2002. Whose history? museummaking and struggles over ethnicity and representation in the Sunbelt. *Critique of Anthropology*. 22(3): 343–379.

Zenker, O. 2011. Autochthony, ethnicity, indigeneity and nationalism: timehonouring and state-oriented modes of rooting individual-territory-group triads in a globalizing world. *Critique of Anthropology*. 31(1): 63–81.

Zhu, Y. 2012. Performing heritage: rethinking authenticity in tourism. *Annals of Tourism Research*. 39(2): 1495–1513.

Zips, W. and Zips-Mairitsch, M. 2007. Lost in transition? The politics of conservation, indigenous land rights and community-based resource management in Africa. *The Journal of Legal Pluralism and Unofficial Law*. 39(55): 37–71.

Zukin, S. 1988. *Loft living: culture and capital in urban change*. New Brunswick, NJ: Rutgers University Press.

Zukin, S. 1995. *The cultures of cities*. Cambridge, MA: Blackwell.

Index

Note: Page numbers followed by "n" denote endnotes.

'Aboriginal Malays' 30
Aboriginal Peoples Act 41, 90
Aboriginal Peoples Ordinance 36
Aboriginal Reserves 90
Aboriginal Tribes Enactment 35
aborigines 27, 32, 106, 109;
  enslavement of 26
activism 8, 10–12, 34, 40, 42–48,
  59, 104, 110, 111, 113 (see also
  Indigenous activism)
activists 10, 17, 21, 44, 45, 58, 84, 85,
  87, 88, 101, 104, 107, 113, 114, 142,
  148, 187, 188
Adat (customs) 46, 70, 144, 159
Adat Tanah (Customary Lands) 106
Adiguru Kraf (Master Craftsman) 63
Adong Kuwau case 105
Advisory Council for Native Affairs
  (ACNA) 38, 39
'Aki Nabalu' 135, 136, 138, 153n5,
  175, 176
Among Primitive Peoples in Borneo
  (Evans) 33
Among the Forest Dwarfs of Malaya
  (Schebesta) 32
Amverton Cove Golf Course and Island
  Resort 81, 82
Anglo-Dutch rivalry 26
anthropology 7, 9, 32
anthropometric measurement 31
'anti-development' 45, 48,
  101, 104
Appadurai, Arjun 14, 65, 66, 191
'appropriate technology' 8
appropriation 20, 72, 73, 111, 188
Ariffin, Jamilah 100, 101, 102
Asian Indigenous movements 44, 45

Asian Indigenous Peoples Pact (AIPP)
  44, 45
assimilation 10, 46, 102, 129
Assistant Protector of Aborigines in the
  Department of Aborigines 61
Association of Southeast Asian Nations
  (ASEAN) 57
'authentic' 23, 50, 62, 68, 75, 80, 97,
  111, 129, 133, 138, 144, 175, 181
authenticity concept 12, 19
autochthony 26, 31, 33, 35, 47, 189
'auto-exoticism' 20, 139, 151

Bambaazon 130, 131, 133
bangkaha 149
berarak (bride parade) ritual 70
Besisi 53
Blagden, Charles Otto 28, 29, 32, 90
bobohizans 126, 127, 130–132,
  134, 135, 137, 139, 140, 150–152,
  189, 190
bohungkitas 126
bobohizans 126, 127, 130–132, 134, 135,
  137, 139, 140, 150–152, 189, 190
Borneo Project 146
British administration 35, 36
British colonial mission 40
British colonial rule 30
British Commonwealth 39
British-led security forces 35–36
British North Borneo Company 37, 38
broker 9, 17, 18, 54, 55, 56, 57, 58, 59,
  64, 71, 72, 73, 74, 75, 76, 77, 78, 80,
  83, 85, 93, 115, 138, 163, 176, 185;
  see also individual entries
brokerage: communication and
  transactions 9; community-based

cultural projects 9; definition of 8; dual dimension to 9; group solidarity 9; key role in 9; politics of 6
Brooke, Charles Sir 28
Brooke, James Sir 28
'brown' race 27
buffalo meat 169
bumiputera policy (same as 'son of the soil' policy) 30, 34, 39
bumiputeras 34, 39, 42
bunga mandi (flower bath) ritual 71

Cambridge Expedition 28
capacity-building 17, 52–88, 91, 113, 147, 185
'capacity to aspire' 191
Carey, Iskander 36
Catholics Student Society 43
Center for Orang Asli Concerns (COAC) 44, 82, 85, 113, 187
Centre for Creative Content and Digital Innovation (3CDI) 66
Chambri people of Papua New Guinea 138
Choo Chee Kuang 91, 92, 96
Christianity 127, 132, 166
Christian social justice movement 43, 141
civilisation 26, 27, 30, 34, 35, 111
'civility' 26
Civil Service 38, 39
climatic control 98
Cohen, Eric 20
colonial civilising mission 17, 41, 52, 58, 87
colonial custodianship 35
colonialism 10
Committee of Village Development 55
commodification 22, 48, 50, 59, 60, 67–69, 87, 129, 136
communicating non-economic values 66
'community:' conceptualisation of 52; notion of 5; settled and unambiguous community 5; *see also individual entries*
community-based approaches 4
community-based cultural projects 1, 9, 52, 66, 89, 90, 97, 117, 154
community-based museum development 52, 55
contemporary anthropological knowledge 11

contestation 4–6, 22, 52, 87, 99, 117–153, 184, 188, 190, 191
contradictory dualism 48, 143, 192; *see also* double-bind
Corporation Asli Selangor Private Limited 54
Country Garden Danga Bay development 103
Crawfurd, John 27, 32
'critical Indigeneity' 12
'critical museology' 3, 10–13, 117
Crown Colony 39
cultural anthropology 26
cultural heritage/heritage 6, 8, 9, 13, 16–18; Indigenous 4, 5, 12, 16, 19 (*see also* Indigenous cultural heritage); intangible 136; Lotud 159; transformation 18, 24, 59, 152, 155; transformation, representation, and interpretation 59–72, 96–99, 124–148; transmit 98; *see also individual entries*
cultural heritage instrumentalisation: anthropological literature 13; constructivist perspective 13; critical approach to 13–16; instrumental value of 13, 14
cultural institutions 96
cultural mapping 146
cultural practices 19, 34; vernacular 19
cultural tourism 6, 96; Indigenous 6
cultural wisdom and integrity 11
culture 1; instrumentalisation of 9, 13; manifestations of 15; re-conceptualisation of 14–15; *see also individual entries*
'culture for development' 1, 4, 5, 75, 92, 117, 119, 155, 192
culture of dependency 1, 5, 6, 17, 18, 52, 59, 87, 96, 115, 117, 123

dakwah programme 40
Danga Bay area 93, 100, 103
Dasar Pemilikan Tanah (Land Ownership Policy) 86
Datu system 37
decentralisation 6
decision-making power 122
decolonisation 4, 5, 10, 191
de-contextualisation/ de-contextualise 20, 117, 135
Dent, Alfred 37
Department of Orang Asli Affairs (JHEOA) 36, 51n2, 62

Department of Orang Asli
    Development (JAKOA) 36, 40,
    51n2, 53, 62, 90
descent, Nuremberg principle of 11
Diana Uju 61, 64, 69
*Dissertation on the Languages and
    Literature of the Indo-Chinese
    Nations* (Leyden) 26
diversity of cultures 12
double-bind 13, 69, 89–116, 129, 186,
    188, 192; *see also* contradictory
    dualism
dramaturgical analysis 19
Dusunic group/people 118, 155
'Dya' 28
'Dyak' 28

Earth Summit in 1992 45
East Malaysia 3, 37; *see also* Indigenous
    people
ecologically noble savages 47, 84, 110,
    111, 115, 143
economic marginalisation 101
economic neo-liberalisation 111
Economic Transformation
    Programme 92
eco-tourism business 17, 89, 93, 95
Eddy bin Salim 93, 99
Eighth Malaysia Plan 48
embodiments 12
'emergent authenticity' 20, 21, 68, 98,
    134, 152
empowerment 8, 21, 24, 85,
    97, 123, 147, 184, 187,
    191, 192; *see also* Indigenous
    empowerment
Enas, Hoessein 61
Enlightenment 27
Escobar, Arturo 7
ethnic tourism 19
'ethnographic capital' 76, 114, 185
ethnographic literature 60, 61
ethnographic museums 3
Eurocentric museology 4
Europe: cultural development 14;
    'negro' race in 27; transatlantic
    slavery in 27
Evans, Ivor 33, 34
evolutionary hierarchy 17, 52, 58, 87;
    see also racial hierarchy
evolutionary schema 30
exoticisation 49, 50, 87, 90, 95, 115,
    118, 130, 152, 186, 188

fascism, struggle against 10
Federated Malay States Museums in
    Malaya 33
Federation of Malaysia 39, 41
Ferguson, James 7, 59, 102, 187, 191
Fifth Exhibition of the Exposition of
    Arts 61
foreign missionaries 34
Forest Enactment 44, 144, 153n6
Forest Rules 44
Free, Prior and Informed Consent
    (FPIC) xiii, 83
The Future of Indigenous Museums
    (Stanley) 4

Gali Adam 63, 66, 69
Gintutun Do Mohoing 119, 149, 150
GIS (Geographic Information
    System) 146
Global Environment Facility (GEF) 91,
    92, 96
'global ecological imaginary' 84
globalisation 12, 60
'global sense of place' 6, 12
global tourism 6
Gontusan, Adam 139–141
governance of the prior 13, 109
GPS (Global Positioning System)
    106, 146
gusi (heirloom jars) 156, 165, 169, 190

Haddon, Alfred Cort 31
Hari Moyang (Ancestor's Day) 61, 66,
    77, 79, 146
headhunting 119, 124, 125, 129, 149,
    152, 189
Herbert Deane Noone 35
heritage dissonance 15, 74, 149, 150
heritage-making 13, 15, 21, 23–24,
    60, 184
A History of Java (Raffles) 26
The History of Sumatra (Marsden) 26
History of the Indian Archipelago
    (Crawfurd) 27
Hose, Charles 30–32
'House of Skulls' 130
human evolution 28
human rights 104
human skulls 125–126, 128

Iban/Sea Dayak 31
'Identity Markers' project 147
India: colonial custodianship 35

Indigeneity 10; articulation of 12;
in Borneo 27–28; concept of 11;
definition of 10; in Malaysia 25–34;
in Peninsular Malaysia 30, 33;
polythetic definition of 11–12;
reformulation of 12; in Southeast
Asia 27; strategic essentialism of 12,
85, 88, 187
Indigenous activism 8, 10, 11, 46, 58,
59, 89, 110, 113, 145, 148
Indigenous community/communities
4–6, 10, 11, 46, 116, 117, 120, 144,
151, 152, 183, 185
Indigenous cultural heritage:
commodification of 22; contestation
(*see* contestation); exhibitionism
and exploitation of 58;
instrumentalisation of 73; Mah Meri
cultural practices 73; mobilisation
of 117; museumification and
disneyfication of 138; representation
and performance of 23; tourism
imaginaries 23
'Indigenous cultural renaissance' 12
Indigenous cultural villages 1, 5, 6, 8,
9, 16, 18, 21, 22, 23, 24, 32, 49, 50,
113, 114, 115, 120, 184, 185; *see
also individual entries*
Indigenous empowerment 53, 58, 59,
88, 97
Indigenous movement 10; in Malaysia
14, 45, 104
Indigenous museums 8, 98, 99, 115,
152, 159, 169, 191; concept of 5;
positive rhetoric of 5; Southeast
Asian perspective 5
Indigenous people: definition of 11;
discursive portrayal of 29; 'double-
bind' for 90, 111; economic and
political agendas 12; empowerment
of 21; at Indigenous cultural villages
22; Indigenous workers 18; in
Malaysia 16, 21, 25; opportunities
for 13; in Peninsular Malaysia 25;
as 'primitive Other' 90; as 'primitive
people' 22; quasi-empowerment for
59; self-identity for 21;
socio-economic development 92;
Southeast Asia 19
Indigenous populations 28;
classifications of 30, 32; *see also*
Indigenous community/communities
Indigenous rights movement 10, 11, 43

Indigenous tourism model 58, 59
Indo-China 53
insider/insiders 117, 120, 122, 123,
151, 185
instrumentalisation 13–16, 23, 152,
184; *see also individual entries*
Instrumentality 14
instrumental value of culture 14
intellectual property 20, 73, 188, 190
International Decade for the World's
Indigenous People 10
international Indigenisms 10
intrinsic values of culture 14
The Invention of Culture (Wagner) 13
The Invention of Tradition (Hobsbawm
and Ranger) 13
Iskandar Development Region (IDR)
90, 93, 96, 104, 107
Iskandar Development Region Agency
(IDRA) 99, 107
Islam religion 3, 40, 42, 127, 132
Islamic religious councils in Malaysia 40

Jakun (same as Proto-Malays) 28, 46
Japanese occupation 35
Jaringan Orang Asal SeMalaysia (JOAS)
44, 45
Jefree bin Salim 92
jerat tupai (squirrel game) 71, 75
Jilan, Datuk Patrick 156–158, 161, 182,
186
Jilan, Margaret 159, 166, 173
Jimis, Winnie 132
JKKK (Jawatan Kuasa Kemajuan dan
Keselamatan Kampung) 55
John Baptist, Judeth 133, 136–139,
175, 178
Johor Bahru 94, 103
Johore Strait 90, 91
Johor State Land Office 107
Jo-oh dance 61
Jumaat Misman 108
jungle survival 32

Kaamatan celebrations (Harvest
Festival) 134, 135
Kadazan: people 42, 118, 119, 122,
125, 129, 135, 136, 138, 152, 189;
language 42, 131, 132, 135, 139;
longhouse 119
'Kadazandusun' 36, 160
Kadazandusun Cultural Association
(KDCA) 133, 181

Kadazandusun Language Foundation (KLF) 130–133
Kalamantan 31
Kampung Bakar Batu 90
Kampung Kuai-Kadazon 118, 119; development of 120
Kampung Rambai 54
Kampung Simpang Arang 90
Kampung Sungai Bumbun 54–56, 58, 63, 66, 69, 74, 77, 85
Kampung Sungai Judah 54
Kampung Sungai Temon 17, 90; eco-tourism development 93, 96; Orang Seletar villagers of 93, 96
Kemi anak Khamis 65
Kenyah-Kayan 31
Kirshenblatt-Gimblett, Barbara 23, 136, 189
Kreps, Christina 4, 8, 99, 127, 169
Kuala Lumpur International Airport 105
Kuper, Adam 11, 12
Kurin, Richard 8

lalavangan 169, 171
land reclamation 97
Lasimbang, Anne 44, 141–145, 147, 148, 187
Lasimbang, Jannie 43, 44
Lasimbang, Rita 130, 131, 133, 148
Lembaga Adat (Tribal Council) 105–106
Leyden, John 26
libabou ritual 168, 180
libabou (spirit medium) 167, 168, 172, 178, 179, 180, 182
liberal-democratic states 11
liberal government technology 13
Liberating Cultures (Kreps) 4
Linangkit Cultural Village 1, 18; community-based cultural projects 154; contexts, personalities, and interests 157–165; financial sustainability of 154; frictions, tensions, and issues 175–182; Lotud-themed weddings 157; unequal power relationships 155
Linangkit technique 160
Lintar, Peter 176
Lotud people 18, 136, 155, 160, 161
Lowenthal, David 26

MacCannell, Dean 19, 95, 132
McDougall, William 30–32

Magang ceremony 126, 130
Magavau ceremony 130, 132, 133, 135
Mah Meri Cultural Village 1, 16, 17, 52, 53; colonial civilising mission 58; commercial folk-art genre of 67; commodification of 69; contexts, personalities, and interests 54–59; cultural representation of 62; frictions, tensions, and issues 72–86; globalisation and modernisation 60; history and cultural traditions of 54; Indigenous empowerment of 53; infrastructure of 54; Mah Meri people 56; national development plan 52; paternalistic approach to 57; 'patron-client' relationship 59; prevailing structure of 59; three-day wedding ceremony 70–71
Mah Meri of Malaysia Art and Culture (Werner) 62
Mah Meri Unmasked 66
Malay 30, 58; *see also individual entries*
Malayan Communist Party (MCP) 35, 40
Malayan Emergency 35, 36, 40
Malay Archipelago 26–28, 31, 34
Malay-Muslim Federal Government 41
Malay-Muslim groups 38, 39, 42, 58
Malay-Muslim leadership of Malaysia 42
Malay-Muslim society of Malaysia 3, 117
Malay-Muslim villages 102
Malaysia: case studies, location of 2; economic and social realities of 42; exhibitions in 61–62; indigeneity, historical conceptualisations of 25–34; indigenous consciousness and activism in 42–48; Indigenous heritage in 16; in Indigenous people 16; indigenous people in 3, 5; indigenous tourism and sustainable development 48–50; neo-liberalisation of 104; political and economic climate in 43; political position, indigenous populations 35–42
Malaysia Handicraft Development Corporation (MHDC) 63
Malaysian Bar Council 47, 106, 186
Malaysian Department of Orang Asli Development (JAKOA) 29
Malaysian eco-tourism enterprise 93, 95
Malaysian Ministry of Tourism, Arts and Culture (MOTAC) 16

Malaysian radio station 91
Malaysian Ringgit (RM) 54
Malaysian Society of Marine Science
(MSMS) 91
2013 Malaysian Student Film and
Video Festival 73
Malaysian-Thai border 40
Mangahau ritual ceremony 156
Mangambai ritual 131
Manickam, Sandra Khor 25, 30, 33
Margaret Jilan 159
marginalisation/marginalise 1, 3,
6, 10, 15, 18, 44, 50, 52, 59, 87,
117, 186, 191
Marsden, William 26
Martin, Rudolf 28
Mat bin Inder 99
mediation/mediate 1, 9, 22, 83, 85, 89,
139
menhir 18, 119, 124, 149, 150, 151
metropolitan civilisation 30
Mimpi Mah Meri (Mah Meri Dream) 73
Ministry of Tourism, Arts and Culture
(MOTAC) 54, 55, 58
Mitchell, Don 14, 15
mobilisation /mobilise 84
modernity 111
Modsuung ritual 140
Mogkodim ritual 131
Mohlukas ceremony 165–170
Momohizan ceremony 127, 128
Monolibabou ritual 168, 178
Monolinsim ritual 173
Monsopiad Cultural Village 1, 18,
117, 118; contexts, personalities,
and interests 120–124; decision-
making power 122; establishment
of 118, 129; frictions, tensions, and
issues 149–151; long-term strategic
management 121; management rights
of 123; non-Indigenous investor 122;
operational model of 121; tourism
industry 120
Monumbul 172
Moujing, Dousia 118, 119, 126–128,
129, 131, 151
Moujing, Wildy 119, 120, 122, 128, 130
Mount Kinabalu 155, 177–178
Moyang (ancestors) 61
Moyang Harimau Berantai (Chained
Tiger Ancestor) 63–64
Muhammad, Mahathir 45
Murutic group 118

museological literature 16, 59, 124, 151
museological phenomenon 3
museology 3, 4, 5, 7, 10–13, 24, 87,
115, 152
museum anthropology 6
Musical instruments and dance
movements 97, 98
Muslim prayers 173

National Museum of Malaysia 62
National Orang Asli Museum 48
national unity policy 42
National University of Malaysia
(UKM) 43
native chief 29, 38
Native Courts 38, 39, 179
native customary lands 44, 47, 69, 81,
82, 84, 104, 117, 164
native customary rights 18, 47, 86,
96, 99, 106, 108, 110, 111, 112,
143–146, 152
*The Natives of Sarawak and British
North Borneo* (Roth) 27
Native Tutorial Programme 39
Nature Classroom 93, 94
'negotiation of expectations' 23, 152,
189
Negritos (Semang) 32–34
The Negritos of Malaya (Evans) 33
'negro' race 27
neo-liberalisation of Malaysia 104
New Economic Policy (NEP) 39
New Zealand: settler-colonial contexts 4
Nicholas, Colin 43, 44, 47, 107, 108, 112
noble savages 11, 22, 45, 50, 69, 189
non-governmental organisation
(NGO) 91
non-Western art 64
non-Western museum models 4
North Borneo Company 125
nyireh (Xylocarpus moluccensis) 61

Odun Badin 170
Odun Lumanjar 179, 180
Odun Sobinting 167, 168, 180
Office of the United Nations High
Commissioner for Human Rights
(OHCHR) 10
Orang Asli 3, 35–37, 40, 41, 53
Orang Asli Entrepreneur Carnival
2014 98
Orang Asli village in Bukit Lagong 55
Orang Laut 108, 116n11

Orang Seletar Cultural Centre 1, 17–18; Choo Chee Kuang 91; community-run cultural institutions 96; contexts, personalities, and interest 92–96; Danga Bay area 100; eco-tourism business 89, 93; establishment of 92; frictions, tensions, and issues 99–114; high-rise waterfront properties development 93; history and lifestyle of 94; in Kampung Sungai Temon 91; lands, clearing of 99; political and social structures for 101; 'primitive Other' 95; public awareness of 93–94
'originality' 26
outsider/outsiders 16, 101, 117, 120, 122, 123, 151, 184, 185, 190
Overbeck-Dent Association 37

PACOS Trust 44–47, 141, 143, 147, 187
Pagan Races of the Malay Peninsula (Skeat) 28, 29
'pagan races'/'tribes' 35; of Peninsular Malaysia 33
The Pagans of North Borneo (Rutter) 33
The Pagan Tribes of Borneo (Hose) 30
'paired opposite' 6
palm oil plantations 69
pangkis (war cry) 134
Panglima Gemilang Darjah Kinabalu (PGDK) 158
Pan-Negritos theory 32
Papers on the Ethnology and Archaeology of the Malay Peninsula (Evans) 33
Parti Bersatu Sabah (PSB) 158
Patanic group 118
paternalism 90
paternalistic approach 43
patong (wooden sculptures) 61
'patron-client' relationship 24, 17, 52, 59
Penampang, District of 118, 130, 135, 136, 147, 160
Peninsular Malaysia 1, 3, 29, 35, 43, 47, 54
Peninsular Malaysia Orang Asli Association (POASM) 43, 113
'performative authenticity' 20, 141
Persatuan Komulakan Lotud Sabah, the Lotud Youth Association (KLOSA) 162, 163
Pesta Kaamatan (Harvest Festival) 133
Phelan, Peter 126

Pion Bumbon 68
'place-based imaginaries' 108–109, 115
political autonomy 3, 41
political ecology 8
politics 1, 3–6, 10, 12, 42, 52, 114, 121, 151; *see also individual entries*
'politics of representation' 21, 22
Polunin, Ivan 91
polythetic 11, 83
positionalities 12
post-colonial Malaysia 34; nation-building projects 5
power: dynamics 5, 12, 13, 23, 147, 177, 192; relations 4, 8, 12, 13, 15, 16, 23, 106, 152
'primitive people' 22
'primitivist tourism' 49, 125, 129
primordiality 26, 31, 33, 47, 109, 189
profit-making mission 119
'Projects for Awareness and Community Organisations in Sabah' (PACOS) 43, 44
pro-Malay-Muslim policies 108
proto-Malays (Jakun) 90, 108
pseudoscientific techniques 28
Pulau Carey (Carey island) 54, 65, 73, 76, 81
Punan 31
'purity' 26
Puteri Harbour 103
Pygmies in Africa 32

quasi-empowerment 59

racial discourses 26, 27, 32, 34
racial hierarchy 33, 34; *see also* evolutionary hierarchy
racial science in India 28
racial theory, Malay Archipelago 27
Raffles, Stamford 26
recognition 6, 7, 14, 36, 46, 108, 109, 186
Reflections of a Culture Broker (Kurin) 8
regeneration plans 14
'regime of representation' 21, 22
region classification 28
're-groupment schemes' 40
The Religion of the Tempasuk Dusuns of North Borneo (Evans) 33
Return of the Native (Kuper) 11
rinait 126, 132, 133, 165, 171–173, 180
River Bumbun 82, 83
The River Must Flow (COAC) 82
ritual cleansing 155, 182, 183

ritual efficacy 80, 155, 166, 168, 175, 190
Roth, Henry Ling 27, 28
Royal Charter 37
Rutter, Owen 33, 125

Sabah State Government 18, 120, 163
Sabah State Museum 178
Sabah Students Association Group 43
Sagong Tasi case 105–106
Sakai 11, 25, 28, 29
Salim bin Palon 99
'salvage paradigm' 32
sambut menantu (reception)
   ritual 71
sandai 169, 171
'sanitisation' process 20
sarong(tube cloth) 138, 140, 167, 173
Schebesta, Paul 32
Seal of Excellence for Handicraft
   Products scheme 64
self-determination 5, 10, 11, 23,
   45, 48, 85, 101, 142, 184
self-identification policy 11
self-representation 21
Semang (Negritos) people 28
Senoi Dream Theory 53, 73
Senoi people 53, 73
'settled and unambiguous community' 5
settler colonialism 4, 5, 13, 28
Shanghai Exposition 2010 63, 68
Skeat, Walter William 28, 29, 32, 90
Smithsonian Institution 8
Society of Malaysian Artists 62
socio-economic development 40, 53,
   92, 95
'sons of the soil' policy (*see also*
   bumiputera policy) 39
Southeast Asia: museological
   phenomenon in 3
Southeast Asian Regional Centre for
   Archaeology and Fine Arts (SEAMO
   SPAFA) 137
Southwest Pacific museums 96
'staged authenticity' 19
staging/staged 13, 16–24, 67–69,
   71, 134, 140, 145, 166, 175,
   188–190; *see also*
   individual entries
Stanley, Nick 5, 96, 98, 169
Statement of Policy Regarding the
   Long-Term Administration of the
   Aboriginal Peoples 37, 39
Stephens, Donald 42

1901 Straits Settlement census 30
Straits Settlements 28
Straits, Torres 31
'strategic creativity' 64
2020 Strategic Plan 40
*Studies in Religion, Folklore and
   Custom in British North Borneo
   and the Malay Peninsula*
   (Evans) 33
subjectivities 12, 21, 109, 147
Subramaniam, Yogeswaran 104,
   111, 112
Suluk Muslim 42
sumazau dance 126, 133, 134, 137
supra-national organisations 10
Sup Tarajun 169
'survivance' concept 13, 23
sustainable development 1, 24

taboos 21, 124, 127, 128, 135, 140,
   169, 170, 190
Tangkob 119
tantagas 156, 165, 169, 173–175,
   178, 181
'tapestry weaving' 159
Temuan people 72
tengkho wood 61
Thailand 132
Tok Batin (Village Headman) 54, 57,
   70, 74, 94
Tompoq Topoh 76
topeng (wooden masks) 61
tourism 21, 22, 68; community-based
   approaches 6
tourism imaginaries 22, 23, 50
tourism industry 120
tourist art 21, 65–68
'tourist gaze' 130
Tuaran, District of 136, 155, 170,
   175, 178
Tumabur ritual 180–183
Tun Mustapha 42
tradition 14–16, 20, 66, 74, 119,
   141, 179
transnational solidarity formation 12
tribal slot 148
tripartite classification 29

UNDRIP Convention 46, 47, 83
unequal power relationships 155
UNESCO 1, 6, 7, 52–53, 63, 119,
   155, 192
UNESCO World Heritage Site 177

United Nations 10
United Nations conferences 104
United Nations Declaration on the
  Rights of Indigenous Peoples
  (UNDRIP) 46
United Nations Permanent Forum
  on Indigenous Issues
  (UNPFII) 46
United Sabah Dusun Association
  (USDA) 158
United Sabah Party 158
United States 4; settler-colonial
  contexts 4
'unity in diversity,' rhetoric of 49
universal cultural rights 7
University Asian Art Museum 62, 66
urbanisation 31, 97

'vanishing savage' 34
Vietnam 132

Village Administration Ordinance 38
Village Headman (Tok Batin) 17, 54,
  57, 70, 74, 94
Volk, concept of 26
von Overbeck, Gustavus Baron 37

'weapons of the weak' 77
wedding ceremony 70–71, 74
Werner, Ronald 62
Williams-Hunt, Anthony 43
Williams-Hunt, P.D.R. 43
Wong Yun Yun 93, 186
woodcarving 61, 62, 65, 66
Working Group of Indigenous Peoples
  (WGIP) 11
World Bank-sponsored Thaba-Tseka
  project 7
World Commission on Culture and
  Development 1
World Wide Fund for Nature (WWF) 44